A Strategy for
EQUALITY

Tralee General Hospital I.

Date

Report of the Commission on the
Status of People with Disabilities

Designed at Language

Printed by Cahill Printers

OpuB Health Inequality

CONTENTS

A Strategy for Equality Report of the Commission on the Status of People with Disabilities

CONTENTS

Foreword

"We, as people with disabilities, are shouldering our responsibility to ensure that disabled people are "included" as full citizens in Ireland. It is now time that everyone else joins this process, so that we can all live and participate together as equal members of society".

- excerpt from a submission

It is with great pleasure that I present the Report of the Commission on the Status of People with Disabilities to Government and so honour the pledge we gave to the many people with disabilities, their families and carers we met at our "Listening Meetings" held throughout the country and to those who made written submissions to us.

From the outset, the Commission made consultation and participation our highest priority. I hope that this approach will become part and parcel of the way in which policy will be formed in the future.

This Report is an equality strategy which will, if implemented, set about removing the barriers which stand in the way of people with disabilities who want to live full and fulfilled lives. It will also benefit greatly the parents and carers of people with disabilities. The Commission's strategy involves legislative solutions, proposals for new policy initiatives and new structures for delivery of equality services within a framework of rights, not charity. The Commission has developed a model of service which places the user of those services at the centre of the process of service delivery, from the planning stage right through to implementation.

While the Commission recommends that a reasonable time frame be set for the implementation of our recommendations, there are, however, a number of recommendations which require immediate attention. These are as follows:-

Recommendations 23.20 - 23.23 in relation to a special programme to replace sub-standard facilities for people with disabilities, with St. Ita's Hospital, Portrane receiving priority attention.

Recommendation 1.24 in relation to the provision of funding to the new Council for the Status of People with Disabilities.

Recommendation 2.5 in relation to the revision of the EU Treaties.

Recommendation 7.31 in relation to the acute shortage of sheltered workplaces

Recommendations 3.6 and 3.7 in relation to the retention and resourcing of the Department of Equality and Law Reform.

Recommendation 13.5 in relation to all new and used rail rolling stock and road vehicles ordered for public transport from January 1st 1997.

I firmly believe that if these recommendations are implemented immediately, then a good start will have been made to tackling the gross in-equalities experienced on a daily basis by people with disabilities, their families and carers.

I would like to thank the members of the Commission for their dedication and commitment to our work and, in particular, to compliment our Secretary, Mr. Pat Wylie and the other members of the Secretariat without whose resourcefulness and forbearance this Report would not have been possible.

The Hon. Mr. Justice Feargus M. Flood

Chairperson to the Commission

Preface

The Commission on the Status of People with Disabilities was established on the 29th November, 1993 by the Minister of Equality of Law Reform, Mervyn Taylor, TD., with the following terms of reference:

1.   To advise the Government on practical measures necessary to ensure that people with a disability can exercise their rights to participate, to the fullest extent of their potential, in economic, social and cultural life.

2.   To examine the current situation of people with a disability and the organisation and adequacy of existing services, both public and voluntary, to meet their needs.

3.   To make recommendations setting out necessary changes, in legislation, policies, organisation, practices and structures to ensure that the needs of people with disabilities are met in a cohesive, comprehensive and cost effective way.

4.   To establish the estimated costs of all recommendations made, and

5.   To report to the Government within a period of two years from the date of its establishment.

The Commission received some 600 written submissions, a majority of them (327) from individuals with disabilities. A further 111 submissions came from parents and others close to people with disabilities while 162 submissions were received from organisations. In addition, the Commission held 30 "listening meetings" at ten centres around the country as well as at a number of locations in and around Dublin. Members of the Commission heard at first hand at these meetings of the frustrations and problems facing people with disabilities. Between the submissions and the listening meetings, the Commission drew up a comprehensive picture of the lifestyles of people with disabilities.

The Commission appointed a number of Working Groups and individuals to examine and develop proposals on various issues. Their reports, a number of which the Commission is making available publicly, provided an extremely valuable input into the Commission's deliberations. These reports represent the views of the Working Groups which produced them, and do not necessarily reflect the views of the Commission. The membership of the individual Working Groups is contained in Appendix E.

Public life does not stand still while a Commission deliberates. During the lifetime of the Commission, several important issues arose which were of great significance to people with disabilities, and these were taken up by the Commission.

A comprehensive submission was made, under the chairmanship of Commission member Dr. Gerard Quinn, to the Constitution Review Group, recommending specific amendments to the Constitution to ensure equal rights to people with disabilities in all aspects of Irish life.

Submissions were made to the Minister for Equality and Law Reform, Mervyn Taylor, T.D. concerning the content of proposed Equality Bill and the Equal Status legislation. As well as making general proposals as to the manner of securing equal rights for people with disabilities, the Legislation Working Group made a technical submission regarding the important matter of the definition of disability which would be appropriate to this legislation.

The Report of the Special Education Review Committee, published by the Minister for Education was followed by the White Paper "Charting our Education Future". The Commission's Education Working Group made a comprehensive submission to the Department of Education, focusing on the need for new education legislation which would ensure equality of opportunity, access and participation for disabled students, by creating entitlements to services and by providing for reasonable accommodation for all disabled students in mainstream schools. Members of this Working Group had the opportunity to meet with senior officials of the Department of Education on this issue.

A delegation from the Commission met with the Irish Minister for European Affairs to stress the importance of including a non-discrimination clause in the E.U. Treaty.

A comprehensive submission was made to the Working Group on a Courts Commission, highlighting the problems which people with disabilities face in securing access to one of the most fundamental rights in a democratic state, the right of access to the Courts and the legal system; proposals were made to the Working Group on Taxicab provision, dealing with this most important aspect of transport provision for people with disabilities; consultations took place with the Insurance Federation of Ireland, in respect of inequalities in the right of access to insurance provision; discussions took place with Aer Rianta and Aer Lingus regarding access to air travel.

The Secretariat of the Commission was provided by the Department of Equality and Law Reform and comprised of:

Mr. Pat Wylie - Secretary
Mr. Breandán O Cathasaigh
Ms. Anne Colgan and
Ms. Ann Casey

The Commission would also like to acknowledge, with thanks, the support and assistance they received from the following:

Ms. Lucinda MacMahon
Ms. May McCarthy
Ms. Irene O'Keeffe
Ms. Eileen Bowden
Ms. Betty Ann Carroll and
Ms. Collette Deely

One of the most important aspects of the Commission itself was the fact that 60 per cent of its members were people with disabilities, their carers or family members. Its members were:

Mr Justice Feargus Flood, Chairperson	Sr. Angela Magee
Mark Blake-Knox	Frank Mulcahy
Jacqui Browne	Seamus Ó Cinnéide
Anne Coogan	Allen O'Connor
John A. Cooney	Kathleen O'Flaherty
Paddy Doyle	Margaret O'Leary
Frieda Finlay	Arthur O'Reilly
Michael Gogarty	Colman Patton
David Leydon	Gerard Quinn
Paul McCarthy	Annie Ryan
Conn Mac Cinngamhna	Fidelma Ryan
* Anne McManus	** Frances Spillane

* replaced by John Bohan who in turn was replaced by Paula Lyons
** replaced by John Collins

Listening Exercises of the Commission

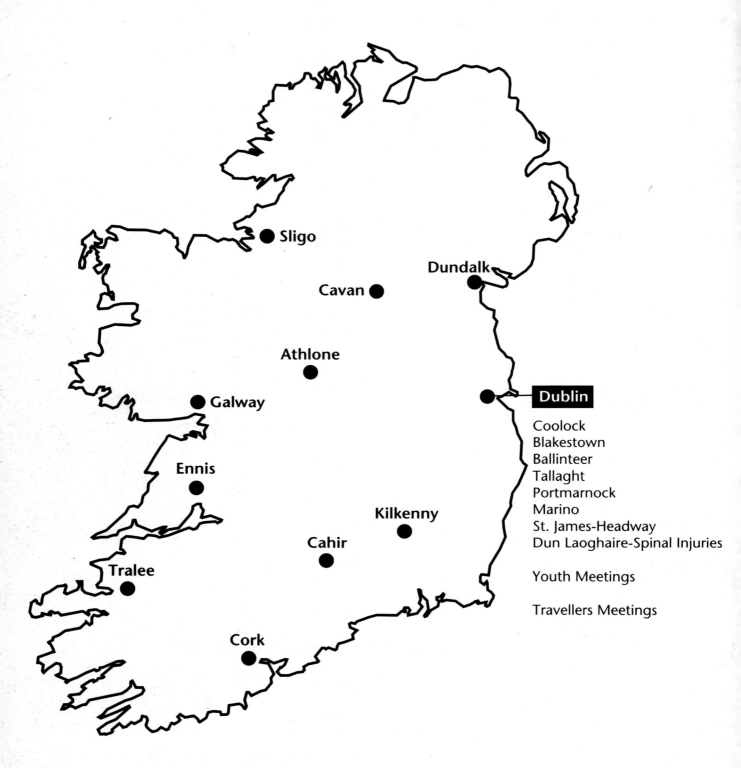

Sligo

Dundalk

Cavan

Athlone

Galway

Dublin

Coolock
Blakestown
Ballinteer
Tallaght
Portmarnock
Marino
St. James-Headway
Dun Laoghaire-Spinal Injuries

Youth Meetings

Travellers Meetings

Ennis

Kilkenny

Cahir

Tralee

Cork

Part One
INTRODUCTION

Chapter One
OVERVIEW

DELIVERING THE
CESSARY SERVICES

INCLUSION OF WOMEN
WITH DISABILITIES

HEALTH

INSURANCE

POLITICAL
RIGHTS

EDUCATION

LEGAL STATUS
OF PEOPLE
WITH DISABILITIES

TRANSPORT
& MOBILITY

SEXUALITY &
RELATIONSHIPS

HOUSING AND
ACCOMMODATION

ARTS &
CULTURE

OVERVIEW

ACCESS

POLICY DEVELOPMENT
& IMPLEMENTATION

TECHNOLOGY
COMMUNICATIO

RELIGIOUS
PRACTICE

VULNERABLE
PEOPLE

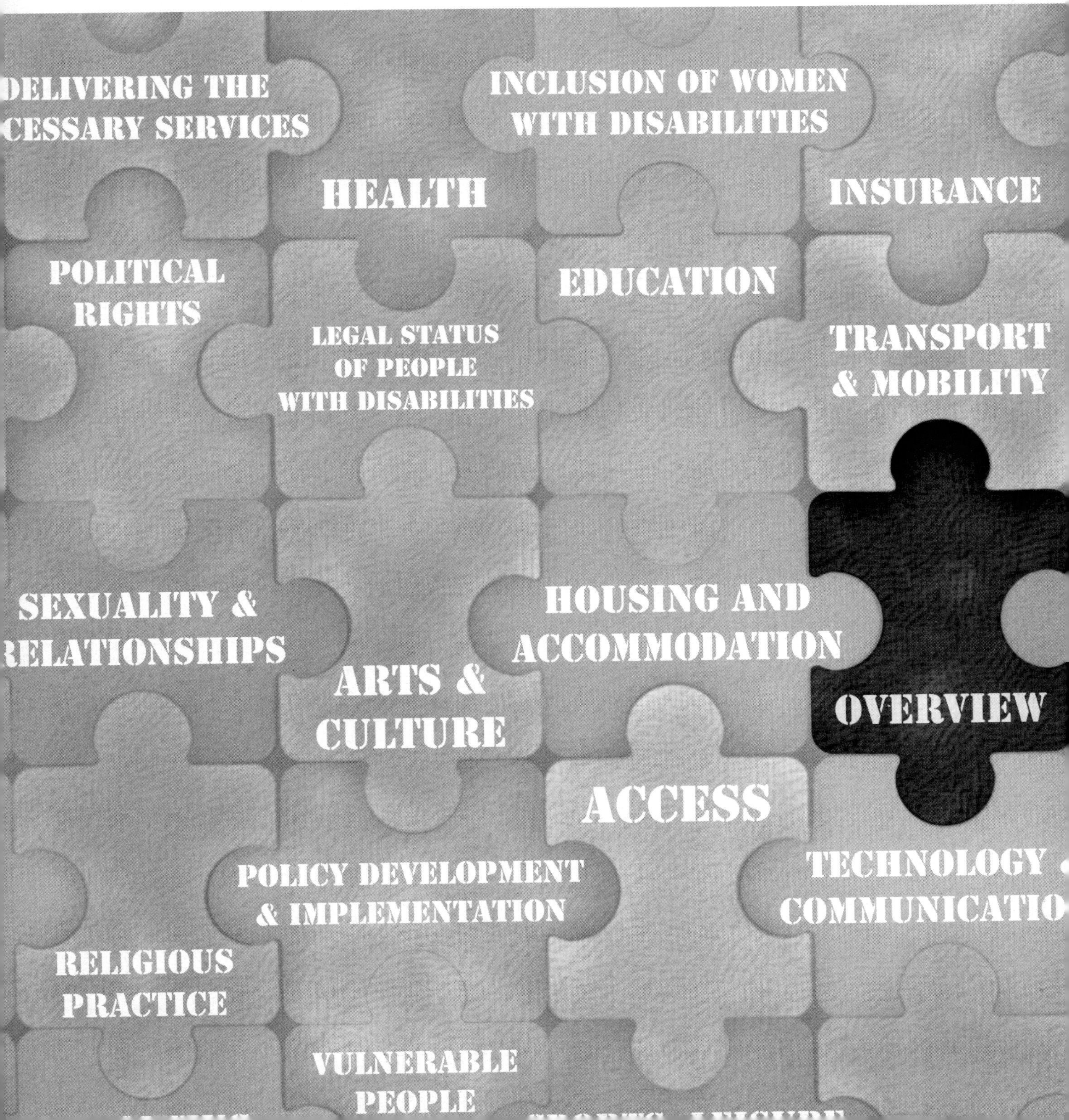

People with disabilities do not want to be pitied nor do they want their disabilities to be dismissed as of little importance. All that is required is a little respect and basic needs and rights. Surely this is not too much to ask?

- excerpt from submission

Overview

KHC 3037
Cprue Health Inequality

1.1   People with disabilities are the neglected citizens of Ireland. On the eve of the 21st century, many of them suffer intolerable conditions because of outdated social and economic policies and unthinking public attitudes. Changes have begun to come about, influenced by international recognition that disability is a social rather than a medical issue, but many of those changes have been piecemeal. Public attitudes towards disability are still based on charity rather than on rights, and the odds are stacked against people with disabilities at almost every turn. Whether their status is looked at in terms of economics, information, education, mobility, or housing they are seen to be treated as second-class citizens.

1.2   People with disabilities are angry, and their justifiable anger was evident in submissions to the Commission and at listening meetings which the Commission held throughout the country over the past two years. The picture that emerged was one of a society which excludes people with disabilities from almost every aspect of economic, social, political and cultural life. People with disabilities and their families made it clear that they want equality, that they want to move from a reliance on charity towards establishing basic rights. They want, and are entitled to, equality and full participation as citizens.

1.3   One of the most striking features of the submissions was the sense of absolute frustration which emerged from them. The frustration did not centre, as some might expect, on personal experiences of physical pain, discomfort or impaired function. Nor did it centre on the incurable nature of many disabling conditions nor on the question of "why me", which is often discussed in relation to the distribution of disability. On the contrary, the frustration revolved around people's sense that they were being put in a position of having to deal with a myriad of oppressive social barriers in addition to their disabling conditions.

1.4   Another theme to emerge clearly from the submissions and the meetings was that of marginalisation. This word took on a stark reality and force from the hundreds of pages of submissions sent in to the Commission from people with disabilities and their families. Many people with disabilities felt that they were being either kept at, or pushed to, the margins of society. They were not being allowed to realise their potential or to participate as fully as they are entitled to in everyday life.

1.5   Disability can have major implications, not only for the individuals who are directly affected, but also for those who find themselves in the role of informal carers. While it is almost always close family members - parents, spouses, or children - who fill this role, friends or neighbours may also be involved in a major way. The Commission received 100 submissions from the family members of people with a disability. This material was also full of strong feelings and emotion and underlined the point that caring for people with disabilities can be an ongoing physical, mental and emotional strain accompanied by a sense of terrible isolation.

1.6   In practical terms, one of the single largest areas of concern raised in the submissions and at the listening meetings was the question of access and transport. Clearly, the built environment and most forms of transport are very inaccessible for people with disabilities. Many of the submissions from individuals referred to the inability to get out and about, the need to plan every trip and the sense of being "a prisoner in one's own home". They criticised the inaccessibility of public transport: as one person put it graphically, "public transport means that when you are disabled you are no longer a member of the public". These problems are not just mechanical ones but ones that have several important consequences. They mean that people are denied full access to education, to employment and training, to cultural and leisure events. They mean that the overall cost of living for people with disabilities is higher than for other people.

1.7   Another of the major failings identified at the listening meetings was the lack of information available to people with disabilities and their carers. And not just the absence of information but the way in which people were treated when they went looking for it. The difficulty of obtaining access to entitlements and services, both public and private, was of major concern. Many submissions emphasised the lack of co-ordination between service providers, the fragmentation of services and the difficulty in getting entitlements. There is no one source of information for people with disabilities and they frequently have to go from organisation to organisation in an attempt to identify their options. The absence of easily accessible information is clearly a major factor in the isolation and marginalisation experienced by very many citizens.

1.8   There was serious concern too about education: a failure to provide comprehensive education for people with disabilities results in their being denied access to employment and training opportunities comparable to those available to people without disabilities. Other areas which attracted a large number of comments in the submissions included employment and training, income support, health and personal support. In addition, many complaints were received from people about the length of waiting lists for services.

1.9   All that said, people with disabilities are not without hope. This hope does not centre on finding a "cure" for disabling conditions, but on the possibility of improving their quality of life through changes in existing attitudes and improvements in services which will, together, allow them to develop their own potential. As one submission put it: "It is our earnest wish that people with disabilities will be given their rightful place in society, the opportunity to participate and to contribute fully in all areas of Irish life."

1.10 The Commission on the Status of People with Disabilities wants to see that hope become a reality and has wide-ranging, even radical, proposals to make it happen. For example, it recommends that a Disability Support Service will be established with resource centres all over Ireland, providing information, advice, advocacy, and practical support to people with disabilities and their families from the minute they need it, either from the ante-natal stage or whenever the need arises later in life. It proposes the establishment of a National Disability Authority, charged with overseeing the implementation of new laws aimed at improving the lives of people with disabilities, and co-ordinating everyone's efforts to do this. It proposes that new ways of thinking about people with disabilities, underpinned by laws and supported by practical measures, will spell an end to the discrimination and exclusion that is their experience now.

1.11 Perhaps one of the most telling indications of the neglect of people with disabilities is the silence of relevant official statistics. Unlike most European Union countries, there are no comprehensive statistics available for Ireland. The opportunity to determine accurate figures was missed again in the 1996 census of population: it should not be lost in future censuses. In addition, the Commission repeatedly came up against an absence of information about people with disabilities in relation to a wide range of issues.

1.12 The Commission itself was not in a position to conduct or commission a major survey of the population because of the complexity of the task, the resources and time it would require and because of its own deadlines. However, it asked the Economic and Social Research Institute to assist it by collating existing quantitative data on disability to help it arrive at some overall estimates. (See Appendix A for a full discussion of the numbers.)

1.13 On the basis of that and reports from other EU countries, the Commission concluded that some 360,000 Irish people, or 10% of the population, have a disability. This number is a conservative estimate and compares, for instance, to 12.5% of the populations across most EU countries.

1.14 Disability is not present in equal proportions among all age groups, tending for obvious reasons to be more common among older people. Recent surveys in Northern Ireland estimated, for instance, that 17.4% of the adult population there have disabilities compared to 3.5% of the child population. Our own estimates suggest that half of all people with disabilities in the Republic are aged 60 and over. When the families of those with disabilities are included - and the Commission specifically included families of people with disabilities in its considerations - a large and significant proportion of the population is clearly affected by disability. There are few families who have not been, are not, or will not be, affected by disability to some extent or other at some time in their lives.

1.15   Pending the next census of population, the Central Statistics Office should carry out a survey of the extent of disabilities in Ireland and establish a system to ensure that relevant data is regularly updated. This survey should be undertaken in the early part of 1997 and updated bi-annually thereafter. All agencies responsible for the monitoring or quality control of services should also ensure that adequate management statistics are collected as a matter of course.

1.16   In drawing up a strategic Irish policy on disability for the first time, it is important to look at the context of change. Attitudes towards disability have changed considerably over the past 15 years, led by a stronger and more vocal movement of people with disabilities throughout the world. The United Nations International Year of Disabled People in 1981 marked a watershed in thinking and led to the World Programme of Action concerning Disabled People adopted by the UN in 1982. In essence, this international movement has changed the approach towards disability. Rather than being seen as a "personal" or "medical" problem which was the result of an individual's physiological, anatomical or psychological impairment and caused by disease, accidents or other "personal tragedies", it is now seen as a "social" problem whereby disability is caused by society's failure to adapt itself to the different ways in which those with disabilities accomplish activities.

1.17   Three key principles have informed recent international legislation and practice:

- The recognition that disability is a social rather than a medical issue.

- The adoption of a civil rights perspective, and

- The recognition of equality as a key principle of the human rights approach.

1.18   These principles have come together in the United Nations' Standard Rules on the Equalisation of Opportunities for Persons with Disabilities which were adopted in 1993 in consultation with organisations representing people with disabilities. The Rules while not legally binding on UN member states do reflect current thinking about disability policy and are intended to provide the basic international legal standard for programmes, laws and policy on disability in the coming years. They are aimed at ensuring that all people with disabilities can exercise the same rights and obligations as other people. To do so, they set out a list of preconditions for equal participation, including awareness raising, support services, and specific targets for equal participation, including access to the physical environment, access to information and communications, public transport, education, employment, income maintenance, family life, culture, recreation and sports and religion. They also set out specific implementation measures and monitoring mechanisms.

1.19   The Commission sees the UN Standard Rules as being a key document in the future development of disability policy and many of the recommendations in this report are aimed at implementing them. It welcomes the change of emphasis away from a medical approach to disability towards a more social approach, especially when a medical or diagnostic approach ignored the imperfections and deficiencies of surrounding society. A given level of impairment or degree of restriction does not necessarily lead to disadvantage: it is the societal response (in terms of attitudes and expectations as well as the services and facilities made available) which has an important impact on the extent to which impairment or disability lead to disadvantage. The impairment may be caused by physical, mental, intellectual, emotional or sensory factors. The fact, for example, that many public buildings are inaccessible to people with mobility impairment is not something which is caused by the impairment. It is perfectly possible to construct buildings which are readily accessible to people who use wheelchairs or have other types of mobility impairment. Inaccessible buildings are caused by society's decision, whether informed or uninformed, to build structures in such a way that they will not be accessible to some people.

1.20   After various stops and starts over the years, the Irish disability movement restarted again towards the end of the UN Decade of Disabled Persons (1981-1990). As the European movement of disabled people grew, more Irish people with disabilities became aware of it and wanted to be a part of it. This led to the establishment and growth of organisations controlled (i.e. with over 51% of their membership) by people with disabilities.

1.21   The core message of politically active groups such as the Forum of People with Disabilities, the Centre for Independent Living and the Advocacy Ireland Movement was and continues to be heard both by the media and by policy makers.

1.22   At the European Non-Governmental Organisation (NGO) level members of various Irish NGOs have contributed at the highest level to the many debates that take place on disability issues. One of the highlights for the Irish disability movement was the impact made by the Irish representatives at the first European Disabled People's Parliament held in Brussels in 1993 and co-chaired by an Irish person. Of the 60 speakers who contributed to the debate that day

14 were Irish, and 34 Irish delegates were among the attendance of 500 people with disabilities.

1.23   The recommendations in this report must also be seen against the background of overall developments in Ireland, in particular the development of measures which recognise the importance of equality and equity. Included in those are measures to deal with poverty as well as efforts to improve the delivery of services to people who need them.

1.24   The Commission welcomes and strongly supports the establishment of a representative Council for the Status of People with Disabilities. It recognises the need to allow the Council to establish itself and to develop its own priorities and ways of working and believes that it will fulfil a central role in lobbying for the implementation of the Commission's recommendations. The Commission recommends that the Department of Equality and Law Reform should provide ongoing core funding at a level appropriate to the importance of the task facing the Council and which takes account of the additional costs which arise in respect of disability, for example, sign language interpreters, brailling, transport and so on. We wish the Council and all its members every success in their work.

1.25   The establishment of the Department of Equality and Law Reform is a significant indicator of the Government's recognition of the importance of equality. This is also recognised in the "Equal Participation" section of the Programme for Government - A Government of Renewal - which states that the Government regards "the work of the Commission for the Status of People with a Disability as being fundamentally important" and commits the Government to taking "specific action to end discrimination and to ensure equal opportunity for participation by all our people in Irish life".

1.26   In particular, the Government has committed itself to introduce a Disabilities Act "to set out the rights of persons with a disability, together with the means of redress for those whose rights are denied". The Government will also "put in place mechanisms for full and equal participation by every citizen with a disability in every aspect of our economic and social life".

1.27   The importance of equality has also been emphasised in a report from the National Economic and Social Forum on Equality Proofing Issues which found that people with disabilities are discriminated against in terms of rights and opportunities which other people take for granted. The Commission strongly endorses the NESF recommendations on "equality proofing" as it refers to people with disabilities. The Commission believes that there is an urgent need for the Government to adopt a policy of "disability proofing" legislation and any public policy initiatives. It recommends that the Minister for Equality and

Law Reform should bring proposals to Government within six months aimed at securing agreement to adopting a policy of "disability proofing".

1.28 Given the connection between poverty and disability, the Government's commitment to draw up a National Anti-Poverty Strategy to address all aspects of poverty and social exclusion is also relevant. Under the Strategy, all government departments and state agencies will be expected to include the reduction and prevention of poverty as key objectives in the development and implementation of their policies and programmes. They will also be required to consult and involve people affected by poverty in this process. As a person with a disability stated: "if you are poor you are likely to be disabled, and if you are disabled you are likely to be poor." Disability is a cause of poverty and social exclusion and it is important that specific measures to respond to the needs of people with disabilities are included in the Anti-Poverty Strategy.

1.29 The Programme for Competitiveness and Work, published in February 1994 contains an important commitment to people with disabilities where it states that:

"The report of the recently-established Commission on the Status of People with Disabilities will be considered in consultation with the social partners with a view to effecting a real advance in the position of people with disabilities in all aspects of life".

1.30 One of the most important facts about the Commission itself is that almost two-thirds of its members are people with disabilities or are carers of, or members of families of, people with disabilities. In their meetings and deliberations over the last three years, they have learned a lot about disability, the many forms it can take and the many hardships that can be imposed on those affected. Those members who have been previously involved in other disability groups readily admit that they, too, have learned a lot. All these experiences underline the Commission's approach to its task and its findings.

1.31 The Commission decided a number of issues early on and adopted guiding principles for its work. Among the issues decided was to use the term "people with disabilities" rather than terms which have been used in the past such as "the disabled" or "the handicapped". It does so in order to emphasise the point that people with disabilities are people first and foremost.

1.32 For the purpose of its work, the Commission understood the term "people with disabilities" to include children and adults who experience any restriction in their capacity to participate in economic, social or cultural life on account of a physical, sensory, learning, mental health or emotional impairment.

1.33   It also decided that it should make recommendations for all people with disabilities rather than attempt to divide them up according to types of disability. In doing so, the Commission fully recognises the specific needs of particular groups but is seeking to address the common sense of exclusion experienced by all people with disabilities. The Commission was also particularly mindful of doubly disadvantaged groups, such as women, children or Travellers with disabilities. It was also conscious of the fact that there is inequality and discrimination between groups of people with disabilities, some of whom for reasons of numbers or history are able to exert greater influence than others. For this reason, too, the Commission has adopted the approach of making recommendations as relevant as possible to all people with disabilities.

1.34   The three guiding principles adopted by the Commission to inform its work were:

- Equality

- Maximising Participation

- Enabling Independence and Choice

1.35   The key principle, the principle which underlies all the recommendations in this report, is the principle of equality. People with disabilities must be recognised and treated as having equal status with all other citizens. The State should provide for programmes of affirmative action and positive discrimination to address the past inequalities experienced by people with disabilities. Equal status can only be achieved if the rights of people with disabilities are upheld.

1.36   It is important to explain what we mean by equality. There are many ways in which equality can be understood, ranging from formal legal equality, to equality of opportunities, to equality of status at all levels of Irish life. Formal legal equality would simply ensure that all existing formal discrimination against people with disabilities was removed. This is obviously a precondition for equality but it is only a beginning.

1.37   There must also be equality of opportunity so that people with disabilities can participate in education, employment, and all other walks of life on an equal basis. This could involve measures to encourage people with disabilities to participate in education, sport, or cultural activities, or disability and equality training for people working in public services. But equality of opportunity would still not ensure equality of status.

1.38   To ensure that people with disabilities have equal status and are widely represented at all levels of Irish life will require affirmative action. Government must take the lead in this but every other sector of Irish life, including local authorities, churches, public bodies, employers, trade union and sectoral organisations, non-governmental, voluntary and community organisations and individuals must recognise that the existing exclusion of people with disabilities from so many aspects of Irish life impoverishes all of us. Examples of affirmative action, or positive discrimination, could include training policies to develop senior management skills among employees with disabilities, or university access programmes for students with disabilities to enable them to participate on equal terms in the university system.

1.39   The second principle - maximising participation - means that people with disabilities have the right to participate in all areas of Irish life to the fullest extent possible, and that individually and collectively (and where appropriate, their families and friends) they have the right to influence decisions which affect their lives. It also means that in the course of all policy making, the State should have regard to the needs and interests of people with disabilities.

1.40   The third principle - enabling independence and choice - means that people with disabilities have the right to be able to achieve their full potential. They have the right to make their own decisions and choices regarding the conditions of life best suited to their circumstances. They also have the right to quality services which meet their needs at all stages of life and they must not be dependent on charity or voluntary effort.

1.41   The State must acknowledge its responsibility to ensure equality of status. In particular, it must assume special responsibility for marginal or vulnerable groups of people with disabilities, and support them, their families and friends to the extent that they cannot do so for themselves.

1.42   The Commission proposes a wide range of measures to ensure that people with disabilities become full participants in society, independent and, above all, equal. It puts forward a detailed plan for the overall structures required to achieve that aim as well as specific recommendations on all aspects of life. When implemented, these recommendations will transform the lives of very many people.

1.43   Recommendations on overall government policy and new structures for state services are outlined in detail in the next section of this report along with costings for all the Commission's proposals. The following section, Part 3, addresses the economic issues raised by disability while Part 4 deals with specific areas of social and civil rights for people with disabilities. Part 5 covers the issues affecting those people with disabilities who are particularly vulnerable and Part 6 covers research. The Appendices include further details about specific aspects raised in the body of the report.

1.44   Arising from its work, the Commission concluded that there are a number of issues on which it is necessary to have minimum ethical standards, based on respect for human dignity and a safeguarding of individual rights, particularly in the areas of medicine, biology, biotechnology, law and administration. The Commission did not consider that such matters came properly within its terms of reference. It recommends that the Government should take appropriate steps to have such matters addressed at an early date.

1.45   Throughout this report, the Commission's intention is that where people with disabilities are mentioned, this will include parents and families of people with disabilities when appropriate.

1.46   This is an ambitious report which, when the recommendations are implemented, should change the world for many people with disabilities, including their families and carers. That is no less than people with disabilities deserve and what they, as equal citizens of this state, are entitled to as of right.

THE COMMISSION'S RECOMMENDATIONS

The Legal Status of People with Disabilities

1. Definitions of disability should use language which reflects the right of people with disabilities to be treated as full citizens: all definitions of disability should be reviewed and inappropriate and offensive language replaced. **(2.2)**

2. The Government should

    • propose that a non-discrimination clause in relation, inter alia, to disability is included in the revision of EU Treaties

    • ensure that the EU's power to provide for, and to take legislative action in relation to, disability issues is clarified. **(2.5)**

3. The Government should support the European Commission Resolution, proposed in its Communication on Equality of Opportunity for People with Disabilities. **(2.6)**

4. The Commission supports the majority recommendation of the Review Group on the Constitution that the following be added to Article 40.1:

    'No person shall be unfairly discriminated against, directly or indirectly, on any ground such as sex, race, age, disability, sexual orientation, colour, language, culture, religion, political or other opinion, national, social or ethnic origin, membership of the travelling community, property, birth or other status' **(2.7)**

5. The Commission endorses the recommendations of the Review Group in relation to personal rights. **(2.8)**

6. The Commission welcomes the Review Group's conclusion that the European Convention on Human Rights and Fundamental Freedoms and other international human rights conventions be drawn upon in the area of rights where:

    (a) the rights are not expressly protected by the Constitution;

    (b) the standard of protection of such rights is superior to those guaranteed by the Constitution;

    (c) the wording of a clause of the Constitution protecting such right might be improved and fully supports the Review Group's view that this requires a section by section analysis of the fundamental rights provisions of the Constitution. **(2.9)**

7.   The Commission supports the majority recommendation of the Review Group that a Human Rights Commission should be established to maintain an overview of the extent to which human rights are protected at both the constitutional and legal levels, to assess the adequacy of this protection and to make recommendations to Government for the better protection of these rights, as appropriate. **(2.10)**

8.   Article 42 of the Constitution should be amended to include

- the right to education

- equality within education

- education at all levels. **(2.12)**

9.   A Disabilities Act should be introduced which sets out the rights of people with disabilities and means of redress for those whose rights are denied. The Act should outlaw all discrimination against people with disabilities and should require public and private bodies, employers and educators to make reasonable accommodation to meet their specific needs. **(2.14 - 2.16)**

10.   Pending the implementation of a Disabilities Act, the outline principles, including definition of disability, of such an Act which are set out in this Report should be reflected in the proposed Employment Equality and Equal Status legislation. **(2.20)**

11.   All Government Departments should review the definitions of disability in legislation under their respective remits. **(2.28)**

Policy Development and Implementations

12.   The Department of Equality and Law Reform should be given prime responsibility for the development, monitoring, co-ordinating and implementation of policy for people with disabilities and should be given the necessary resources for its tasks. **(3.6 & 3.7)**

13.   A Disability Equality Unit should be established within that Department headed by an official at Assistant Secretary level to:

- provide a focal point for disability equality policy and legislation development

- operate an interdepartmental co-ordinating mechanism

- monitor the implementation of government decisions in relation to disability policy

- monitor the achievement of the quota for the employment of people with disabilities in the public sector. (3.7)

14. The Department of Health should be renamed the Department of Health and Social Services. (3.8)

15. Health Boards should be described as Health and Social Service Authorities with appropriate changes in their internal structures. (3.8)

16. An interdepartmental committee should be established at a senior level, under the aegis of the Department of Equality and Law Reform, to co-ordinate government strategy for people with disabilities. (3.9)

17. Each government department should carry out a physical access review and plan to ensure, within five years, that all their premises are accessible to people with disabilities. (3.10)

18. Government Departments and State agencies should provide disability awareness training for all staff. (3.11)

19. A National Disability Authority (NDA) should be established, reporting to the Department of Equality and law Reform. Its key functions would be:

- to monitor compliance with the recommendations of this Commission and other relevant EU and international agreements that have been accepted by government

- to serve as a national focal point to co-ordinate disability policies

- to undertake and commission research on disability issues

- to advise on and develop standards in relation to disability programmes and services

- to require the creation of appropriate standards for services provided to people with disabilities and to ensure their observance

- to monitor and evaluate programmes and services for people with disabilities

- to provide grievance and redress procedures

- to publish an annual report to be laid before each House of the Oireachtas and special reports as considered necessary

- to provide a Disability Support Service at local level

- to organise Community Acton Plans at local level. (3.12 - 3.14)

20.   Membership of the NDA should be balanced and representative. At least 60% of the membership should be people with disabilities or their families. (3.15 - 3.16)

21.   The NDA should co-ordinate the development of local Community Action Plans. (3.17 - 3.22)

22.   Local planning groups should include users and carers and should consult widely with users and carers in the community before drawing up the plans. (3.21)

23.   The role of the National Rehabilitation Board will need to be reviewed in the light of the Commission's recommendations. (3.23 - 3.27)

24.   Non-governmental and voluntary organisations may need to re-evaluate their current structures and functions and to consider how closer working relationships and even merging with similar organisations may help them to provide the range of services required. (3.31)

25.   Services to people with disabilities should have in-built systems of quality assurance, continual dialogue with users, and performance feedback. (3.35)

26.   The NDA should draw up guidelines for statutory and non-statutory organisations on effective ways to involve people with disabilities in all aspects of service planning and delivery. (3.39)

27.   Each statutory organisation should include a set of objectives for involving people with disabilities as part of their annual targets. (3.40)

28.   People with disabilities should be directly represented on relevant boards. (3.40)

Delivering The Necessary Services

29.   A Disability Support Service (DSS), which would be the focal point of collection and distribution of information, should be established, and a national network of Disability Resource Centres set up. The Resource Centres would be a simple point of contact for information, advice, support and advocacy. Support Co-Ordinators would be trained to guide individuals or their families through the range of services they might need at different stages in their life. The Disability Support Service would be accountable to the National Disability Authority. (4.3)

30. People with disabilities should be included in preparing, monitoring and evaluating information. (4.5)

31. An assessment of needs should be made at the onset of disability, resulting in a Statement of Needs which identifies the full spectrum of services required by the person concerned from a range of agencies, as well as their financial needs. (4.6)

32. Education and training in self-advocacy should form an integral part of the curriculum followed by people with disabilities. (4.7)

33. Independent advocacy services should be mandatory in residential care settings or similar services. (4.7)

34. The Disability Support Service should have two main components - Support Coordinators and Resource Centres. It should provide outreach activities and should utilise existing structures, personnel and other resources, where possible. (4.9)

35. Support Coordinators should be a valuable source of information to statutory and non-statutory bodies in relation to local needs and adequacy of services. They should be represented on Community Planning Groups. (4.14)

36. Programmes to train Support Coordinators should be provided through third level colleges. (4.16)

37. An independent evaluation of the Support Co-ordinatior's function should be carried out after two years. (4.17)

38. In addition to providing up-to-date information on the services available, Resource Centres would provide access to the Internet and to Handynet, the computerised database on technical aids and appliances. (4.19)

39. The right to information should be included in legislation relating to all public services. (4.23)

40. The obligation to provide accessible information on a proactive basis should be included in conditions governing public funding to non-statutory organisations. (4.23)

41. Assessments should go beyond a medically based procedure to a comprehensive, multi-disciplinary, person-centred assessment of disability, utilising self-assessment to the maximum extent possible. (4.30)

42. Measures should be undertaken to harmonise assessment of eligibility. These include the carrying out of assessment by a single agency and the introduction of a 'passport system' whereby qualification for one payment or service would lead to automatic entitlement to a range of other benefits and services. In order to achieve this, an inter-Departmental working group should be set up comprising senior representatives from the Revenue Commissioners and Departments of Health, Social Welfare and Education by the Minister for Equality and Law Reform. **(4.32 & 4.33)**

43. It is the Commission's view that in relation to each person with a disability the following system should be in place: there should be a new Assessment of Needs process, underpinned by law, with adequate arrangements made for its enforcement and monitoring and for an appeals procedure, and it should lead to a Statement of Needs. **(4.34)**

44. A person with a disability who requires an assessment of needs should be able to arrange it directly or with the assistance of the Disability Support Service. **(4.35)**

45. The end result of the assessment process should be a Statement of Needs. The prioritisation of needs should reflect the relative importance of each need in enabling the person to exercise his/her rights to participate to the fullest extent of his/her potential in all aspects of society. **(4.37 - 4.38)**

46. Advocacy services should be independent of service providers. **(4.47)**

47. Self advocacy should, where appropriate, be supplemented by the provision of citizen's advocacy. Funding for such a service should be provided by the Department of Health/Social Services. **(4.49)**

48. In certain situations, the provision of independent advocacy services should be mandatory. The provision of advocacy should be incorporated into any legislation dealing with particularly vulnerable people in residential settings. **(4.49)**

49. Funding should be provided by the Legal Aid Board to ensure that people with disabilities can employ an advocate to access expert legal representation, where necessary. **(4.49)**

50. Adequate appeals and complaints procedures should be established in respect of all services. **(4.50 - 4.51)**

Income and Disability

51. Further research should be carried out into income support provided to people with disabilities. **(6.5)**

52. A comprehensive system of income support for people with disabilities should be established which would apply national standards to payments. **(6.11)**

53. Two types of payments should be established:

- a payment to compensate for loss of income due to an incapacity for full-time work, or work to full potential, to be called a Disability Pension

- a graduated payment to meet the additional everyday costs associated with disability. This payment, which would be made irrespective of whether the person is at work or not, would be called the 'Costs of Disability Payment' **(6.12)**

54. The current disability benefit payment relates generally to illness rather than disability: it should be renamed 'Sickness Benefit'. People with disabilities who have been receiving this payment for two years or more should be given the choice of transferring to the new Disability Pension. **(6.14)**

55. All disability payments should be provided for in legislation to make it clear that there is a legal right to payment. **(6.15)**

56. The Disability Pension should be a pension payable to all people with disabilities, including those who live full-time or part-time in residential settings, who meet the qualifying conditions. **(6.17)**

57. The Disability Pension should not be means-tested: the qualifying conditions should protect against misuse. **(6.18)**

58. The rates of payment recommended by the Commission on Social Welfare should be achieved as a matter of priority in relation to all income replacement payments. **(6.19)**

59. Incentives to undertake employment should be available to people in receipt of disability pension, taking particular account of the extent to which a person is allowed to work without losing their entitlement and the extent to which the pension is reduced on the basis of such income. **(6.20)**

60. The State should, as a matter of principle, acknowledge its role of supporting people with disabilities and their families in meeting the additional costs arising from disability. **(6.25)**

61. The Department of Health and Social Services should introduce a variable and non-taxable Costs of Disability Payment where services are not or cannot be provided. (6.26)

62. There should be a nation-wide assessment procedure based on needs, and an independent appeals system in relation to such assessments (6.27)

63. The existing domiciliary care allowance should continue but its administration should be transferred to the Department of Social Welfare. (6.32)

64. A Carers Allowance should be paid to all carers. Persons caring for people who require full-time care or attention should be eligible for this payment. (6.34 - 6.35)

65. Persons qualifying for the domiciliary care allowance should automatically qualify for the Carers Allowance when the person being cared for reaches age 16 unless he/she goes into a full-time residential setting. (6.35)

66. Carers of more than one person or of a person in a five day residential setting should be paid on a pro-rata basis. (6.35)

67. Carers should not be disqualified from payment if they are engaged in other work outside their home. A certain level of earnings should be disregarded for qualifying purposes (6.35)

68. Carers should be credited with contributions which entitle them to social welfare benefits (6.35)

69. Subject to the introduction of the new Carers Allowance, existing tax allowances should be phased out for new claimants. (6.37)

70. The means test should be related to the carer's means only and should not include those of his/her spouse/partner. (6.38)

71. The Carers Allowance should not be taxable. (6.39)

72. Specific regard should be given by Government within any Anti-Poverty Strategy to combating the disproportionate impact of poverty on people with disabilities. (6.40)

Work and Training

73. Appropriate legislation, which should take account of the experience of similar legislation in other jurisdictions, should be introduced as soon as possible to outlaw discrimination on the grounds of disability in employment and training. (7.6)

74. The Minster for Equality and Law Reform should bring proposals to Government within six months aimed at securing agreement to a policy of 'disability proofing'. (7.7)

75. There should be increased Government expenditure on creating sustainable employment for people with disabilities. (7.8)

76. An appropriate proportion of the 1% employment levy should be allocated to the provision of work opportunities for people with disabilities. (7.9)

77. The Safety, Health and Welfare at Work Act should be properly enforced in such a way as to ensure that it is not used to impede the employment of people with disabilities. (7.10)

78. State and representative organisations in the agriculture sector should develop additional disability prevention programmes. (7.11)

79. Overall government responsibility for vocational training and employment of people with disabilities should be assigned to the Department of Enterprise and Employment.

That Department should produce a strategy paper on the employment and training of people with disabilities within six months of responsibility being assigned. (7.12)

80. The Department of Enterprise and Employment should arrange for the collection, collation and publication of comprehensive labour market statistics in respect of people with disabilities from an early date. (7.13)

81. The 3% quota of public service jobs reserved for people with disabilities should be fully attained within three years. There should be strict monitoring of quota compliance within the civil service and all statutory bodies and annual publication of the situation. (7.16)

82. All exchequer supported organisations established to provide services to people with disabilities should attain an 8% quota within four years. (7.17)

83. The Commission does not recommend the introduction of a mandatory quota in the private sector at this time but recommends that the position be reviewed after three years. Should less than 3% employment of people with disabilities have been achieved within that period, a mandatory quota should be introduced. (7.19 - 7.20)

84. In awarding business contracts, State bodies should, subject to compliance with national and EU regulations, give positive consideration to suppliers of goods or services who comply with the employment quota and/or the NRB Positive to Disability Scheme. (7.21)

85. Programmes such as disability awareness, access audits, disability equality training and disability prevention should be developed and implemented across all sectors of the economy. (7.22)

86. Funding for the NRB Employment Support Scheme should be expanded to achieve a minimum annual target of 500 jobs for people with disabilities over the next three years. (7.23)

87. Additional funding should be provided to the NRB Workplace and Equipment Adaptation Scheme with a minimum target of 500 jobs for people with disabilities over three years. (7.23)

88. IBEC and ICTU consultative committees on disability issues should seek to include people with disabilities. (7.25)

89. The framework of actions by social partners in the Declaration of European Businesses against Exclusion and in programmes such as HELIOS II economic integration should be supported. (7.26)

90. Social partners in national, sectoral or industrial agreements should implement an equality clause which promotes the recruitment and retention in employment of people with disabilities. (7.27)

91. The Department of Enterprise and Employment, in conjunction with the Co-Operative Development Unit in FÁS, should establish a pilot programme of worker co-operative employment by people with disabilities with a target of 100 jobs over the next three years. (7.28)

92. The Department of Enterprise and Employment in conjunction with the Department of Arts, Culture and the Gaeltacht, should initiate programmes to identify and promote employment opportunities for people with disabilities within these sectors. (7.29)

93. Government funding should be provided in the 1997 Budget to provide 500 additional sheltered workplaces to meet the current acute shortage of places. (7.31)

94. The Department of Enterprise and Employment should establish a resource to advise and assist agencies, communities and individuals to develop new employment opportunities, including sheltered workshops. Such support should include help with market research, product development, marketing, financial management. (7.32)

95. The status and rights of people with disabilities in sheltered work settings should be defined and appropriately protected. (7.33)

96. Standards should be introduced for the establishment and operation of sheltered workshops. (7.33)

97. All public employment services should be fully accessible to people with disabilities. (7.35)

98. Occupational guidance should be available to all people with disabilities who seek it. (7.35)

99. People with disabilities should be eligible, without restriction as to period of unemployment, to participate in all government employment measures directed at those who are unemployed. (7.36)

100. People with disabilities participating in government sponsored training programmes should be paid an appropriate training allowance and retain their secondary benefits. (7.42)

101. Matching funding for ESF-supported training should not be dependent on attracting persons who are availing of disability-related income. (7.42)

102. An immediate review of mainstream vocational training programmes should be undertaken with a view to maximising their accessibility to people with disabilities. (7.43)

103. The range of training choices for people with disabilities should be extended by inviting properly accredited training providers outside the specialist agencies to offer relevant and suitable programmes. (7.44)

104. New, innovative and more flexible models of training should be encouraged. (7.45)

105. There should be a greater concentration on job placement activity. (7.45)

106. Priority might be given to training which integrates people with and without disabilities (7.46)

107. Employer-based training models should be further developed. (7.47)

Insurance

108. The Ombudsman's office should investigate, and publish its report, before the end of July, 1997, on any loading by insurance companies of drivers with disabilities.

109. Legislation should be introduced in respect of the following:-

(i) An insurer should not discriminate against any person or group of people with a disability on the basis of their disability, when quoting for or issuing insurance cover, provided, however, that cover for specific disabilities and diseases may be excluded or provided subject to a higher charge, and benefits with respect to specific disabilities and diseases may be limited in amount,

(ii) An insurer should not discriminate against any individual, company or body when quoting for or issuing insurance cover for any event involving people with disabilities, provided, however, that cover may be excluded or provided subject to a higher charge,

(iii) An insurer should not discriminate against any individual, company or body when quoting for or issuing motor insurance, provided, however, that cover for specific disabilities and diseases may be excluded or provided subject to a higher charge, and benefits with respect to specific disabilities and diseases may be limited in amount, if the party providing insurance cover can establish the permissibility of such an exclusion, higher charge or limitation.

For purposes of establishing the permissibility of any exclusion or limitation, the party providing insurance must establish by clear and convincing evidence that the exclusion, higher charge, or limitation: **(1)** is not based on stereotype or prejudice; **(2)** is supported by sound and current actuarial data; and **(3)** is necessary to the realisation of a fair and reasonable rate of return on investment by the party providing insurance. **(8.7)**

Access

110. A national committee, resourced by the Department of the Environment, should be set up to develop policy and practice and to monitor progress in relation to the universal right of access to the built and external environments. **(9.18)**

111. The Department of the Environment should ensure that the universal right of access for all citizens becomes the over-arching principle which guides all relevant legislation, policy and practice in Ireland. The planning laws, fire regulations, health, safety and welfare legislation and all other legislation and guidelines which refer to any aspect of the built and/or external environments should also be reviewed by the Department from this perspective. **(9.19)**

112. The Building Regulations, 1991 should be reviewed in the Department of the Environment to:

- eliminate inconsistencies from the Technical Guidance Documents which work to the detriment of people with disabilities

- ensure that each local authority establishes an efficient building control department with responsibility for implementing the Building Regulations (and the Road Traffic Acts) fully and immediately

- make building inspections mandatory

- ensure that Part M is enforced vigorously. **(9.20)**

113. The Department of the Environment should bring forward legislation to introduce access certificates, along the lines of existing fire certificates, specifying that buildings are safe and appropriate for use. **(9.21)**

114. The proposed Disabilities Act should ensure that all premises in public ownership or open to the public in any way (including employees and customers) and the services and facilities they contain should become accessible to all citizens over a short time scale. **(9.22)**

115. The Department of Justice should also propose amendments to all legislation pertaining to the granting of licences to premises open to the public - including licences to places of entertainment and public assembly, public houses and restaurants - to require the District Court to have regard to the adequacy of access by people with disabilities. **(9.23)**

116. The Department of Equality and Law Reform should introduce Equal Status legislation concerning access to goods, facilities and services as soon as possible, ensuring that the legislation and any accompanying regulations and/or guidelines define what is reasonable and what constitutes undue difficulty in such a way as to minimise derogations which mitigate against the universal right of access. **(9.24)**

117. The Department of the Environment should introduce a public awareness campaign to educate all citizens about the universal right of access. **(9.25)**

118. The Royal Institute of Architects of Ireland and the Society of Designers in Ireland should ensure that the universal right of access becomes a key criterion in all their courses, competitions and activities. **(9.26)**

119. FÁS should give consideration to extending its training for building control personnel to other interested participants, particularly facilitating people with disabilities to become involved. Training on access issues, starting from the principle of the universal right of access of all citizens, should be included on all vocational training courses, including in-service and continuing training, for design and building management professionals, such as planners, architects, engineers, fire/safety officers, interior designers, graphic designers, building managers and all allied service providers. **(9.27)**

120. The Department of the Environment should seek authorisation from Rehabilitation International to award the International Symbol of Access. That Department should draw up, in consultation with appropriate bodies, clear criteria and conditions governing the award of the Symbol. The scheme should then be relaunched, with all previous recipients invited to re-apply. **(9.28)**

121. State funding mechanisms, including the National Lottery, should introduce accessibility to all citizens as a key criterion for the projects they fund. **(9.29)**

122. The Department of the Environment should introduce legislation to regulate and enforce standards for roads, pavements, parkways, signage, etc. **(9.31)**

123. The prohibition of parking on pavements should be rigorously enforced and planning permission should be required for placement of street furniture. Local authorities should ensure that all pavements are dished and have tactile paving by the year 2000. Where pedestrian zones are created using cobblestones, a smooth path should also be provided. Wheelchair users should be entitled to use bicycle lanes. **(9.32)**

124. Each local authority should employ a Local Access Officer to co-ordinate and promote access activities in their areas. **(9.33)**

125. The formation of an umbrella organisation for local access groups should be facilitated. Local Access Officers should support groups with training, technical information, advice on campaigning and group development. **(9.35)**

126. Local authorities should provide funding for local access groups and consult with access groups throughout the construction of new developments in the built and external environments. **(9.36)**

127. The Department of the Environment should fund local authorities to improve accessibility in their areas on foot of agreed community based action plans. **(9.37)**

Health

128. Hospitals and other settings in which services are provided should be accessible externally and internally. **(10.5)**

129. Relatives of people with disabilities who are attending a specialist service which is a long distance from their home should receive support in making regular visits to them. This is especially important in relation to children with disabilities. Such support may include free travel, crèche facilities, etc. **(10.8)**

130. Ambulances for both routine and emergency admissions should be equipped to transport all persons including those in electric wheelchairs. **(10.8)**

131. When a diagnosis, the impact of which is disabling is being given to a person, doctors should be required to advise the individual, or their family as appropriate, of the Disability Support Service and the location of the nearest Resource Centre. A hospital based key worker should be allocated to each person who can facilitate communications between hospital staff, family and the person with a disability. This key worker would also be responsible for making arrangements to inform all relevant community services prior to the person's discharge. **(10.9)**

132. Close liaison is required between hospital maternity units and all community services for children with disabilities. The hospital key worker should ensure that on discharge, parents of a child with a disability are allocated a key worker in their local Health Board to facilitate the effective delivery of services. **(10.10)**

133. Hospital staff at all levels should receive disability awareness training which addresses basic customer service and basic skills in dealing with people with disabilities. **(10.11)**

134. Special service programmes should be organised for people with disabilities to provide rapid and convenient access to relevant services designed to improve the overall quality and independence of their lives.

In doing so, the service should reach out in a pro active way to ensure that such a person is never inadvertently excluded because of his or her disability. **(10.12)**

135. All surgical and medical appliances should be supplied free of charge to holders of the Long Term Illness Card. Health Act procedures for the supply of technical aids should be redefined ensuring that there is an adequate definition for technical aids and equipment and standard procedures for assessing requirements. The provision in the Act which allows refunds for medical and surgical appliances should be implemented. Additional funding is required to ensure that there is a comprehensive supply of technical aids, as well as rapid, efficient assessment procedures. Money should also be provided by the Department of Health for repair services for technical aids. (10.16)

136. Research into the development of technical aids and equipment should be encouraged by government, and people with disabilities should be involved in the design of such research. (10.16)

137. Day activity centres should be further developed nationwide on a permanent basis with appropriately trained staff and access to all modern therapies, including music, art, drama and alternative therapies like aromatherapy and reflexology etc. (10.17)

138. The present home help scheme should be extended to provide more comprehensive care, including personal care as well as household duties and care at unsociable hours, where that is needed. Home help assistants should receive a basic training which includes disability awareness training as well as education about proper personal care assistance. (10.20)

139. Respite care services should be expanded for persons with physical and/or sensory disabilities. (10.21)

140. The Department of Health should develop minimum standards for respite care facilities and ensure that all new and existing units comply with those standards. (10.21)

141. Personal assistance services should be provided for people with significant physical disabilities. (10.22)

142. Further ongoing support and development of peer counselling and peer support services for deaf people should be given by the Departments of Health and Social Welfare. (10.22)

143. Additional revenue funding should be provided over a five-year period to address current shortfalls in services for people with disabilities including:

- day services
- therapy services such as occupational therapy, speech therapy, and physiotherapy
- respite care
- personal assistant services for people with severe disabilities
- peer counselling and peer support
- counselling including genetic counselling
- residential care **(10.23)**

144. GP premises should be adapted where necessary to make them accessible to people with disabilities. The cost of such adaptation could be met from the general practice development fund and the indicative drug target scheme. The practice of having specialist outpatient clinics in general practice settings should be promoted and expanded. (10.24)

145. Units specialising in continuing therapeutic care for people who have been discharged from medical rehabilitation centres (e.g., for paraplegia due to road traffic accident) should be developed throughout the country. Such units would be staffed by teams consisting of physiotherapists, occupational therapists, nurses and social workers, who would have ongoing supervision from the relevant specialised centre from which a patient had returned. In the central unit they would have regular refresher courses, training in new techniques, and opportunity to familiarise themselves with the individual treatment needs of any patient destined to return to their area. (10.25)

146. The training of health care staff should include a comprehensive disability awareness module designed in consultation with the Council for the Status of People with Disabilities. (10.26)

147. National standards should be set by the Department of Health for services provided to persons with a disability in the community. These should apply to medical, nursing, and paramedical staff. A review of selection criteria for health care training should be undertaken with an increased emphasis on choosing candidates with interpersonal skills: this should involve assessing attitudes and personality via an interview prior to selection. A postgraduate course for medical and paramedical personnel should be devised to improve their communications with people with disabilities. (10.27)

148. General practitioners and other community care personnel should receive up-dated training in screening and detection of persons at risk. (10.28)

149. Genetic counselling services should be made available nationwide as a matter of urgency. (10.29)

150. Ways of maximising choice of service should be examined. For example, people with disabilities or their carers could be given control, either direct or indirect, of part or all of their allocation of resources for the purchase of services. (10.30)

151. Case conferences concerning a person with a disability should include the person and his/her family, as appropriate, as well as professionals from community and hospital services. (10.31)

152. Medical and paramedical education should actively address patients' rights. The right to hear one's diagnosis in a sensitive and humane manner should be recognised. Medical personnel should be obliged to inform patients of all significant effects of therapy, including pharmaceutical preparations, surgical and investigative procedures, electroconvulsive shock therapy and psychological interventions. (10.32)

153. All persons, having been fully informed of their rights, may refuse to undergo treatment. This right of refusal must be respected by professionals and such a refusal should not interfere with the right of people to receive any other form of recommended treatment to which they give informed consent.

The Department of health should issue a code of practice to deal with situations where it is legally possible to institute treatment without consent. Legal safeguards should exist to prevent abuse of people receiving such treatment. (10.33)

154. Patients must give full and free consent before participating with doctors/nurses in medical tutorials, examinations or case conferences. (10.34)

155. No person should be overlooked for treatment or have treatment delayed or curtailed because of a disability. (10.35)

156. Effective complaint procedures should be developed and operated by each Health Board. Rights Advisers should be employed in every psychiatric hospital and there should be a Patient Advocate, not employed by the Department of Health, in every hospital. (10.36)

157. The families of people who are mentally ill or experience emotional difficulties should be provided with counselling and education by the Health Boards. (10.39)

158. A sign language interpreter service should be available to facilitate deaf persons in accessing health services. (10.40)

159. Each Health Board should review existing levels of services with reference to the principles of equity, accountability and quality of service and draw up five year plans to provide comprehensive community-based services for people with disabilities. These plans should be submitted to the Minister for Health by July 1, 1997, for approval. (10.41)

160. The policy report for mental health services, Planning for the Future, and for mental handicap services, Needs and Abilities, should be reviewed urgently. (10.42)

161.   The government should implement forthwith its policy to appoint advisory committees to each health authority in line with the recommendation of the national health strategy. Such committees should comprise consumer groups including people with disabilities and should have access to senior management levels. (10.43)

162.   Complaints procedures should be developed and there should be a statutory obligation on each health authority to provide feedback on consumer opinions to the Minister for Health. (10.44)

163.   Health Boards should take a consistent approach to the changes expected of them as a result of the Health Strategy, to ensure an equitable service nationwide. (10.45)

Education

164.   The Department of Education should be the accountable authority in relation to all educational matters of concern to people with disabilities and their families. (11.5)

165.   The Commission asserts the following principles in regard to the education of every citizen with a disability. The Commission further asserts that the rights explicit and implicit in these principles should be incorporated in all education policy, and should be enshrined in any legislation:-

- Every child is educable. All children, including those with disabilities, have a right to a free and appropriate education in the least restrictive environment. Appropriate education for all children with disabilities should be provided in mainstream schools, except where it is clear that the child involved will not benefit through being placed in a mainstream environment, or that other children would be unduly and unfairly disadvantaged.

- Every individual has an equal right to educational provision, which will enable him or her to participate in all aspects of economic, social, cultural and political life, to the fullest extent of his or her potential.

- The unique needs of the individual person must be the paramount consideration when decisions are being made concerning the appropriate provision of education for that person. In so far as is practical a continuum of services must be available to meet those needs close to the person's home and family.

- It is the responsibility of the State to provide sufficient resources to ensure that pre-school children, children of school-going age and adults with disabilities have an education appropriate to their needs in the best possible environment.

- Parents have primacy in the decision-making process as soon as their child with a disability has been identified as having particular educational needs. They [and the child whenever appropriate] must be entitled to make an Informed choice on the educational placement of their child.

- There shall be an accessible appeals procedure on educational enrolment recommendations. This will have due regard for the rights of the child, the rights of the parents and the educational rights of other children.

- All schools have a responsibility to serve children with disabilities in the least restrictive environment. Each school plan must strive to make schools inclusive institutions. To facilitate inclusive education, due recognition must be given to the rights and needs of teachers for resources, initial education, and continuing professional development.

- Flexibility and formal linkages should be built into educational provision at local level. It must be a statutory duty of all existing or new management structures to secure access to high quality and appropriate education for all children and adults with disabilities.

- Priority should be given to the needs of people with disabilities, within the broad framework of educational provision, and this should be reflected in the allocation of resources. (11.8)

166. An inclusive Education Act should enshrine and stimulate further progress towards inclusion while increasing support to specialist schools. It should facilitate co-ordination and linkages between mainstream and specialist schools and between specialist vocational training centres and centres offering adult education opportunities. (11.10)

167. The Act should also set out clearly the entitlements of students and the rights of parents. (11.11)

168. All people with disabilities should be offered an appropriate education in the environment of their choice. The concept of an "appropriate" education needs to be clearly defined in legislation. In this regard, the Commission favours the definition of "appropriate" which is contained in the American Individuals with Disabilities Education Act (IDEA). It states that for a programme to be "appropriate" it must be based on and responsive to the child's individualised educational needs as identified in the evaluation process. The IDEA requires that a written Individual Education programme (IEP) is developed for the adult and child with disability. (11.12)

169. Legislation must create a strong presumption that students will be placed in the least restrictive environment. The onus of proof in demonstrating the inappropriateness of a placement in a mainstream school should be placed on the school authorities. It should be rebutted only by demonstrating objective

impossibility, or that such placement would not be in the best interests of the child, or that placement would unduly hinder the education rights of other children. (11.13)

170.   Legal provision is also required for individual assessments of need and the development of an individual education plan which would give effect to the student's educational requirements. This legal provision should take the form of a statutory instrument and should contain provision for enforcement. The individual plan should assess the resources required to meet the students' needs and make recommendations for placement. Assessments should be carried out by an independent agency, ideally under the auspices of the proposed Regional Education Boards, and should be holistic in nature. Education plans should be reviewed annually and revised in the light of a child's changing and developing needs.

The legal rights, roles and responsibilities of parents must be clearly outlined in relation to any assessment or decision-making process and should reflect the constitutional rights of parents in the matter of their child's education. (11.14)

171.   A second opinion should be available in relation to decisions about placements and an appeal to an independent body should be available to the parent, pupil or school authority. (11.15)

172.   Schools and educational establishments should be required to make every reasonable accommodation to meet the educational needs of a student, in line with the choice of the student, or where appropriate, the parents. The right to refuse entry must be allowed only in very exceptional circumstances: refusal should not be possible solely on the grounds of resources. (11.15)

173.   The National Disability Authority, in collaboration with the Department of Education, would be the appropriate body to monitor and enforce the disability provisions of the Education Act. (11.16)

174.   Local policy issues should, as far as possible, be decided locally, within the overall policy framework. The proposed Regional Education Boards will create greater opportunities for local planning and greater opportunities for parents and students with disabilities to influence the shape of local services. (11.17)

175.   Regional Education Boards should have a statutory duty to ensure that every child with special educational needs is provided with an appropriate education. They should be required to provide:

- assessment facilities
- access to independent appeals procedures in relation to placement recommendations;

- consultation with parents and children in the planning of local services;

- information to parents, people with disabilities, the Disability Support Service and the public about all aspects of services in the area. (11.18)

176. Parents should be acknowledged as full and equal partners throughout the educational process and be provided with guidance and support, full information about their child's progress, and be allowed to contribute meaningfully to it. (11.19)

177. Consultation with people with disabilities and their representative organisations should be a key feature of future policy formation. A permanent committee on the educational needs of children with disabilities should be established. (11.20)

178. The proposed permanent committee should have direct links with the Co-ordinating Group of Secretaries and the Council for the Status of People with Disabilities. (11.21)

179. The Education Act should require the Department of Education - and the Regional Education Boards when established - to draw up Community Education Plans to meet the needs of students with disabilities on a regional basis. The Act should also impose a legal obligation on the Department of Education through the Regional Education Boards to assess the education needs of all people with disabilities who request an assessment, including those who live in residential settings. (11.22)

180. The core provisions of the Community Education Plans should be contained in the Education Act and should include:

- Speech and occupational therapy;

- Physical education;

- Support and counselling for parents;

- Psychological support;

- Technical aids and supports;

- Communications support;

- School transport, including an escort where necessary;

- Classroom assistants;

- Resource and remedial teaching;

- Personal assistants. (11.23)

181. The Education Act should require the Department of Education (and Regional Education Boards) to take into account the needs identified in the assessment procedures in drawing up the Community Education Plans. The Department should also be statutorily required to take into account the needs identified in deciding both the level of funding and the type of services for which funding is provided. (11.24)

182. The school psychological service should be increased significantly in strength and its role and operation broadened. (11.26)

183. The provision of therapy supports should be a matter of right rather than choice if access to them is essential to enable a child to achieve his or her educational potential. (11.27)

184. Essential supports should be provided in a coherent and co-ordinated basis within each local area. Specialist support personnel should be brought together into cohesive local teams. They would provide information and support to local schools and teachers' centres as well as students and parents and assist in drawing up school plans for the inclusion of students with disabilities. There should be strong links and networking at local level between the teams and the local Disability Support Service. (11.28)

185. Education support services should be available to all children with disabilities and their families from the earliest possible point, namely the point of diagnosis of disability. The measures required to meet an individual's needs could be identified at the stage of the individual Needs Assessments. (11.29)

186. The provision of support services should be the subject of joint action between the Health Boards and the educational authorities. A technical aids and appliances' fund should be set up at local level, funded jointly by educational and health budgets, from which the necessary appliances would be purchased. (11.30)

187. Support teaching services - remedial, resource and visiting teachers - should be extended to cover all children with disabilities in both special and mainstream schools, especially in their early years when support and guidance is essential. Due recognition of the contribution of these teachers and appropriate time-tabling is recommended to allow them fulfil their roles. (11.31)

188. Where local school transport is not an option for a child with a disability, alternative supports must be provided. (11.32)

189. The present review of the school transport service offers an opportunity to examine imaginative possibilities for the provision of an integrated local

transport service which would provide accessible transport services in a local community. (11.33)

190.   Transport or alternative support should also be available to students who wish to advance to further education or third level education. (11.33)

191.   To accommodate students with disabilities in mainstream schools, curricula should allow for flexibility, additions and adaptations. Where necessary, students with disabilities in mainstream settings should have specially adapted teaching methods, materials, curricula and examination regulations. (11.34)

192.   The National Council for Curriculum and Assessment should establish curriculum development projects for pupils at primary and post primary levels. Special emphasis should be placed on education for creativity, appropriate testing and examination procedures, and upon adequate and appropriate extracurricular activities. (11.35)

193.   Curriculum flexibility is particularly important in second level education where the academic focus and the high level of emphasis on language skills can create difficulties for many students with disabilities. New models utilising specialist classes, special and mainstream schools and the sharing of school facilities are urgently needed so that all students are enabled to achieve a recognised educational qualification. (11.36)

194.   The curricular needs of all pupils in specialist settings should be reviewed, based on ages, abilities, needs and aspirations. (11.37)

195.   Special national schools should be reclassified as primary and post-primary schools to recognise the fact that students attend such schools up to the age of eighteen years. Post primary special schools should attract all of the facilities, improved teacher ratios, posts of responsibility, and additional capitation that applies to mainstream post primary schools. (11.38)

196.   In relation to assessment, greater flexibility is required from the State, individual schools and examining bodies in their approach to, and methods of, examining students with disabilities. A fair and appropriate system of examination testing and of assessment should be provided for the student with a disability. All examinations should be offered in a place and manner appropriate and accessible to people with disabilities. (11.39)

197.   A system of standards should be applied to all specialist schools. The option of access to mainstream certification should be available to those in specialist education settings. (11.40)

198.   A greater emphasis should be placed upon forming links between vocational training centres and local post primary schools. This is especially important for students whose abilities are more skill based than academically based. **(11.41)**

199.   The Department of Education should provide high quality, appropriate pre-school services to children with disabilities. Teaching personnel should have a background and training which equips them to respond to the particular needs of young children with disabilities. Every encouragement and practical support, including financial support, should be given to community playgroups and pre-school groups who wish to include young children with disabilities in their services. **(11.42)**

200.   The needs of the deaf child and his/her absolute right to a specialist education whether in a specialist school or a designated setting attached to a mainstream school should be respected. Adults who wish to have access to further education options through sign language should be enabled to have such educational options met at local level. **(11.44)**

201.   In order to remove the duality of the special and mainstream systems, a series of actions will be needed:

- possibility of enrolment in more than one school at any time;

- closer curriculum linkages with joint planning between specialist and mainstream schools for individual students;

- bridging the gulf between teachers in the separate systems;

- practical supports for closer linkages, such as flexible transport arrangements;

- a funding strategy in which funding is linked to the student rather than to any school.

Innovatory or pilot programmes should be initiated in a number of local areas in the short term to achieve the necessary linkages. **(11.45)**

202.   The development of the network of supports proposed in this report and in the report of the Special Education Review Committee (1993) will take some time to put in place. For these reasons, there is a need for a systematic plan to develop a clear specialist role for special schools in the longer term. That role will involve catering for children with very special needs who cannot be accommodated within the mainstream system. Work done in the specialist schools should be developmental, innovative and capable of dissemination to the wider educational community in order to facilitate greater levels of inclusion. **(11.46)**

203. To facilitate these specialist roles the schools concerned should have a core multi-disciplinary staff, which is free of the constraints imposed on staffing ratios by changing student numbers. It should be in the nature of the specialist role of these schools that numbers fluctuate as students move between them and the mainstream as individual needs change and develop. All specialist schools should be required to have in place a policy and a programme to support their students in linking into the wider community in all possible ways. **(11.47)**

204. The availability of a designated school should not be seen as justification for not spending resources to provide accessible transport or support services. The child's right to the least restrictive placement, and the parental right of choice cannot be frustrated on the grounds that a cheaper option exists.

An in-depth evaluation of the concept of designated school should be carried out before any further developments in this area occur. Local parents should be consulted fully if consideration is being given to the development of a designated school in an area. **(11.49)**

205. The Commission supports the general recommendation of the Report of the Committee on Access and Participation of Students with Disabilities in Higher Education that "there should be full integration of persons with disability in the higher education system, and that appropriate funding provisions should be put in place to support this policy". **(11.50)**

206. The Department of Education should fund pre-university and college education courses which prepare people with disabilities for university and third-level colleges. While such preparation may be achieved within secondary schools in the long-term, there is currently a substantial need for this service. **(11.51)**

207. The Commission commends the work presently being undertaken around the specific inclusion of adults with learning disabilities on a university campus. The development of research into the educational needs of people with learning disabilities, the development of appropriate curricula and teaching methods, and greater access over time by people with learning difficulties to different levels of education appropriate to their needs is essential. **(11.52)**

208. All initial and continuing teacher education programmes should include modules on meeting the needs of pupils with disabilities. Elements on disability awareness and appropriate curriculum design should be included. Sign language or braille should be taught as part of all teacher training courses. **(11.53)**

209. The specialist education element should be taught within the general context of child development and educational psychology. Specialist modules should incorporate obligatory components on the identification, assessment and teaching of pupils with disabilities and special educational needs. Emphasis should also be placed upon working with and including parents, special needs classroom assistants and visiting teachers, as well as on the principles of guidance and counselling. **(11.54)**

210. More advanced courses and more alternative methods leading to qualifications in aspects of specialist education are required. **(11.55)**

211. Induction programmes should be organised for any teacher, visiting teacher or special needs assistant who is taking up for the first time a post with defined responsibility for the teaching or care of children with special educational needs, whatever the stage of his or her career. **(11.56)**

212. All in-service courses supported by the Department of Education should have an input on disability awareness, as is the case with gender equality. In addition to in-service courses, booster courses and one-day conferences should be held regularly in order to give teachers the opportunity to update their skills and access to best practice. **(11.57)**

213. In-service education and training for guidance counsellors should be provided to ensure that they are aware of all of the options, including specialist training and further education facilities, that are accessible and available to young people with disabilities leaving school. **(11.58)**

214. Physical education teachers should be encouraged to develop alternative strategies and games that are inclusive of all the children enrolled in their school. **(11.59)**

215. More opportunities should be created for people with disabilities to become teachers in both specialist and mainstream schools. **(11.60)**

216. Entry procedures to teacher training courses for deaf candidates should use subject suitability as the criterion. Ability in the area of sign language and an aptitude for teaching should be central to selection for training. The teacher training course should meet the educational needs of deaf teachers and their students. **(11.61)**

217. One per cent of the education budget (i.e. approximately £20 million at current rates) of additional expenditure should be allocated annually to meet the educational needs of pupils/students with disabilities.

Funding should be linked to the student and should follow the student as he or she moves to appropriate educational settings. The level of funding or other supports must relate to need, rather than to diagnostic categories, since there is no necessary link between them. **(11.62 & 11.63)**

218. School managements should be encouraged to move towards inclusiveness by a range of incentives and supports which would enable them to develop programmes and support structures for inclusion. Support should not be provided in the form of non-specific grants: it should be given for specific planned reforms, development of materials, appropriate in-career programmes, and physical adjustments to buildings. School managements who make good progress towards being an inclusive school should be awarded a "Positive to Disability" symbol of excellence, analogous to the scheme for employers. **(11.64)**

Housing and Accommodation

219. The Department of the Environment should formulate and publicise in accessible form a policy on housing for people with disabilities. This would provide information for planners, consumers and housing suppliers about the situation and requirements of people with disabilities and the options available. **(12.10)**

220. As part of its policy formulation, the Department of the Environment should collate information about the demand for, and the take up of, housing for people with disabilities. It should commission further analysis of the 1996 assessment of housing needs to establish the requirements of people with disabilities and the reasons for the low level of assessed need to date. All future national assessments of housing needs by local authorities should explicitly address the housing requirements of those living long term in residential centres. **(12.11)**

221. Ongoing information on access features and the suitability of housing for people with disabilities should be made available by those involved in supplying housing whether in the commercial or non-profit sectors. People with disabilities should be invited to contribute to the reviews underway in the Department of the Environment on the various measures introduced under a plan for Social Housing. **(12.12)**

222. Data should be collected on the role of the non-profit and voluntary housing sector in meeting the requirements of people with disabilities and on the relative merits of the various models of support housing which are now operational. **(12.13)**

223. To enable this sector to make a greater contribution, adjustments should be made in the capital assistance available and a properly defined scheme of

funding for support housing services should be put in place. Funding from the Voluntary Capital Assistance Scheme should only be granted to housing agencies which are building to the standards of Lifetime Adaptable Housing. (12.14)

224. A policy of building Lifetime Adaptable Housing as the norm in all housing sectors should be adopted.

This new policy should be implemented through the assimilation of Part M of the Building Regulations into all other parts of the Regulations. An education and awareness programme should be put in place to promote understanding of the concept among developers, designers and builders. (12.15 - 12.16)

225. Standards for Lifetime Adaptable Housing should be phased in with the immediate adoption of those aspects of adaptability which are relatively easy to apply and are based on a greater awareness of design requirements. The next phase, the application of more adequate space standards for full Lifetime Adaptable Housing, should be provided for in legislation and become operational within three years. (12.17)

226. Section 23 type incentives should be adjusted to allow a higher rate of allowances (between 10% and 20%) for units which meet the Lifetime Adaptable Housing specifications. The financial incentives to seaside resorts should require a specified proportion of all eligible dwellings to be built in accordance with the new standards. (12.18)

227. In order to improve existing houses, the Disabled Person's Grant should be modified to cover up to 95% of approved costs. The grant should be extended to the occupants of new houses and to those renting in the voluntary/non-profit housing sector who have security of tenure. (12.19)

228. There should be greater uniformity in the implementation of the Disabled Person's Grant by housing authorities. Information about the grant and its appeals procedures needs to be made available more widely. (12.20)

229. Local housing authorities throughout the country should be proactive in building up a supply of suitable housing. Schemes now available under A Plan for Social Housing should be utilised in a strategic manner. (12.21)

230. Three new schemes should be put in place to improve the prospects of people with disabilities on low incomes of home ownership and to help offset the additional costs of suitable housing. Each of the proposals builds on an existing scheme.

- A new grant to incorporate the Disabled Person's Grant and the first time purchaser's grant should be introduced where a first home is being purchased by a person with a disability and where additional housing costs are likely to be incurred.

- The Shared Ownership System should be widened to allow house purchasers with a disability on low incomes to receive the enhanced first time purchaser's grant.

- A financing arrangement should be developed to allow approved voluntary and non-profit housing bodies to provide an equity sharing tenure based on a 50% ownership by people with disabilities on limited incomes. (12.22)

231. Statistics on the numbers of people with physical and sensory disabilities inappropriately placed in institutions should be compiled immediately. A plan of action to ensure that those inappropriately placed be moved to a more appropriate setting should then be put in place and no person with a physical or sensory disability should be inappropriately placed in these institutions in the future. (12.23)

232. A range of successful accommodation options already exists in very limited numbers which encourage a full and active lifestyle. These and other new and innovative options should be encouraged. (12.24)

233. Housing options for people with disabilities should include a mix of different arrangements. Single houses, houses capable of accommodating four or five people; bungalow units clustered together; a group of three or four town houses with a communal garden - all of these options must be included. They should be situated close to amenities and retail outlets in order to maximise independence and they must have the appropriate support staff. (12.26)

234. Consideration should be given to the special accommodation needs of people with disabilities and their partners. (12.27)

235. A review should be undertaken of people with disabilities in residential centres to establish accurately their numbers, locations and living conditions. There should also be a review of people on waiting lists for residential centres to see if these lists could be reduced substantially by the provision of other services. The information obtained from these reviews would also help the planning of housing and accommodation options for the future. (12.28)

236. Action should be taken to ensure that the rights of people living in residential centres are protected. The following are particularly recommended:

- All residential establishments should publish an operational policy.

- A Bill or Charter of Rights (see below) should set parameters for the operational policy.

- An Independent Ombudsman should oversee residential centres, resolve grievances and ensure that proper consideration is given to the views and concerns of residents. (12.29)

237.   Residents should be actively encouraged to participate in the running of residential centres and a target set of 50% representation by them or their advocates on management boards within five years. Residents should be trained in preparation for management roles and in the skills necessary to live independently. Disability equality training should be provided for residents, staff and management. (12.30)

238.   Income supports should be provided in a way which promotes autonomy and choice with payments made directly to individuals rather than to institutions. Payments should be clearly defined as between accommodation, personal assistance, and care elements. (12.31)

239.   People living in residential centres should have access to an Independent Living Fund which should be established to allow the employment of personal assistants and to train people with disabilities in the management of personal assistants. The Disability Support Service should also assist residents to obtain the best value and the most appropriate mix of services. (12.32)

240.   A Charter of Rights for residents of residential centres should contain the following essential elements:

- Specific provisions setting out the detailed services provided by the institution.

- Quality standards of services to which the person is entitled.

- The right to information and the manner in which that will be provided.

- The manner in which records will be maintained and the right of access to records.

- The right of access to complaint procedures and the manner in which the complaint procedures will operate.

- The right to an independent appeal.

- The right to advocacy and representation.

- The right to participate in management and monitoring, and

- A system of review and amendment of the Charter taking into account the views of service users. (12.33)

241.   A system of overseeing and monitoring of standards in residential accommodation should be set in place by the Departments of Health and Environment (to be reviewed by the National Disability Authority). (12.34)

Transport and Mobility

242.   All new and used rail rolling stock and road vehicles ordered for public transport (including those ordered by private operators) from January 1st, 1997 should be accessible to all users. The Government should take measures to ensure that no licences will be issued for the transportation of people unless these vehicles meet the accessibility criteria. In addition, at least 80% of all transport and transport services purchased by Health Boards from 1st January 1997 for transporting clients should be wheelchair accessible. (13.5)

243.   The Department of Transport, Energy and Communications should provide an information centre on the accessibility of all services. It should be available through a freephone number, on Aertel teletext and in alternative media to print. All terminals and stations should also provide visual, audio and, ideally, braille information on arrivals and departures as well as the accessibility of specific services. A clear map of stations or terminals and their facilities should be sited at their entrances and at ticket offices. The buildings, of course, should all be made fully accessible. (13.6)

244.   A public awareness programme as well as staff training programmes on customer care should be developed and implemented. (13.7)

245.   A National Mobility Training and Advice Centre should be established to offer advice on mobility aids for all categories of people with a disability as well as training and orientation for people with disabilities themselves. Local training could be sub-contracted out to non governmental organisations but minimum standards should be set by the National Disability Authority. Such training should include the use of public transport and the rules of the road to prepare a person with a disability for using whatever aid they require. (13.8)

246.   Community Action Plans should include a local structure for the planning and implementation of accessible transport services. (13.9)

247.   The Department of Social Welfare should introduce a standard Disabled Persons Public Transport Travel Pass which should automatically cover a companion and should not restrict days and times a person can travel on public transport. (13.11)

248.   The Mobility Allowance should be increased to a minimum of £40 per week and index linked. (13.12)

249. Every CIE, Bus Eireann and Dublin Bus depot should have at least one accessible bus by June 1, 1997. The Department of Transport, Energy and Communications should subsidise the additional cost of such vehicles: thereafter, the bus companies should bear the cost of replacement vehicles. Ireland should ensure that the forthcoming EU directive on buses and coaches requires them to be accessible to all citizens. **(13.21)**

250. The Department of Transport, Energy and Communications and Dublin Bus should provide the necessary funding to ensure a viable Omnilink pilot project by advertising and running it properly. Each should provide £250,000 towards the cost and the results of the pilot should be published. **(13.23)**

251. A limited amount of seating should be included in the design of bus shelters. In addition, there should be discussions with the Council for the Status of People with Disabilities about providing destination and timetable information in braille in shelters. Consideration should also be given to erecting bus shelters in rural areas. **(13.24)**

252. An adaptation programme should be started in 1997 to make school buses accessible to all students. EU funds should be sought for the programme which should be completed in five years. **(13.25)**

253. Research should be carried out into the possibility of using school buses outside times when they are required for transporting students. They could be used to take people with disability and others to day care centres, day activity centres, shops and so on. This research should examine the improvements in the quality of life that the use of these buses could bring to many individuals. The results should be published. **(13.27)**

254. Where possible, all transport which caters for children and/or adults with disabilities should have an escort on the bus as well as the driver. Both the escorts and drivers should be properly trained and have Garda clearance before they are employed. **(13.29)**

255. There are a number of other options for providing transport services for people with disabilities which could be examined. These include:

- Vantastic: set up in Dublin in 1995, this involves two accessible vans and eight trained drivers and can be booked for regular or one-off trips.

- Service Routes: bus services open to everyone but specially adapted for people with mobility impairments. Using smaller than average vehicles, the routes usually go into housing estates and up narrow roads. They could be of particular benefit to rural areas where the basic problem with public transport is its unavailability. Service routes could be set up as joint ventures between private operators and voluntary or statutory groups.

- Post Buses: these collect and deliver mail and carry passengers, using vehicles like estate cars, Land Rovers and mini-buses. They run on a published route and to a timetable and could also provide a valuable service for people in rural areas and people with disabilities if accessible vehicles were used.

- Social Car Schemes: they provide volunteer drivers (who receive a petrol allowance) for people with disabilities, usually for short trips. (13.30)

256.   The Council for the Status of People with Disabilities should investigate the feasibility of setting up, in conjunction with the Northern Ireland authorities, a Driver Assessment Centre to make available to people throughout Ireland the latest technology in these areas. (13.32)

257.   The present VAT and VRT rebates on cars for drivers with disabilities should be retained and the maximum rebate increased from the present limit of £7,500 and linked to the Consumer Price Index. (13.33)

258.   The medical criteria governing eligibility for drivers' concessions should be examined in consultation with the Council on the Status of People with Disabilities and the National Disability Authority. This examination should review the present regulations and bring forward proposals for future regulations. The Disabled Drivers Medical Board of Appeal, currently administered by the National Rehabilitation Board, should be continued. (13.34)

259.   The present disabled drivers badge should be replaced by one that is acceptable within the E.U. It should be issued to the driver concerned and should be transferable when travelling in a car other than his/her own.. (13.35)

260.   The Department of Social Welfare should replace the present motorised transport grants operated by the Health Boards with a new first-time grant for motorists with disabilities. This should:

- be payable to first time purchasers who qualify under the criteria governing eligibility for drivers with disabilities;

- be sufficient to cover 75% of the net cost of a standard new car (after rebates);

- restrict any means test to the driver only. (13.36)

261.   Present VAT and VRT rebates on cars for passengers with disabilities should be retained at the present limit of £12,500 and linked to the Consumer Price Index. (13.37)

262. The Commission welcomes the 1996 Finance Act amendment of the rule "that an adaptation of a car/van for the use of a disabled passenger must amount to 20% of its cost" to 10% of the original cost of the car and recommends that the percentage be reduced to zero over the next three years. Those not eligible under the criteria above should be entitled to a rebate of duty on 200 gallons of petrol/diesel in a calendar year on journeys on which they are a passenger, provided they are registered with the Council for the Status of People with Disabilities. (13.38)

263. The medical criteria governing eligibility for concessions to passengers should be examined in consultation with the Council for the Status of People with Disabilities and the National Disability Authority. A badge for passengers with a disability should be introduced for people who qualify under any of the above schemes and should be transferable to any car in which they are a passenger. (13.39)

264. The Department of the Environment should produce a three year plan for the introduction of country-wide regulations on street and local authority parking spaces for people with disabilities. They should cover the dimensions, number and siting of spaces and should exempt holders of the new badges for drivers and passengers with disabilities from payment of parking fees. Local authorities should provide a ratio of 1:25 of on street parking spaces for drivers/passengers with disabilities by the end of 1998. Penalties for improper use of these parking spaces should be severe and strictly enforced. All regulations introduced by the Department of the Environment should be compulsory on all local authorities. (13.42)

265. Planning laws should specify that a minimum of 1:50 parking spaces be set aside for drivers/passengers with disabilities in private developments. (13.44)

266. All local authorities should take cognisance of the needs of people with disabilities when issuing new licences. Taxi drivers should not be licensed without taking a training programme in the care of passengers with disabilities. (13.47)

267. All aircraft should have an onboard chair available to allow people with disabilities to access the facilities. All safety announcements on board planes are made by voice and some thought should be given by airlines to including people with a hearing impairment in these procedures. (13.50)

268. The completion of a medical form should not be requested of people with disabilities by airlines unless a person is undergoing medial treatment. Irish airlines should propose to IATA that separate forms be used for people with disabilities and for people suffering illnesses to ensure that only the

information required for ensuring a smooth passage for people with disabilities is requested. (13.53)

269.   All ferry terminals should be fully accessible. (13.54)

270.   Only ferries which are accessible to all should be licensed to carry passengers. (13.57)

Technology and Communications

271.   The Department of Social Welfare and the Department of Transport, Energy and Communications should introduce legislation to ensure access to assistive technology and telecommunications, in line with the UN Standard Rules. Access this technology should include financial access. (14.7)

272.   A single existing agency should be responsible for all assistive technology and for disseminating information about new technological developments. Services should continue to be provided by a mixture of state and voluntary organisations but voluntary sector services must be properly funded and regulated.

   This agency should also provide an adequate assessment service of the most appropriate technical aids for people with disabilities. (14.8 - 14.9)

273.   The overall agency should set up nominated assessment centres and support them with appropriate funding for equipment, staff and training. There should also be a county network of 'feeder' or 'outreach' centres to provide primary assessments and training. All assessment must be based on a person centred approach. (14.11)

274.   The Department of Transport, Energy and Communications should ensure that all companies licensed to provide telephone services should provide text telephone, a relay service and other special or adapted equipment required by people with disabilities. These services should not cost more than conventional telephones. All new public payphones should be accessible to everybody, including people in wheelchairs. (14.14)

275.   Drivers with disabilities who qualify for concessions should also qualify automatically for free mobile phone rental and a number of call units to cover any emergencies when they are travelling alone. (14.15)

276.   RTE and other television stations with national licences should expand the number of hours and the range of programmes which are sub-titled. There should be a minimum of 50% of all programming hours captioned by 1998

and this should increase to all programming as soon as possible afterwards. (14.16)

277. Interpreting support should be available in public services such as hospitals, garda stations, courts and schools. Most information and public documents are available only in written text, with major consequences for people with sight impairments. Reader Services should be made available to people who need them and on conditions that are not so stringent that they exclude a large number of people. (14.18)

278. People who are deaf and deaf/blind have communication skills which require some patience and training to understand. Such training is not available at present and should be provided in an approved centre. Interpreters should also be trained and available to people with speech impediments. (14.19)

279. There is a need to recognise sign language which is not currently recognised in Ireland. (14.20)

The Law and the Legal System

280. All public documents, such as legislation and regulations, should be provided in a range of appropriate formats, including large print, braille and computer disc. (15.3)

281. All legal documents should be as clear and easy to understand as possible. An information leaflet should be enclosed with documents in relation to court proceedings which would give specific advice in relation to access to the court for people with disabilities and other relevant information. Court staff should be aware of disability issues and should be able to deal with inquiries from people with disabilities. (15.4)

282. The Legal Aid Board should examine all its offices and make them fully accessible to people with disabilities. It should also assess the accessibility of its services in relation to people with visual and hearing disabilities in order to ensure that appropriate facilities (such as sign language translation) are fully available. (15.6)

283. The Department of Justice should make all court buildings accessible over a period of five years. Information in relation to accessibility of court buildings (accessible parking, entrances, toilets, facilities for persons with hearing disabilities, etc.) should be provided for all people with disabilities using the court system. (15.7)

284.   Sign language interpretation should be available, where required, in all courts and in respect of all services provided by the Legal Aid Board, including court appearances. Similar provision should be made for people with speech disabilities who require interpretation facilities. **(15.8)**

285.   The Law Reform Commission has proposed that the oath should be abolished and replaced by an affirmation. In relation to people with learning disabilities, it has also proposed that a test of competence to give evidence should be introduced and that such persons should not be required to affirm. However, these do not apply in relation to the civil law where the old rules still apply. It is particularly important that all efforts should be made to ensure that people with intellectual disabilities are facilitated in giving evidence in court. In particular, the court needs to be sensitive to the particular needs and abilities of such persons. Consideration should be given to extending the changes in criminal law to all types of case. **(15.10)**

286.   Some people with disabilities are specifically excluded from serving on juries under the Juries Act 1976. The First Schedule to that Act, which sets out a list of persons ineligible to serve on a jury, includes two types of people with disabilities:

*   people who have insufficient capacity to read, deafness or other permanent infirmity, and

*   people who suffer or have suffered from mental illness or mental disability and, on account of that condition, are either (i) resident in a hospital or other similar institution or (ii) regularly attending treatment by a medical practitioner.

These provisions should be repealed. **(15.11)**

287.   There is need for a new public review of mental incapacity and the criminal law to be carried out by the Law Reform Commission or by an inter-departmental committee. **(15.13)**

288.   The Council for the Status of People with Disabilities should enter into discussion with the Law Society, the Bar Council and the Kings Inns in relation to the provision of legal services to people with disabilities. These discussions should also cover access by people with disabilities to their professional training courses. **(15.14 - 15.15)**

289.   Research should be carried out on people with disabilities as victims of crime. **(15.17)**

290.   Further research into the specific problems faced by people with disabilities in relation to abuse should be carried out and the relevant authorities should

draw up policies and guidelines in this area drawing on best practice. (15.18)

291. The relevant public bodies (including the Departments of Justice and Health, Health Boards, Gardai) should review existing policies in order to ensure that adequate protection and support is provided for people with disabilities. (15.19)

292. Disability awareness training should be provided to all Gardai and other persons working in this area as part of their general training. All Garda stations should be fully accessible to people with disabilities and Gardai and other personnel who are able to communicate in sign language should be available. (15.20)

293. A significant proportion of children who come in contact with the Juvenile System are described as having general learning difficulties. However, they often suffer from a range of disadvantages and it is difficult to distinguish the effects of learning difficulties from the other disadvantages. Accordingly, it is suggested that the most appropriate way to develop policies in relation to such children is to see them as children with a range of difficulties (including general learning difficulties) rather than highlighting their disability. (15.21)

294. The Child Care Act should be implemented as a matter of priority to ensure that a system of child welfare services is in place to prevent, where possible, children coming in contact with the juvenile justice system. (15.22)

295. The juvenile justice system should be reformed urgently so as to put in place a child centred system of juvenile justice. (15.22)

296. Appropriate services should be provided for all children and young people with disabilities who become involved in the juvenile justice system, including education, training and accommodation. (15.22)

297. The issue of people with disabilities in the prison system should be the subject of further long-term research. Such research should investigate the extent to which people with different types of disability are to be found in the prison population and the extent to which the current prison system meets their specific needs. (15.24)

298. The Department of Justice should review the accessibility of prisons for people with disabilities. All new prison buildings should comply with the building regulations in this regard. (15.25)

299. The Department of Justice should ensure that all educational and training courses and materials provided are appropriate to the needs of people with disabilities. Prisoners with learning disabilities should be identified; special

programmes, with the emphasis on remedial education, should be set up; continuous assessment should be carried out in all cases with a view to suitable placement following release. (15.26)

300.   All prison staff should receive disability awareness training. (15.27)

Political Rights

301.   All polling stations, booths and procedures should be made accessible for people with disabilities. This would include the printing of photographs of the candidates on ballot papers in order to assist people in voting; the design of polling booths; and the production of voting papers appropriate to the needs of people with disabilities (e.g in braille). (16.1 - 16.5)

302.   People with disabilities who are unable to attend at a polling station should be entitled to be registered on a postal voting register and should be entitled to a postal vote. (16.6)

303.   All political parties should establish affirmative action programmes to encourage people with disabilities to participate fully in local, national and European politics. (16.7)

Chapter Seventeen

The Inclusion of Women with Disabilities

304.   The National Women's Council of Ireland should address the impact of disability on gender equality. Specific action and research should be undertaken to combat the reality of the double exclusion experienced by women with disabilities. (17.1 - 17.4)

305.   Women with disabilities should be consulted in developing policies for them and they should remain sufficiently resourced to maintain their status within the family and within the local community. (17.5)

306.   In order to ensure that women with disabilities are enabled to participate at all levels of society it will be necessary to:

- provide structures and spaces in which women with disabilities can meet together to discuss matters of common concern and to find ways of improving their situation;

- ensure that policy makers and others are informed and aware of the issues arising from women's experiences of disability, based on the social understanding of disability rather than over-relying on the medical and individualistic model of disability;

- provide disability equality and awareness training to enable non-disabled women to learn, understand and reflect upon their own attitudes to disability. Such training should be facilitated by women with disabilities;

- have all women's groups, when they are developing projects at local level, to consider the accessibility of such projects to women with disabilities through consultation with local women with disabilities;

- develop an equality proofing mechanism so that the impact of a particular project or proposal on women with disabilities is always considered. (17.6)

Sexuality and Relationships

307.   The Department of Health should develop policies (including delivery structures) in conjunction with the Council on the Status of People with Disabilities in relation to the sexual rights of people with disabilities. These policies should cover the following areas:

- the right to privacy and dignity,

- the right to accessible information and guidance,

- the right to counselling as appropriate,

- the right to their bodily integrity and how this can be protected, in accordance with their ability to protect themselves,

- the right to information on family planning, contraceptive services, sex therapy services, sexual equipment, and on the prevention and investigation of sexual abuse. (18.1 - 18.9)

308.   Consultations with people with disabilities should be undertaken to establish priority areas for research. These consultations should be carried out by the Health Research Board under the auspices of the National Disability Authority and funded by the Department of Health. (18.10)

309.   Disability and sexuality awareness should be included in the professional and academic training of all those who work with people with disabilities whether they are paid staff or volunteers. (18.11)

310.   All service providers, particularly residential providers, should have regard to the right of the individual and practices involving segregation rather than education which deliberately prevent informed, consensual relationships should be ended. (18.17)

311.   Access to support services for adult individuals and families, where required, could be provided through the Disability Support Service, and would thereby

be available in all residential centres as well. (18.18)

312.   Counselling in sexual and reproductive health could be particularly useful for people with disabilities who face a wide range of barriers to expressing their sexuality. (18.20)

313.   People with disabilities and parents clearly want and need access to appropriate genetic and medical counselling services, in order to make informed personal decisions about having children. (18.21)

314.   All women are entitled to ante and post natal health care free of charge but the facilities offered through the public health service are often inaccessible and inappropriate for women with disabilities. Some units do offer tailored services such as the ante-natal classes with a sign interpreter in the Rotunda Hospital in Dublin. However, there are insufficient examples of such initiatives. (18.22)

315.   Programmes relating to sex education should be available in accessible formats, and include positive images of people with disabilities. These programmes should be provided as appropriate in all schools, training centres, workshops and residential centres for people with disabilities. (18.24 - 18.25)

316.   The legal system should be reformed so that it is better able to deal with cases of abuse involving people with disabilities. This may include mandatory reporting and addressing the issue of people with disabilities, especially those with learning disabilities, being credible witnesses. Sex offenders with previous convictions should not be given positions of trust with people with disabilities. (18.26)

317.   There is no precise information about the extent of sterilisation of people with disabilities in Ireland. Although men are also sterilised, this issue more often concerns women. It is assumed that the sterilisations which do take place are authorised on the basis of medical and psychological opinion and with parental agreement. It is not known to what extent people with disabilities are consulted about such decisions. This is a profoundly complex question with ethical, social, economic and legal implications. It is a question to be faced in the future, given the developing emphasis on people's rights and changing attitudes. (18.27)

318.   There is less discussion of hysterectomy, whether consensual or non-voluntary, but such practices do exist and need to be investigated. (18.28)

319.   There is evidence of non-consensual use of contraception by women with disabilities. While contraception does not have the same permanency as sterilisation, people with disabilities must be protected from non-voluntary and unnecessary medical interventions. (18.29)

320. All counselling services should be accessible to people with disabilities. Care should be taken with the perception of counsellors about the lives of people with disabilities to ensure they do not encourage abortion in the case of foetal disability. **(18.20)**

321. Sterilisation of people with disabilities on the grounds of their disability alone should be legally prohibited. In any situation where sterilisation is being considered, every effort must be made to ensure that informed and free consent exists. Where informed consent is not possible, strict legal criteria must be adjudged to exist by a court of law before sterilisation can be carried out. These criteria should include the requirement to show:

- just and necessary cause;

- that other methods of contraception are unworkable;

- that fair procedures are observed, including medical and psychological assessment of the person's welfare and rights;

- independent advocacy on behalf of the person and full consultation with parents and carers where appropriate. **(18.31)**

Religious Practice

322. People with disabilities should be made to feel welcome and should be fully involved in every aspect of congregational life. To this end,

- every religious community should set up a small task force or working group, which should include people with disabilities, to look at anything which could be a barrier to the inclusion of all in worship and to develop an action plan to eliminate those barriers;

- disability awareness should be included in the formation of religious leaders at every level. **(19.1 - 19.4)**

Arts and Culture

323. The recommended review of the Building Regulations 1991, should include all arts venues and aim to make them as accessible as possible to as many people as possible. Among the facilities that should be available in all theatres, cinemas, auditoriums and concert halls are transfer places (which allow wheelchair users to sit in a seat) and wheelchair spaces (where the user can stay in their wheelchair). Induction loop systems, which amplify sound for hearing aid users, should be installed in all auditoriums, especially those in receipt of grant-aid, while infra-red systems are preferable in music venues. Stages may also require loop systems to facilitate deaf performers. **(20.8)**

324.　Box-office desks should be located at heights accessible to both wheelchair-users and ambulant people and should incorporate a counter loop system and a minicom or other text telephone system. Audio description systems - through which people with visual impairments can hear during pauses in dialogue descriptions of action taking place on stage or screen via a headset - should be installed in all cinemas and buildings where performances take place. The same equipment can be used for such services as simultaneous translation. (20.9)

325.　Super-titling equipment should be available for use in the Abbey Theatre, Siamsa Tire, the Municipal Theatre, Galway Wexford Theatre Royal; Waterford Theatre Royal, Cork Opera House and any commercial theatre with more than 800 seats. (20.10)

326.　The Department of Arts, Culture and the Gaeltacht should draw up a code of practice for all the national cultural institutions and the heritage services to provide facilities and information at their institutions, sites and visitor centres for people with disabilities. (20.11)

327.　Strategies should be developed by the Arts Council, the Heritage Council and the National Monuments and Historic Properties Service to find ways of making accessible those arts and heritage activities which take place in existing buildings, including listed buildings. Operating in a building which cannot easily be made wheelchair-accessible should not prevent arts organisations from providing access features for people with sensory or other disabilities. (20.12)

328.　The Arts Council should disability proof the Arts Plan 1995-1997. (20.13)

329.　The joint action research project by the Arts Council and the National Rehabilitation Board, mooted in the plan, should be expanded to include the Council for the Status of People with Disabilities as a third partner. Meanwhile, organisations in the field of disability should develop and implement arts policies in order to encourage and support access and opportunity in the arts for people with disabilities. (20.15)

330.　In order to increase access to, and participation in, the arts for people with disabilities, relevant state agencies should devise systems of incentives for them, both financial and otherwise. Along with local authorities, the Arts Council should provide adequate and clearly ring-fenced funding as a temporary strategic tool to increase access and opportunity in the arts for people with disabilities through grants to:

- encourage the development of both disability arts and arts and disability practices, including integrated provision;

- ensure that venues become accessible to audiences and practitioners with disabilities. (20.16)

331.   The Arts Council should develop a concessionary card system, through which people with disabilities in receipt of state benefits could obtain admission to arts venues and courses at concessionary rates. Priority seating in certain parts of auditoria (e.g. with level access for wheelchair-users, aisle seats for physically disabled people, near the stage for visually impaired people, in good view of sign interpreters or super-titling for deaf people) should be offered to people with disabilities who need it, at the cheapest rate on offer. This is an access requirement which should be fulfilled at all times and should not be subject to the same conditions as financial concessions. (20.17)

332.   The Arts Council, local authorities, arts and disability organisations should introduce a system of bursaries for people with disabilities, with the aim of increasing their representation in all art forms and methods of cultural expression. (20.18)

333.   All children with disabilities should be given the opportunity to participate in a range of arts activities as part of their general education, including at pre-school level. (20.19)

334.   People with disabilities who have missed out on arts education should be offered compensatory education through adult education programmes run or funded by the VECs. Providers of adult, second-chance and continuing education should ensure that arts education is made widely available to students with disabilities. (20.20)

335.   The training, including in-service training, of primary school teachers and secondary school art and music teachers should have an arts dimension. (20.21)

336.   All arts organisations should institute disability equality training for their staff, members and volunteers. Disability equality training is particularly vital for front-of-house and box office staff, whose offers of assistance, pro-activity, information-giving skills and knowledge are of paramount importance in dealing with customers with disabilities. (20.22)

337.   Arts awareness courses should be run in disability organisations, including for access experts. This is intended to ensure that disability organisations develop awareness of the arts and encourage their membership and client groups to seek involvement in the arts at all levels. (20.23)

338.   The Council for the Status of People with Disabilities should develop models and mechanisms for the identification of talent, leading to professional training

in areas of disability arts or arts and disability practice where few role models exist and/or where the appropriate language and aesthetic are only in the process of development. The training itself should take place in mainstream settings. **(20.24)**

339. Training in music, art and theatre for people with disabilities should be open in its entry policies, modular in structure, and lead to clearly-specified, national qualifications. **(20.25)**

340. Artist-in-residence schemes should be organised to ensure that:

- artists with disabilities work as artists-in-residence in both inclusive and disability-specific settings;

- artists-in-residence working with people with disabilities are of the same standard of excellence as those who work with other people. **(20.26)**

341. The Irish Writers' Centre should develop training and standards for live and recorded audio description. **(20.27)**

342. Theatre-in-education companies and others involved in outreach work in schools should ensure that their performances and workshops can be accessed by all children with disabilities in any class or school they work with. **(20.28)**

343. Arts and cultural organisations should strive to make information on their facilities, services, events, or performances available in a wide range of formats (e.g. large print, tape, Braille, computer disk, signing). The Department of Arts, Culture and the Gaeltacht and the Arts Council should lead by example in providing information. **(20.29)**

344. Information on arts and cultural facilities, events and performances should state clearly their arrangements for people with disabilities. This should include access information, pricing policy and any special features (such as the use of a strobe light or glitter ball which can have adverse effects on some people with epilepsy). Events and courses should be publicised by the widest possible range of media including Aertel, local radio, teletext, magazines for deaf people, specialist TV and radio programmes aimed at people with disabilities, the disability press and newsletters, and via disability organisations such as Deaf Clubs to ensure that the maximum number of people with disabilities have access to the information. **(20.30)**

345. Arts and cultural organisations should provide scripts, precis, introductory talks, taped programmes, audio and sign language interpreted tours, touch tables, thermoforms and other means of ensuring maximum access for people with disabilities to venues, performances, exhibitions and events. **(20.31)**

346.   The Council for the Status of People with Disabilities should appoint an arts officer. This would ensure that arts and cultural matters assume a central position within the Council's work from the beginning. The Arts Council should nominate a professional member of staff to act as a link between artform officers and people with disabilities and their organisations. (20.32)

347.   The Council for the Status of People with Disabilities should set up a talent bank of interested and suitably qualified people with disabilities to be recommended to the Minister for Arts, Culture and the Gaeltacht for consideration as nominees to state boards. The Arts Council should also have access to this talent bank and should ensure that people with disabilities are included as nominees to boards of management of arts organisations. (20.33)

348.   The Arts Council should commission the production of resource packs for arts organisations to assist them to implement ways of involving people with disabilities as audiences, participants or employees. (20.34)

349.   CAFE (Creative Activity for Everyone) should be developed as a central independent source of expert advice on arts and disability issues. CAFE and APIC (Awareness Publishing Information Communications) should co-operate more closely in order to facilitate such developments as the disability access coding of CAFE's extensive database. CAFE should also consider the establishment of a system of arts animateurs to facilitate the interface between arts and disability organisations. (20.35)

350.   County arts officers should conduct an immediate disability audit/inventory of all venues and arts organisations in their areas, reporting to the Arts Council, relevant city/county managers and regional authorities. This process should be repeated and updated in 1999 as part of a review of progress. (20.36)

351.   Application forms issued by the Arts Council, the Ireland Funds and other funding bodies for arts organisations should include a section requesting information about facilities for people with disabilities and arrangements made to ensure their full participation in the applicant organisation. As well as tracking progress made, this mechanism should also enable the Arts Council and other funding bodies to make disability-specific grants from time to time in respect of staffing and recruitment and numbers and types of exhibitions. (20.37)

352.   A touring "hothouse" roadshow should be developed by Very Special Arts to provide opportunities for people with disabilities, including those who live in institutions, to sample arts approaches in workshops and developmental projects. (20.38)

353. The Arts Council should revise its handbooks for exhibition organisers to include sections on display, particularly as it affects people with disabilities. Exhibitions should be mounted in such a way that exhibits can be clearly appreciated by both wheelchair-users and ambulant people, with cord barriers, if used, at heights which do not present a trip hazard. All exhibition rooms and galleries should include seating to enable ambulant people with disabilities to rest. (20.39)

354. The Minister for Arts, Culture and the Gaeltacht should propose an amendment to the Arts Act, 1951, Section 1, recognising "creative communication in sign language" as a specific artform. This would ensure the recognition of deaf arts and culture at the most formal level, alongside drama, literature and music. The drama officer of the Arts Council should provide a list of all sign interpreters qualified to work in theatre to all theatres and theatre companies. (20.40)

355. Moltar don Roinn Comhionannais agus Athchóirithe Dlí, i gcomhar le hÚdaras na Gaeltachta, staitisticí maidir leis an líon iomlán de dhaoine le mí-chumais sa nGaeltacht a chur le chéile, agus cláracha a fhorbairt chun cuidiú le daoine le mí-chumais bheith páirteach i saol cultúrtha agus soisialta na Gaeltachta tríd is tríd. (20.41)

356. The Department of Enterprise and Employment should ensure that the legislation currently in the course of preparation by, its Copyright Unit exempts from liability for copyright infringements any reproduction in formats other than print of copyright works, which are made for the use in education, or otherwise for the personal use, of people with visual impairments. Where the extent of such reproduction might conflict with a normal exploitation of the work, or risk prejudicing the legitimate interests of the author, the legislation should provide for the payment of equitable remuneration to a body representative of the rightsholders affected. (20.42)

Media

357. Research into the effects of media representations of disability should be funded jointly by the Department of Equality and Law Reform and the Department of Arts, Culture and the Gaeltacht. (21.4)

358. In post-primary schools, a section on the portrayal of people with disabilities should be included in media studies from the junior cycle onwards and in the film studies section in Leaving Certificate English. In-service training for teachers should provide the appropriate material and teaching strategies for this. (21.5)

359. All courses and training in the media, journalism and public relations should include specific strands on disability issues. For those already working in the media, there should be workshops and seminars on disability issues. A style

book to provide guidelines about negative, offensive and limiting language should be commissioned and published by the Department of Equality and Law Reform. (21.6)

360. People with disabilities should be helped to participate in media and journalism courses by bursaries established by the Department of Education and the Department of Equality and Law Reform. They should also be given resources to enable them to attend training courses in public relations, lobbying and media management. (21.7)

361. A database of available contributors and sources should be drawn up by the relevant officer of the National Union of Journalists. (21.8)

362. RTE, the Independent Radio and Television Commission and the National Newspapers of Ireland should provide ongoing funding for an independent Media and Disability Unit. This Unit would provide training and expertise to media organisations t ensure the full participation of people with disabilities in media services. It would provide advice about the portrayal of people with disabilities, the coverage of disability events, making programmes specifically for people with disabilities, and disability awareness training. (21.9)

363. Media coverage of disability issues should be brought into the mainstream by, for instance, having them covered by general correspondence rather than by health correspondents. RTE should look at ways in which people with disabilities can be made more visible on television both as presenters and participants. The Advertising Standards Association of Ireland should stringently enforce the Guidance Note on the Portrayal of Disabled People in Advertising, lending particular weight to the views of people with disabilities. (21.10)

364. Public funding to RTE and any other media funding should be dependent on the development by the funded organisation of an appropriate policy concerning people with disabilities. All media institutions and professional organisations should undertake positive measures to facilitate participation and membership by people with disabilities. (21.11)

365. RTE and other television stations with national licences should expand the number of hours and the range of programmes which are sub-titled. There should be a minimum of 50% of all programming hours captioned by 1998 and this should increase to all programming as soon as possible afterwards. (21.12)

366. The National Rehabilitation Board or its successor should initiate a feasibility study into the establishment of a Disability Programmes Unit in association

with appropriate partners such as RTE, the IRTC, FÁS, local radio stations and education institutions. Research should identify potential sources of funding and resources, whether it should operate within RTE or another organisation or as an independent company, and define its functions. **(21.13)**

367.   RTE should specify how it envisages using new information technologies as distribution mechanisms, feedback systems, and alternative media for people with disabilities. In the context of the Green Paper on Broadcasting, the establishment of any broadcasting authority should incorporate clear and accountable methods for dealing with complaints about programmes for or about people with disabilities and include appropriate enforcement mechanisms. **(21.14)**

368.   The use of the Internet as a forum for discussing Irish and international media and disability issues should also be examined. Disability groups should set up World Wide Web pages on the Internet to provide links to other relevant Web pages, to Television, Radio, Print and other news services. This site should also include online archives of text-based documents relevant to radio and TV productions as well as software resources for computer-users with disabilities (such as text to speech conversion software and help files for people with visual difficulties using MAC and Windows operating systems). **(21.15)**

369.   The establishment of a Disability and Perception film or television programme should be initiated jointly by the Irish Film Board and RTE as part of their continuing commitment to and extension of equality principles. This could form a section of the "Short Cuts" initiative. **(21.16)**

Sports, Leisure and Recreation

370.   Lottery funding should be made available to the governing bodies of sporting organisations which represent athletes with disabilities so that Irish athletes will be able to compete internationally on an equal footing with those of other countries. **(22.4)**

371.   Adequate funding should be made available to ensure that Ireland could host the Special Olympics early in the next century. **(22.5)**

372.   Major sports venues should be accessible to people with physical and sensory disabilities. It should not be acceptable to have only a corner of stadiums set aside for wheelchair users and no facilities at all for people with other disabilities. **(22.6)**

373.   Planning permissions should not be granted to any sporting body for renovations or new buildings unless they include proper facilities for people with disabilities.

Elsewhere in Europe, these include commentaries in sections of stands to assist those with visual impairments. (22.7)

374.   The Council for the Status of People with Disabilities should commission a survey of all beaches in the country and try to ensure that only those that are accessible should qualify for the Blue Flags. (22.8)

375.   Bord Failte and the regional tourism authorities should ensure that all tourist information includes details of facilities for people with disabilities. Tourist information centres should only receive state funding if they are accessible to all. All information in them must be available in alternative media and all staff should receive disability awareness training. (22.9)

376.   Government should ensure that all libraries under the control of local authorities are accessible and carry a range of books in large print or talking books. Within five years every public library should have an optical scanner. (22.10)

377.   Voluntary clubs should be fully supported and have a mix of voluntary and paid staff to enable them to operate during holiday seasons, a time when many people with disabilities most need the social outlets they provide. (22.11)

378.   Workshops and other centres catering for people with disabilities, who need more structured leisure time, should be encouraged to open their facilities and centres in the evenings and at week-ends, and to develop a policy on sport, leisure and recreation. (22.12)

Vulnerable People with Disabilities

379.   For those highly dependent people with severe or profound disabilities who are living at home, high quality day activity services, with accessible transport, are an essential part of the necessary services. Day activity services tend to have a low priority and their availability differs widely between Health Boards and within Health Boards. The Commission has already recommended that day activity services should be part of the core personal support services to be provided as part of the Community Action Plan. The entitlement of a person with a severe disability to this service should be no less than that or more able people with disabilities to, say, work or vocational training. Health Boards should be adequately funded by the Department of Health to enable them to secure the development of the necessary quality day services for their area. (23.6)

380.   The well-being of people with severe or profound disabilities who are living at home is bound up inevitably with the well-being of their carers. Financial support for carers is an essential part of an equality strategy which aims at

maximising independence for people with disabilities. Respite care is a requirement in every Health Board area. (23.7)

381.   Where a carer is providing care for a family member in receipt of Disability Allowance he or she should qualify for any allowances or benefits for which they would otherwise be eligible. (23.8)

382.   The following have a special relevance for highly dependent people:

- a system of advocacy: it is important to put in place additional supports to maximise the independence and possibilities for choice for the residents of long-stay services. The sense of powerlessness of this group requires an investment in such measures. The post of advocate needs to be established by statute. Each Health Board should be required to appoint at least one trained advocate on behalf of residents in long-stay services.

- complaints procedures: every agency should be required to have a complaints procedure and to make it known to families and advocates.

- the right to a personal income: many people in residential care receive only a nominal discretionary payment and some receive no income at all, a situation which was strongly criticised by the Ombudsman in his 1992 report. The person with a disability in residential care should have the same entitlement to an income as the person living in the community. The personal income of a person with a disability in residential care should be paid directly to the individual, or an advocate or trustee on their behalf. A reasonable amount should then be charged to them for rent and board.

- the right to other services: the needs of people with disabilities living in residential institutions tend to be seen sometimes only in terms of accommodation or shelter. Individual service and support requirements - for day activity, employment, leisure, therapy or other services - must have equal standing with the service needs of people with disabilities living in the community. The person with a disability in residential care should have appropriate access to the local Disability Support Service and a personal support co-ordinator.

- overseeing and monitoring standards: all types of residential services need a comprehensive and adequately resourced monitoring service with sufficient powers to ensure that standards are implemented in practice. Visiting committees should be established for residential care institutions. The National Disability Authority should have a clear brief in relation to the monitoring of standards in residential care services. (23.10)

383.   The allocation of a place to a person with a severe disability in a particular service should be done on foot of an independent assessment in which the

person's family or advocate would participate fully. There should be statutory entitlement to this assessment process. (23.11)

384.   Where a recommendation has been made for a specific placement, any proposal to refuse admission to an individual should have to be referred to an arbitration process within the Health Board. Arbitration should be carried out by independent third parties with appropriate expertise. There should be a similar procedure for any proposal to terminate a particular placement against the wishes of the person with a disability or their family. (23.12)

385.   The Commission welcomes the proposals in *Shaping a Healthier Future* (the Department of Health's strategy document) for funding service agreements between the voluntary sector and the health authorities. Within this framework, it is necessary to link funding to the service needs of individuals with disabilities. The Commission recommends a two-tier funding structure in order to achieve this. The first tier should be a graded capitation grant which would take account of the level of severity of the person's disability. This grant should follow the person, irrespective of the source of the service.

The second tier should be related to the overhead costs of providing a particular service. It should be based on a formula which would take account of the size of the service, thus protecting smaller services or those with variable numbers from unreasonable fluctuations in their income. (23.13 - 23.14)

386.   Revenue budgets of Health Boards should be structured in such a way that personal support services for people with disabilities should be ring-fenced. Such services should not have to compete with other areas like hospital services. (23.15)

387.   Funding restrictions in the past resulted in significant variations in the quality of services for people with severe and profound intellectual disabilities. Cuts in the late 1980s and early 1990s made it extremely difficult for Health Boards to implement the Planning for the Future policy. As a result there are still more than 1,200 people classed as having mental handicap in psychiatric hospitals. The transfer of such people to voluntary agencies envisaged in the Needs and Abilities Report did not happen.

In the main, the Health Boards have not been able to develop an appropriate service of their own although they are obliged to provide a "last resort" option for people with the most difficult and challenging behaviour. This option does not only apply to people with intellectual disabilities but also to people with multiple disabilities such as those who are deaf/blind.

The proposals in Planning for the Future should be implemented in full as a matter of urgency. (23.16 - 23.17)

388. A special programme and capital fund should be introduced urgently to replace sub-standard facilities for people with disabilities. This programme should be protected from normal competition for scarce funds and should be managed by a special group of experienced professionals from within the Department of Health and the Health Boards. The fund should be directed on a priority basis to the replacement of the worst facilities throughout the country. The total programme should be completed within five years. The replacement facilities should reflect current thinking about design in terms of the lifestyle of the people with disabilities concerned.

Because of the large numbers of people in St Ita's Hospital, Portrane, the Commission is especially anxious that it should be among the first to be replaced under this programme. (23.20 - 23.23)

389. A National Centre for Rare Disabilities should be established and located in a modern teaching facility such as the new Tallaght hospital. It should have satellite centres, linked by computer, in different parts of the country.

The main functions of the National Centre should be:

- to improve the quality of life of people with rare disabilities;

- to provide counselling and advice to families from the moment of diagnosis (and to help families searching for diagnosis);

- to build up a national reservoir of knowledge about rare disabilities and to disseminate information about such conditions, their symptoms and consequences;

- to inculcate a high degree of consciousness and sensitivity among professional staff towards such disabilities; to act as a resource for professionals, especially in, relation to diagnosis and course of treatment.

The National Centre should also encourage more awareness among and between families, to ease the isolation of those affected by rare disabilities, and assist the formation of mutual support groups.

In some cases, it may be necessary to provide families with intensive training to help them cope with aspects of the disability. Such training should be available free at the National Centre and its satellite centres. (23.25 - 23.27)

390. There should be a fundamental review of entitlements to benefits such as medical cards and free transport and to family supports to make sure that no form of long-term or life-long disability is arbitrarily excluded from them. A national

database of rarer disabilities would clearly be a valuable aid to policy in this area. (23.28)

391. Many people with rare forms of disability have shorter life expectancies. All forms of counselling and support in such cases should therefore include the preparation of families for bereavement. This is especially important because of the emotional investment that families make in cases where the disability is not recognised sufficiently. (23.29)

392. Individual planning should take place before the discharge of people with spinal injuries from hospital.

A full assessment of their requirements should be made with their involvement and reasonable accommodation made to enable them to return home and live as they choose. Disability awareness training with particular emphasis on spinal injuries, including their affects on sexuality, should be made available to medical and paramedical staff. A team comprising medical, nursing and paramedical staff with special training in spinal injuries should be available in each Health Board region. Training should also be given to public health nurses on treating people with spinal injuries. (23.30 - 23.31)

393. The Department of Health should fund the establishment of a transitional housing facility, possibly linked to the National Rehabilitation Hospital in Dun Laoghaire and similar to the Transhouse model in the UK. Annual funding should be provided to run such a facility. (23.32)

394. There is a need to provide information to families and carers of people affected by head traumas or brain damage. More counsellors should be trained and made available at Beaumont Hospital in Dublin and other acute hospitals where brain injuries are treated as well as at the National Rehabilitation Hospital. Adequate supports and trained staff should also be made available in regional hospitals and at community level. The Department of Health should ensure that an adequate number of neuropsychologists are trained and available. (23.34)

395. Public awareness of the situation of people with head traumas needs to be increased by the National Rehabilitation Board and other appropriate agencies. Hospitals, GPs and public services generally should be targeted in this regard. It is important, for instance, that teachers in schools should be aware of the adverse effects on pupils who have somebody suffering from a head trauma in the family. (23.35)

396. The Department of Education should draw up a policy for the future education of children with head traumas, including readmission to mainstream education

if appropriate. Suitable supports in the classroom and counselling should be provided at local levels. **(23.36)**

397.   People who have survived head traumas and are judged to be mentally incapable of managing their own affairs are taken into wardship by courts. In this situation, independent advocates should be available, if required, to represent their rights. **(23.37)**

398.   Research into the long-term needs of people with head traumas should be funded by the Department of Health and should inform decisions about compensation arising from accidents. In the interim, the statute of limitations in relation to claims for compensation for head traumas should be extended to ten years to allow assessments of longer term affects which were not foreseen when the initial diagnosis was made. Any compensation due should be awarded in such a way that spouses have conditional access to it. **(23.38)**

399.   The Department of Health should make annual funds available for the establishment of a "Headway House" to provide counselling, telephone helplines, day and visiting services. Suitable respite care facilities should also be established and funded separately by the Department. **(23.39)**

400.   Health and personal support services for elderly people with disabilities and for travellers have been reviewed and are the subjects of development planning. There has been no similar focus on the concerns of young people with disabilities: there is a need to explore the special issues affecting them. Health Boards should address their personal support needs within the framework of the health development sector programme which targets services to particular groups or areas. The Commission urges the National Youth Council, in conjunction with the Council for the Status of People with Disabilities, to undertake in-depth consultation with young people with disabilities to document their concerns and bring them to the attention of policy makers and service providers. In doing so, particular attention should be paid to young people with disabilities in rural communities and in institutional care. **(23.41)**

Research

401.   The proposed National Disability Authority should be empowered to conduct and commission research on disability issues and adequate funding should be allocated to extend both the scope and volume of current research. **(24.1 - 24.4)**

402.   A Research Co-ordination Group should be established under the auspices of the National Disability Authority to provide a forum in which interested bodies could exchange information, agree priorities, avoid overlaps and help to construct joint projects, streamline the dissemination of results and identify and pursue funding options at home and abroad. **(24.5)**

Part Two
POLICY AND STRUCTURAL CHANGES

Chapter Two
LEGAL STATUS OF PEOPLE WITH DISABILITIES

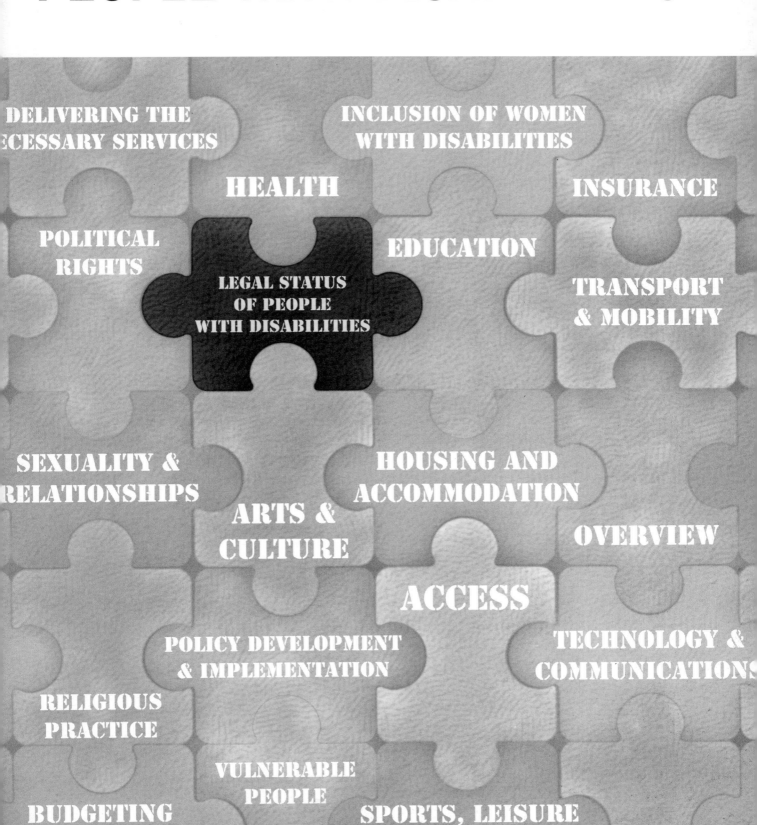

In roughly 200 years they have abolished slavery, sending children down the coal mines at the age of five, knocked down the Berlin Wall and dealt the death blow to apartheid... this leaves the disabled having trouble getting their rights.

- excerpt from submission

2.1   In order to achieve the aims defined by the Commission and to implement its recommendations, the present legal position of people with disabilities under European law and Irish law will require some changes. The law clearly plays an important role in the manner in which people with disabilities are defined and constituted. It is important that it should do so in a positive way and one which is in keeping with the guiding principles of the Commission. Unfortunately, the way in which the law presently defines and constitutes people with disabilities frequently uses archaic and offensive language, relies heavily on a medical concept of disability; and reinforces the dependency and stigma associated with disability.

2.2   It is important that definitions of disability should use language which reflects the right of people with disabilities to be treated as full citizens and to be included in all aspects of society. All definitions of disability should be reviewed and inappropriate and offensive language replaced. In the light of the Commission's view that disability is primarily a social rather than a medical construct, it is inappropriate that definitions of disability should rely solely or mainly on medical definitions or on medical evidence. Finally, definitions of disability should encourage the self-determination and autonomy of people with disabilities rather than reinforce dependency.

2.3   In this chapter, we look at the need for changes in European Union law, in the Irish Constitution, and in existing legislation through the introduction of a Disabilities Act.

European Union Law

2.4   At present there is no reference to disability in the Treaties of the European Union. The European Commission has proposed that in the revision of the European Treaties which is under way in the Inter Governmental Conference (IGC), provisions should be incorporated into the Treaty to ban discrimination of any kind. Such an amendment to the Treaties would require EU institutions to take account of the specific needs of people with disabilities in proposing legislation, EU Programmes and Initiatives. It is important that the Treaties of the European Union should ensure that the EU itself does not discriminate against people with disabilities and a specific amendment to this effect should be adopted in the course of the IGC. Such proposals should be guided by the approach set out in the UN Standard Rules.

This Commission welcomes the recent European Commission Communication on the Equalisation of Opportunities for People with Disabilities which endorses and expands the UN Standards Rules; it also endorses the rights based approach that is taken in this Report. We welcome and fully endorse this Communication from the European Commission and look forward to its adoption.

2.5   The Commission welcomes the fact that the Irish government in its White Paper on Foreign Policy has proposed to seek treaty changes in this area, particularly during the course of its Presidency of the European Union in the second half of 1996. The Commission recommends that the Government should:

- propose that a Non-Discrimination Clause in relation to, inter alia, disability is included in the revision of the EU Treaties, and

- ensure that the EU's power to provide for, and to take legislative action in relation to disability issues is clarified.

2.6   The Commission recommends that the Irish Government support the European Commission's resolution, contained in the Communication on Equality of Opportunity for People with Disabilities entitled "A New European Disability Strategy", when it reaches the Council of Ministers.

The Irish Constitution

2.7   The Commission fully supports the majority recommendation of the Review Group on the Constitution that the following should be added to Article 40.1:

"No person shall be unfairly discriminated against, directly or indirectly, on any ground such as sex, race, age, disability, sexual orientation, colour, language, culture, religion, political or other opinion, national, social or ethic origin, membership of the travelling community, property, birth or other status". *(Articles 40-44 — Page 230 (Para. 8))*

2.8   The Commission endorses the recommendations and conclusions of the Review Group in relation to Personal Rights. *(Article 40.3.1" - 2" — Pages 245 - 272)*

2.9   The Commission welcomes the Review Group's conclusion that the European Convention on Human Rights and Fundamental Freedoms and other international human rights convention be drawn upon in the area of rights where:

(a)   the right is not expressly protected by the Constitution;

(b)   the standard of protection of such rights is superior to those guaranteed by the Constitution; or

(c)   the wording of a clause of the Constitution protecting such right might be improved and fully supports the Groups' view that this requires by section analysis of the fundamental rights provisions of the Constitution. *(Articles 40 - 44 — Page 219)*

2.10   The Commission supports the majority recommendation of the Review Group that a Human Rights Commission should be established to maintain an overview of the extent to which human rights are protected at both the constitutional and legal levels, to assess the adequacy of this protection and to make recommendations to Government for the better protection of these rights, as appropriate. The preferred view of the majority of the members of the Review Group is that a Human Rights Commission should have legislative rather than constitutional status and that, if a legislatively-based commission is established and performs well over a number of years, the possibility of affording it constitutional status should be further considered. The Commission endorses this conclusion.

2.11   The Commission sees the right to education as being fundamentally important. Because of this, we believe that amendments in relation to the Article in the Constitution on Education (Article 42) are essential. At present, Article 42 of the Constitution is largely concerned with regulating the control of education rather than providing a substantive right to education. Recent case law has suggested that the courts may be prepared to develop substantive understandings of the right to education from the existing text. However, the position in this regard is unclear and the Commission believes that amendment of the text to make clear the substantive right to education is essential.

2.12   The Commission recommends that Article 42 should be amended to include the following points:

- The right to education.

    There is a need to spell out the right to education in substantive terms separately from the control of education. There are many precedents for such wording in, for example, the UN Covenant on Economic, Social and Cultural Rights which Ireland has ratified or in the UNESCO Convention on Discrimination and Education.

- Equality within education.

    The right to education should be informed by the core principle of equality. All children (including children with disabilities) should be guaranteed the right to an appropriate education and everything that is necessary to ensure equal access and equal participation in that education.

- The scope of the Article.

    The right to education should be stated to apply to all students at primary, secondary and third levels. This would simply recognise existing reality.

    Consideration should also be given to the insertion of a clause dealing with the educational rights of adults. Education should be defined broadly to include intellectual, social and physical dimensions.

2.13   The Commission recommends that the All Party Oireachtas Committee examining the Irish Constitution endorse the above and propose that these changes be made in the Constitution.

A Disabilities Act

2.14   The Commission welcomes the Government's commitment to introduce a Disabilities Act which will set out the rights of persons with a disability together with means of redress for those whose rights are denied. This legislation is necessary to give practical effect to the recommendations of the Commission. While the constitutional provisions set out the general principle of equality, a detailed Disabilities Act should set out the practical measures by which this can be achieved.

2.15   Many countries have now adopted specific legislation on the rights of people with disabilities. These include the USA (Americans with Disabilities Act 1990), Australia (Disability Discrimination Act 1992), Italy (Law for the Care, Social Integration and Rights of People with Disabilities 1992) and the UK (Disability Discrimination Act 1995). Such legislation is consistent with and required by Ireland's ratification of international agreements on people with disabilities and human rights.

A Disabilities Act should outlaw all discrimination against people with disabilities. Earlier discrimination legislation aimed to ensure only formal equality and equality of participation. However, we need to go beyond a narrow understanding of non-discrimination measures in order to ensure equal success in participation.

2.16   A Disabilities Act should rule out all discrimination in relation to

- Services provided by public bodies

- Services provided by private bodies

- Employment

- Education.

2.17   A Disabilities Act should highlight the following key features:

- A social understanding of the concept of disability rather than an overly medical approach.

- Allowing for difference. The Act must go beyond a formal approach to equality to recognise that true equality requires a recognition and acceptance of difference. Therefore, the Act should require public and private bodies, employers and educators to make 'reasonable accommodation' to meet the specific needs of people with disabilities.

- The core importance of equality. The Disabilities Act should override other general legislation so as to ensure that the principle of equality is achieved.

- Enforcement and access to alternative forms of dispute resolution. Legislation is only as good as its enforcement mechanisms. The Disabilities Act should be enforced by the National Disability Authority (see Chapter 3) and mechanisms for alternative dispute resolution should be established so that individuals can have easy access to mechanisms which can resolve any disputes under the Act.

2.18 The Commission recommends that the Disabilities Act be published and introduced as a matter of immediate priority. Such legislation is absolutely crucial to the strategy for equality set out in this report and without such legislation the strategy for equality cannot succeed.

2.19 The outline principles of a Disabilities Act are contained in Appendix C. This is not presented as definitive, but is nevertheless indicative of the kind of issues which require careful attention when introducing legislation in this area.

Individual Legislative Changes

2.20 We note the Government's commitment in the Programme for Competitiveness and Work to the introduction of an Employment Equality Bill and an Equal Status Bill. Pending the implementation of a comprehensive Disabilities Act, we recommend that the aforementioned principles should be reflected in this more general equality legislation.

2.21 The Commission welcomes the publication of the Employment Equality Bill, 1996, which, for the first time recognises people with disabilities within an inclusive Employment Equality Framework.

2.22 The Commission believes that the Bill should reflect the principles contained within this Report.

2.23 The Commission believes that all provisions within the Bill, insofar as they apply to people with disabilities, should reflect the reality of social gain and should include the principle of reasonable accommodation, in order to facilitate full, fair and equal opportunities for people with disabilities within the areas of training and employment.

2.24 The Commission believes that the definition of disability in the published Bill is wholly inappropriate.

2.25   The Commission regrets that the published Bill does not reflect the submissions made by the Commission to the Minister, prior to publication of the Bill.

2.26   The Commission requests that the Government amend the Bill.

2.27   It would be neither possible nor desirable for the Disabilities Act to contain all the measures relating to people with disabilities. For example, provisions relating to social welfare payments for people with disabilities will be contained in the Social Welfare Acts and health care entitlements will continue to be provided for under the Health Acts. Amendments to, and in some cases the introduction of, legislation in a wide range of areas will be essential in addition to the introduction of the Disabilities Act. A range of amendments to existing legislation including the Juries Act 1976 and the Mental Treatment Act 1945 are also required (see Chapter 15: The Law and The Legal System). These legislative changes are just as essential to the strategy for equality as the introduction of the Disabilities Act itself.

2.28   Individual Departments (including the Departments of Social Welfare, Education, Health and the Environment) should review legislation falling within their remit to ensure that the definitions of disability used (and the practices in relation to the implementation of these definitions) are in accordance with the principles set out by the Commission in this Report.

Chapter Three
POLICY DEVELOPMENT AND IMPLEMENTATION

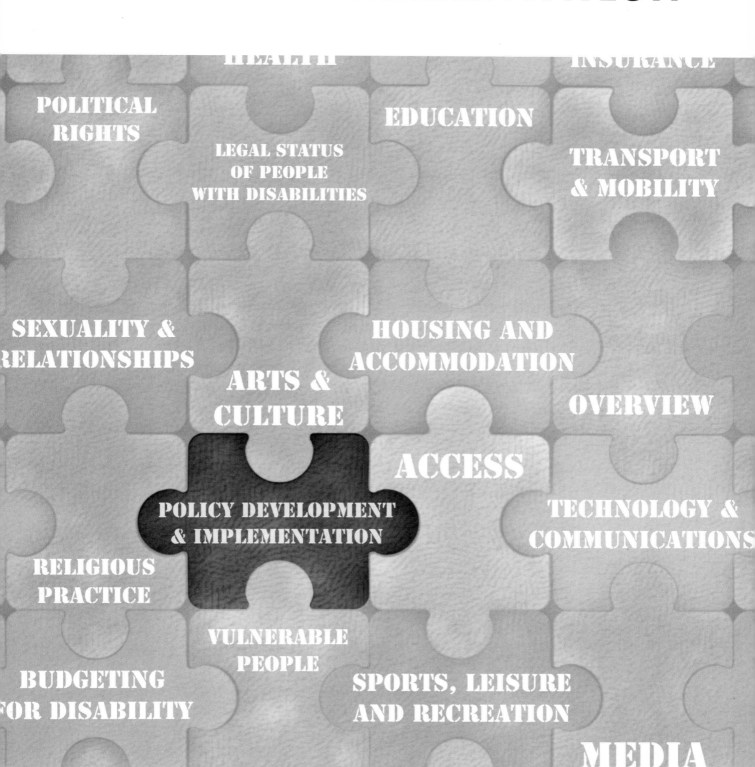

HEALTH

INSURANCE

POLITICAL RIGHTS

EDUCATION

LEGAL STATUS OF PEOPLE WITH DISABILITIES

TRANSPORT & MOBILITY

SEXUALITY & RELATIONSHIPS

HOUSING AND ACCOMMODATION

ARTS & CULTURE

OVERVIEW

ACCESS

POLICY DEVELOPMENT & IMPLEMENTATION

TECHNOLOGY & COMMUNICATIONS

RELIGIOUS PRACTICE

VULNERABLE PEOPLE

BUDGETING FOR DISABILITY

SPORTS, LEISURE AND RECREATION

MEDIA

WORK AND TRAINING

My daughter and her school have been disgracefully let down by the State whose officials engage in a shameful game of buck-passing which ensures that no State body ever accepts responsibility for the child, her well-being and her education.

- excerpt from submissions.

3.1 To change the lives of people with disabilities for the better requires a concerted and organised response from the whole administrative machinery of state. The deep anger already noted amongst people with disabilities is based not solely on the inadequacy of particular services: it is based primarily on a sense of helplessness and frustration in the face of a system which they experience as complex, passive, incommunicative, bureaucratic, reactive, fragmented and not focused on their needs.

3.2 This is a theme which is not exclusive to people with disabilities but is being heard throughout Irish life as an educated society articulates its wishes more forcibly. These wishes are for a user-friendly system and also one in which relations between those providing services and those using them are conducted on a more equal and participative basis rather than on one of subservience between clients and professionals.

3.3 The Commission has come to the conclusion that the State needs to make proper provision for people with disabilities in order to give them a realistic hope of equality of access to the benefits of society. To do so will require major changes in the structures and approach of state services as well as the legislative changes outlined in the last chapter.

3.4 There are already signs of a new sensitivity in the public service, an example of which is the Department of Health's strategy document Planning for a Healthier Future which includes many of these themes. Such a development is necessary across the whole spectrum of administrative bodies. These measures need institutional, political and legal expression and a change in the system and the culture which drives it, in order to provide a pro-active service.

3.5 To achieve this and to eliminate the administrative dysfunction which impacts unfavourably on people with disabilities, the Commission proposes a number of radical and far reaching measures at both central and local government level. These will address the absence of co-ordination and the lack of focus in the present arrangements: there is, for example, no single agency at present which attempts to develop an overview of the needs of people with disabilities and how they fare across the whole spectrum of services. These measures will provide a positive ethos and culture in the administration of public services for people with disabilities and provide the necessary statutory basis from which this renewal will arise. Finally, there is a need to establish a practical mechanism to enable people with disabilities at crucial times in their lives to obtain the best result possible from the available services.

3.6 In order to achieve this, the Commission recommends that the Department of Equality and Law Reform be given the prime responsibility for the development, monitoring and implementation of policy for people with disabilities. The decision to establish a Department responsible for equality is fully vindicated in the light of the situation revealed in this report: it should be maintained in existence and its influence strengthened in relation to social, economic, cultural and political policy for people with disabilities.

3.7   The Department of Equality and Law Reform should be given any necessary resources for its task as national co-ordinator of disability policy. It is further recommended that a Disability Equality Unit be established within the Department headed by an official at Assistant Secretary level. The function of this unit should be:

- to provide a focal point for disability equality policy and legislation development

- to operate an inter-departmental co-ordinating mechanism

- to monitor the implementation of government decisions in relation to disability policy

- to monitor the achievement of the quota for the employment of people with disabilities in the public sector

3.8   The Department of Health and its agencies currently provide a range of services such as respite care, home helps, personal assistants, technical aids and appliances. These services are not primarily health services at all. However, the Department of Health and the health boards have built up a wealth of experience in the provision of these services and there is little justification for changing departmental responsibilities in these areas. The Commission believes, however, that it is important to make it clear that these services are social rather than health services. This is not just a change of terminology but underlines the need to change from a medical and caring model of services towards one based on meeting the social needs of people with disabilities. For these reasons, the Commission recommends that the Department of Health should be renamed the Department of Health and Social Services; the section of the Department which currently deals with a range of non-health services (including child care services and services for the elderly) should be renamed the Social Service Section. The health boards (which are, in any case, to be restructured under the Health Strategy) should be described as Health and Social Service Authorities with appropriate changes in their internal structures.

3.9   An interdepartmental committee should be established at a senior level, under the aegis of the Department of Equality and Law Reform, to co-ordinate government strategy for people with disabilities. All major government departments should be asked, as an integral part of the Government's

Strategic Management Initiative, to identify their strategic objectives in relation to providing public services to people with disabilities, and to develop and publish a five year plan for achieving those objectives.

3.10   Each government department should also carry out a physical access review and plan to ensure that, within five years, all their buildings are made accessible to citizens with disabilities. Many offices throughout the public service are still not accessible: many health centres, for example, have no wheelchair access.

3.11   Government departments and state agencies should provide disability awareness training for all staff. Specific staff members should be assigned responsibility as 'key workers'. These 'key workers' would act as points of contact within their agencies for people with disabilities, their families, carers and Support Co-ordinators.

The National Disability Authority

3.12   In order to achieve the primary aim of ensuring equality for all citizens, the Commission believes it is necessary to create an executive body which will monitor the impact of public policy and services on people with disability. This body should not only be in a position to monitor the system at local level but should have the power to intervene in particular cases in order to ensure equity. The Commission therefore recommends the establishment of a National Disability Authority which would report to the Department of Equality and Law Reform.

3.13   It is important, when setting up a new body, to be able to offer a cogent logic for its creation and to be sure that there is no overlap or duplication of functions. The Commission understands that the devolution of executive functions from departments of State to executive agencies is part of the Strategic Management Initiative. It supports this devolution but considers that a new body is required in order to redress the imbalances which work against people with disabilities. The Commission sees the National Disability Authority as having a clearly separate and independent role, one focused on audit, co-ordination of best practice, and in a position to intervene and evaluate. It will be important to ensure that other roles and functions which would blunt its effectiveness are not loaded on to the National Disability Authority.

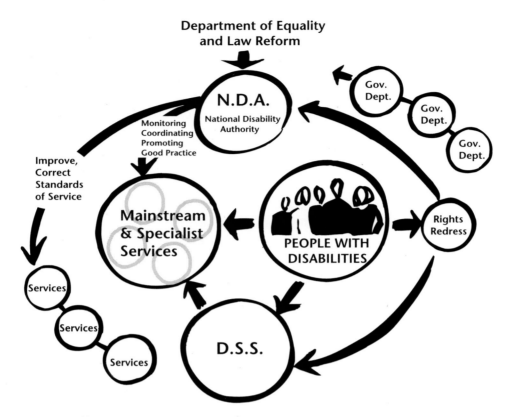

3.14 The overall role of the National Disability Authority will be to empower and enable people with disabilities to achieve and exercise their economic, social, cultural, political and civil rights. Its key functions will be:

- to monitor compliance with the recommendations of this Commission and other relevant EU and international agreements that have been accepted by government

- to serve as a national focal point to co-ordinate disability policies

- to undertake and commission research on disability issues

- to advise on and develop standards in relation to disability programmes and services

- to require the creation of appropriate standards for services provided to people with disabilities and to ensure their observance

- to monitor and evaluate programmes and services for people with disabilities

- to provide grievance and redress procedures

- to publish an annual report to be laid before each House of the Oireachtas and special reports as considered necessary

- to provide a Disability Support Service at local level (see Chapter 4: Delivering the Necessary Services)

- to organise Community Action Plans at local level.

3.15   The membership of the National Disability Authority should include a wide range of interests and represent a balance between key stakeholders (government departments, local authorities, health boards, other state and voluntary agencies) and independent users, carers and specialists. It should be made up of the following and reflect a balance between the genders, geographical areas and the different types of disability:

- 1 representative of the Department of Equality and Law Reform

- 1 representative of the National Rehabilitation Board (or its successor)

- 1 representative of Non-Governmental Organisations

- 1 representative of the chief executives of the Health Boards

- 1 representative of the County Managers

- 2 members to be nominated by the Minister of Equality and Law Reform

- 5 members to be nominated by the Council for the Status of People with Disabilities

- An independent Chairperson unconnected with any of the foregoing.

3.16   In all circumstances, at least 60% of the membership of the National Disability Authority should be people with disabilities, or their families.

Community Action Plans

3.17   The extent to which managers, professionals, users and carers work and plan together across organisational boundaries is a vital element in improving services for people with disabilities. To facilitate and increase that level of co-operation, the Commission recommends the creation of local Community Action Plans. They should be three year plans which involve a wide range of agencies in planning improvements to the lives of people with disabilities.

3.18   In establishing the Community Action Plans, the Commission suggests the following guidelines:

- new arrangements should not duplicate current initiatives. If good inter-agency planning already exists, this should be integrated into a comprehensive approach.

- the planning process should be as simple as possible, recognising the amount of time, resources and energy that many individuals may be asked to commit to it. Agreement should be reached on a small number of strategic priorities. Meetings should be well structured and participants should have sufficient authority to enable rapid progress towards decisions.

- the National Disability Authority should be responsible for co-ordinating Community Action Plans at local level and within a set timescale.

- consultation with, and involvement of, users, families and carers and a diverse range of agencies should be real and involve two-way communications, constant feedback and on-going dialogue.

- the plans should avoid becoming 'wish-lists' which simply set out desirable but unrealistic proposals. They should represent a real commitment of resources by the organisations involved and should be aimed at achieving defined goals.

3.19   The National Disability Authority should be responsible for convening local planning groups which would include local authorities, health boards, relevant Government departments, arts and leisure services, voluntary sector and user groups. As well as being responsible for delivering Community Action Plans within the proposed timescale, the National Disability Authority should organise planning groups within appropriate geographic areas such as those designated for community care.

3.20   There is a difficult tension to manage between the need to plan for holistic services for users and the different concerns and issues of importance to various providers. Inter-agency working achieves different levels of success in different locations. For these reasons, the National Disability Authority should not be expected to plan on behalf of other agencies; it should be responsible simply for initiating the planning process by bringing relevant organisations and service providers together at local level. It would then be up to local stakeholders to agree the best way forward. Different organisations and providers could then take responsibility for acting on recommendations. For example, local authorities should assume responsibility for planning and implementing accessible transport services, local education services should plan educational matters and so on. Government departments responsible for the other agencies involved should issue directives requiring local staff to participate actively in the Community Action Plan groups

3.21   Each local planning group should include users and carers and should consult widely with users and carers in the community before drawing up the plans. The draft plan should then be subject to further consultation. Each planning group should try to ensure that a range of perspectives from users and carers with different needs is represented. Local plans should be published and should be available in an accessible format and use the minimum of jargon.

3.22   Each planning group should develop a three year rolling strategy to improve the quality of life for people with disabilities in the local area. It should include

- strategic objectives and priorities for the next three years;

- objectives in terms of outcomes for users and carers, as well as in service terms;

- specific targets and timetables for implementation;

- service proposals linked to resource and budget commitments;

- collectively agreed objectives which are reflected in the priorities and plans of participating agencies;

- a review of how effectively objectives from previous plans have been met.

3.23   The establishment of the National Disability Authority - and other recommendations of the Commission - will have implications for existing bodies, including the National Rehabilitation Board and voluntary agencies.

National Rehabilitation Board

3.24   NRB was set up under the National Rehabilitation Board (Establishment) Order, 1967. This legislation delineated NRB's functions as follows:

(a)   with the consent of the Minister for Health, to supervise or operate or arrange for the operation of services for the welfare of persons who are disabled as a result of physical defect or injury, mental handicap or mental illness. The services shall be regarded as including:

- the co-ordination of the work of voluntary bodies engaged in the provision of rehabilitation and training services for disabled persons;

- the giving of medical treatment to disabled persons;

- the provision of a service for the assessment of disability and the giving of vocational guidance to disabled persons;

- the training of disabled persons for employment suitable to their condition of health;

- the provision of a service for the placement of disabled persons in employment;

- the making of arrangements with other bodies for training disabled persons;

(b)   with the approval of the Minister for Health, to co-operate with, or assist companies or associations formed for the purpose of performing functions similar to any or all of the functions of the Board, and to enter into such contracts or agreements as may facilitate the provision of the services;

(c)   with the approval of the Minister for Health to do all things necessary, either directly or in co-operation with other bodies, for making available a service for the provision of prostheses and appliances including artificial limbs and hearing aids;

(d)   to furnish advice, information and assistance in relation to any aspect of the services to the Minister for Health, or to any Health Authority;

(e)   with the approval of the Minister for Health to organise and provide courses of training in the treatment, training or placement in employment of disabled persons;

(f)   with the approval of the Minister for Health to provide courses of training for students of occupational therapy.

3.25   While NRB has devolved some its original functions to others over the years, the organisation has also been given responsibility through the Department of Health for the management and monitoring of EU funding in the area of specialised vocational training for people with disabilities, for the operation of the Disabled Drivers Board of Appeal, and other services. NRB operates through a regional structure and a national network of 18 centres.

3.26   NRB is governed by a Board of twenty members appointed by the Minister for Health. The organisation works largely through the process of consultation, both on an individual basis and with other organisations, both statutory and non-governmental. Formal dimensions to this process include mechanisms such as the National Advisory Committees.

3.27   The role of the National Rehabilitation Board will need to be reviewed in the light of the Commission's recommendations. It will in any event be necessary to examine the staffing implications of these recommendations so that the changes can be accomplished without significant additional net costs if possible.

Non-Governmental and Voluntary Organisations

3.28   The Commission's intention for this and the following section, is that where people with disabilities are mentioned, this will include parents, families and individual carers of people with disabilities.

3.29   Non-governmental and voluntary organisations play a key role in the provision of services for people with disabilities and in advancing disability issues. Many of them provide services in the areas of education and training, health, rehabilitation, housing/accommodation, and cultural and sporting activities. People with disabilities and organisations of people with disabilities must be central to a partnership approach. Only by concerted action from all the partners involved can we make good the statement that no community is complete unless all its citizens can play their part.

3.30 In our view, the independence of non governmental and voluntary organisations is an essential element of any dynamic and creative pattern of services. The achievement of the Commission's objectives will lead to far greater partnership between the statutory and non-governmental sectors and the development of mutual relationships.

3.31 In the light of Commission's recommendations on the structure and method of delivering services to people with disabilities and the emphasis on self-advocacy and collaboration, non-governmental and voluntary organisations may need to re-evaluate their current structures and functions and to consider how closer working relationships and even merging with similar organisations may assist them to provide the comprehensive range of quality services that will be required, within the limited funding that will be available. The Department of Health should facilitate a dialogue to explore these issues and possibilities. One way this dialogue might be facilitated would be to convene a national working conference to explore ways to promote collaboration and co-ordination across the sector.

3.32 The remit of umbrella bodies, which represent the interests and concerns of service providers, parents, carers and people with disabilities, may also need to take account of the changes recommended by the Commission, especially in view of the fact that people with disabilities will have their own structures through which they can articulate their views. A review of the current workings of the umbrella bodies, in the light of new developments, would also offer them an opportunity to examine ways of strengthening the links among themselves and of promoting their common interests.

Developing Partnership

3.33 The most important change in thinking required by the principles set out in this report is the emphasis on a comprehensive strategy, one which recognises that people with disabilities are at the centre of all services and supports, and changes the relationship between service providers and people with disabilities to one of active partnership.

3.34 People with disabilities should be able to expect a high quality of service, courteous treatment, understanding and empathy from the staff with whom they deal, and responsive and efficient arrangements for the services they require. The approach of the Strategic Management Initiative, the recommendations of the NESF Quality Delivery of Social Services report and the recommendations of the Commission all emphasise the need for 'customer care'. There is also strong governmental support for changes to service provision across departments which enhance the quality of services provided to consumers.

3.35   To achieve this, the following processes must be in place:

- **Quality assurance:**
  All services to people with disabilities should have quality assurance systems in place. All service providing organisations should also be asked to produce clear quality standards for the services they offer and to put in place performance monitoring systems, including feedback from people with disabilities. Each organisation should also be required to offer disability awareness training to all staff.

- **Continual dialogue with people with disabilities:**
  People with disabilities must be seen as experts in their own lives who can offer important information and ideas in any dialogue with service providers. Person-centred services require the full and active participation of people with disabilities. Better communications will help to identify gaps or overlaps in services.

- **Performance management systems:**
  As feedback from people with disabilities is sought, and good quality systems are built, organisations will understand more clearly how and why services sometimes fail to meet expectations; this will help them to make further improvements.

3.36   In line with the Commission's guiding principle of maximising the participation of people with disabilities, we believe that participation and consultation must be a key principle in the formulation and implementation of all policies which impact on their lives. Any proposals for changes designed to improve the lives of people with disabilities must involve and consult people with disabilities at all stages: 'nothing about us without us' as one group of people with disabilities stated. For partnerships to be successful, however, partners must have common agreed aims. These can only be achieved when all members of the partnership have an equal say in deciding what should happen, how it should happen and why. This is not always an easy process. People with disabilities and providers may have different starting points, different constraints and perhaps different interests. Real partnerships will involve people with disabilities understanding the problems and standpoints of service providers, as much as it will involve professionals and managers understanding and learning from the perspectives of those who use services.

3.37   A number of common obstacles face users who try to get involved:

- professional barriers: a reluctance on the part of providers to risk abandoning 'expert' roles and boundaries in order to involve people with disabilities as equal partners

- complex organisational systems and hierarchies that make it difficult for users and carers to find a way into participation and involvement

- decision making bound up in bureaucracy which is not responsive to new ideas and information

- organisational confusion about involving people with disabilities - who to involve? how to involve them?

- initiatives that involve people with disabilities in planning meetings but then fail to follow up with feedback or the implementation of recommended changes and thus break off a potential on-going dialogue

- initiatives that only involve some types of service users while overlooking others or assuming that they cannot know what is best for them.

3.38   The creation of partnerships where none have existed requires mutual trust and respect and an ongoing commitment to maintaining communications and appropriate responses. In order to engage people with disabilities successfully in planning improvements in services, their participation must be supported and resourced: government departments and agencies should take account of this in drawing up their five-year plans.

3.39   In putting in place effective mechanisms of participation and consultation it will be necessary to overcome environmental and attitudinal barriers. The development of a real process of consultation is one which makes demands on all participants. The National Disability Authority should draw up a set of guidelines for statutory and non-governmental and voluntary organisations on effective ways to involve people with disabilities in all aspects of service planning and delivery.

3.40   In addition, each statutory organisation should include a set of objectives for involving people with disabilities as part of their annual targets. These objectives should be specific, agreed, measurable, achievable and time-limited. Formal requirements for involving people with disabilities should be included in the guidelines for lead agencies responsible for drawing up Community Action Plans. People with disabilities should be directly represented on relevant boards.

Chapter Four
DELIVERING THE NECESSARY SERVICES

DELIVERING THE NECESSARY SERVICES

INCLUSION OF WOMEN WITH DISABILITIES

HEALTH

INSURANCE

POLITICAL RIGHTS

EDUCATION

LEGAL STATUS OF PEOPLE WITH DISABILITIES

TRANSPORT & MOBILITY

SEXUALITY & RELATIONSHIPS

HOUSING AND ACCOMMODATION

ARTS & CULTURE

OVERVIEW

ACCESS

POLICY DEVELOPMENT & IMPLEMENTATION

TECHNOLOGY & COMMUNICATION

RELIGIOUS PRACTICE

VULNERABLE PEOPLE

BUDGETING

SPORTS, LEISURE

It appears to us that the parents of a disabled child face a lifetime of fighting each and every agency and department for their rights and those of their child,

- excerpt from submission

4.1 Existing supports and services for people with disabilities are poorly co-ordinated. People with disabilities and their families have great difficulty and experience serious frustration getting information about their entitlements and accessing these from the multiplicity of agencies which are involved in undertaking assessments and providing services. Professionals working in the field waste much time and energy on duplication.

4.2 The Commission believes a fundamental change in attitudes, procedures, and structures is required to give people with disabilities and their families easily accessible information and support that will empower them to make decisions about their lives.

4.3 A service to be known as the Disability Support Service (DSS), which will be the focal point of collection and distribution of information, should be established, and a national network of Disability Resource Centres set up. The Resource Centres will be a single point of contact for information, advice, support, and advocacy. Support Co-ordinators will be trained to guide individuals or their families through the range of services they might need at different stages in their life. The Disability Support Service will be accountable to the National Disability Authority.

4.4 These structures will deliver to people with disabilities information on all the supports they need whether medical, educational, work, training, housing and so on throughout their lives. The new structures will also ensure that the views of the person with a disability are fully taken into account. The keys to providing this support are:

- information,

- assessment of needs, and

- advocacy,

4.5 The Disability Support Service will be the focal point for gathering and distributing all relevant information for and from people with disabilities. All public bodies will have to adopt a culture where providing information is the norm, and public funding of non-governmental organisations should be dependent on their providing accessible information. People with disabilities should be included in preparing, monitoring and evaluating information.

4.6 The Disability Support Service, Disability Resource Centres, and Support Co-ordinators will all be crucial to ensuring that a proper assessment of needs is made at the onset of disability, an assessment resulting in a Statement of Needs which identifies the full spectrum of services required by that person from a range of agencies, as well as their financial needs.

4.7   Advocacy - self-advocacy and citizen's advocacy - will also play a critical part in giving individuals control of their lives. To this end, education and training in self-advocacy should form an integral part of the curriculum studied by people with disabilities. Citizen's advocates, independent of service providers, should be trained to help people not in a position to defend their rights. Independent advocacy services should be mandatory in residential care settings or similar services.

4.8   The structures and services created to deliver a person-centred continuum of support to every one with a disability or their families are all based on the philosophy that disability is a rights issue, that it is not medical conditions but society which handicaps people with disabilities and that it is society which needs to change. These support structures are designed to give people with disabilities the opportunity to grow, and most importantly, to give them the freedom and ability to access supports at an individual level and to decide what happens in their own lives.

4.9   The Disability Support Service should have two main components - Support Co-ordinators and Resource Centres. It should provide outreach activities to those in maternity and other hospitals, residential settings, remote areas or to those who otherwise might be unable to access the system. It should utilise existing structures, personnel and resources, where possible.

Support Co-ordinators

4.10   Improvements in information and advocacy, and more co-ordinated service provision, will make it easier for people to find and access what they need. Even with such improvements, however, some may still need assistance in finding their way through statutory and other procedures. No one should fail to receive a service they need and to which they are entitled because of bureaucratic or other barriers, real or perceived.

4.11   There are many organisations, both statutory and voluntary, that offer information and advice. None of these bodies has, however, the function or authority to guide and support individuals and/or their families through the range of services they might need at different life stages. The Commission proposes that this type of support should be made available to those who need it through Support Co-ordinators. Their role will be that of a supporter or enabler with the skills to negotiate with statutory and non-governmental organisations and make sure that the right package of services is provided to meet the need identified. Co-ordinators would not act as needs assessors or resource allocators: rather, their role would be to work with people with disabilities to help them understand their needs, entitlements and eligibility and to identify and help to negotiate appropriate provision for each individual.

The role would vary according to the services and programmes needed by an individual to support maximum independence and a holistic lifestyle.

4.12   Services relating to personal/family supports where people might require assistance from a Support Co-ordinator in planning and securing a service include:

- advocacy

- community nursing

- counselling

- day care

- home help, home care attendance and home support

- personal assistance

- personal reader

- recreation, leisure and sports

- residential care

- respite care

- sign language interpreting

- technical aids and appliances

- escorts (buses, etc)

4.13   Other services such as transport, education, training/employment and so on may require less direct involvement by Support Co-ordinators: their involvement in these areas is likely to centre on providing information and support. The individual would, if he or she wished, deal directly with the appropriate agencies to identify specific needs and services required. However, if difficulties develop the Support Co-ordinator may intervene to help resolve them.

4.14   A Support Co-ordinator should be a valuable source of information to statutory and non-statutory agencies regarding local needs and adequacy of services: they should be represented in the Community Planning Groups proposed in the previous chapter.

4.15   To carry out this work, Support Co-ordinators will need access to detailed information on a wide range of services and an understanding of systems, processes and eligibility requirements. They will require considerable skill in communication, negotiation, network building, assertion, problem solving, team-working, facilitation. An appropriate training programme will need to be designed and provided. To facilitate a local small-team approach, Support Co-ordinators should be drawn from a range of relevant professional and experiential backgrounds and should include people with disabilities.

4.16   The training programme for potential Support Co-ordinators should be developed by the Regional Technical Colleges, Universities and other Third Level education institutions in consultation with the Council for the Status of People with Disabilities and other relevant bodies. The programme should be available through the RTC's, Universities and other Third Level Institutions and should commence no later than 1997.

4.17   There should be clear performance measures and careful evaluation of the 'value added' by the co-ordinators. Performance standards and measures should be developed with the full involvement of users. It is suggested that an independent evaluation be carried out two years after the co-ordinators have been appointed and that appropriate funding should be provided for this evaluation.

Disability Resource Centres

4.18   Empowerment requires access to information. It should be possible for any citizen to get whatever information they require and to use it to identify and obtain the services they need and to which they are entitled. Some people may need the assistance of a Support Co-ordinator in this process: many will not. What they should have, however, is a single point of contact for information, advice, contacts/linkages and if necessary, support. These essential points of contact should be a national network of Disability Resource Centres. These Centres should be fully accessible and easily located. Sharing existing suitable premises should be explored in this context in due course.

4.19   In addition to providing up-to-date information on services available from government departments, health boards, local authorities, other statutory and voluntary bodies, the Centres would provide access to the Internet and to Handynet, the computerised database on technical aids and appliances. Centres should display a selection of technical aids of most general interest, such as security devices, etc., together with documentation in accessible formats. Individuals should, of course, continue to have direct access to agencies providing services.

4.20   The Disability Resource Centres will provide information, support and advocacy in areas including:

- rights, entitlements, services
- community nursing

- counselling

- day care

- home help, home care attendance and home support

- personal assistance

- personal reader

- recreation, leisure and sports

- residential care

- respite care

- sign language interpreting

- technical aids and appliances

- transport

- education

- training/employment

- independent living/skills training

Information

4.21   One of the clearest messages coming through to the Commission from people with disabilities has been the problem of access to information. People have expressed serious frustration with several aspects of the availability of information. In particular, there is frustration with its fragmentation, the absence of certain types of information, the absence of a timely source of information, and the absence of a single local centre where most information needs could be satisfied with minimum hardship. The vital questions of access to information including - who keeps it? how can I get it? what format is it in? - has come into even sharper focus with the advent of user-friendly computing and the information superhighway.

4.22   Information is essential to empowerment. Access to relevant, accurate and up-to-date information is a universal right of all people. Walsall Information Federation defined some of the barriers to information for people with disabilities as follows:

- people who are unaware of the existence of a particular service do not know that they need information and so are unable to ask for it

- information is often available in the wrong form, e.g. print when people need voice recordings or Braille

- many people with disabilities have low expectations and so are unlikely to try to seek out information or ask for help

- mobility barriers inhibit people with disabilities from chasing after information

- many people lack time and/or money to go chasing after information. In addition, many professionals appear reluctant to give access to information freely, appearing to defend institutions rather than prioritise customer satisfaction

- information is sometimes presented in a way that makes it difficult to understand

- those people who are not familiar with using information can find it particularly complicated and may not see its relevance

- some people feel reluctant about approaching strangers or official organisations for help or may take great pride in being independent.

4.23   The Disability Support Service will disseminate information to people with disabilities, providing both technical and administrative support in relation to information systems or processes. The right to information should be included in legislation relating to all public services. The obligation to provide accessible information on a pro-active basis should be included among the conditions governing public funding to non-governmental organisations.

4.24   Improved physical access is needed to public and private organisations providing information, such as libraries and citizens' information centres. The information itself should be readily accessible and available if required, in different formats, such as braille, tape, computer disk and most of all in jargon free language.

4.25   Mainstream services will need to be supported in moving towards a culture where providing information to all citizens is the norm. Good sign posting, trained reception staff (including training in sign language and disability awareness), with positive attitudes to responding to requests for information and clear information about the services being offered are basic requirements.

4.26   People with disabilities should be included in the preparation of information and in its monitoring and evaluation. For example, the consumer panels planned by the Department of Social Welfare should include people with disabilities, as should the Telephone Users' Council and other user groups.

4.27   Public bodies will need support (like disability awareness training and handbooks) to implement the necessary changes required of them under any new legislation, policies or practices.

Assessment of Needs

4.28 The Commission has been impressed by the cogency of the case put forward by many individuals with a disability at their listening meetings, for a more orderly, formal, sensitive and comprehensive response to their difficulties in their local setting. The Commission believes that the onset of disability should be met by an assessment process which identifies the total ramifications of the situation for that person, his/her family and those caring for him/her.

4.29 This response is presently unsatisfactory either because of the absence of assessments, or their inadequacy, or the manner in which they are organised and held. The situation is made worse by the presence of many agencies each acting without reference to the others.

4.30 At present, disability-related assessments are heavily reliant on a medical view of disability. In line with the Commission's view of the need for a rights based approach, it is recommended that assessments should be broadened beyond a medically based procedure, to a comprehensive, multi-disciplinary, person-centred assessment of disability, utilising self-assessment to the maximum extent possible. A multi-disciplinary approach could involve disciplines like occupational therapy, rehabilitation psychology, occupational psychology, compensatory education, medical services, counselling and social services.

4.31 Key issues which arise in relation to welfare for people with disabilities, their families and carers are the lack of a single assessment procedure and the lack of co-ordination between agencies in relation to assessments, providing services and making payments. Particular concerns in this regard have been highlighted in a recent report on means testing by the Comptroller and Auditor General, which identified no less than 42 means tested schemes operated by public bodies. There are a further range of schemes of relevance to people with disabilities including social insurance payments from the Department of Social Welfare, discretionary personal social services from the Health Boards and the Disabled Drivers Scheme and other tax rebates from the Revenue Commissioners. In addition to the general qualifying conditions which apply to all claimants, people with disabilities have to undergo an assessment of their degree of disability. This can result in people being assessed by several different agencies for basic entitlements. This often causes undue hardship to people with disabilities, their families and carers and gives rise to much frustration and despondency.

4.32 The Comptroller and Auditor General recommended a number of measures which would harmonise assessment of eligibility and achieve a more efficient service. These included the carrying out of assessments by a single agency and the introduction of a 'passport system' whereby qualification for one payment or service would lead to automatic entitlement to a range of other benefits and services. The qualifying conditions should, however, ensure against any misuse of the various schemes available to people with disabilities.

4.33   The Commission strongly supports these recommendations. It recommends as well that an inter-Departmental working group be set up, at assistant secretary level, by the Minister for Equality and Law Reform, comprising senior representatives from the Revenue Commissioners and the Departments of Health, Social Welfare, and Education to pursue the development of a single assessment procedure which would provide the person with a disability with a "passport" for a range of benefits. The group should in the course of its deliberations consult the Council for the Status of People with Disabilities and those agencies involved in the assessment of needs. The Commission recommends that the group be set up forthwith and report in six months.

4.34   The Commission recommends that in relation to each person with a disability the following system should be in place: there should be a new Assessment of Needs process, underpinned by law, with adequate arrangements made for its enforcement and monitoring and for an appeals procedure, and it should lead to a Statement of Needs.

4.35   A person with a disability who requires an assessment of needs should be able to arrange it directly or with the assistance of the Disability Support Service. Where the Disability Support Service is requested to support any individual in securing an Assessment of Needs, it should have the authority under the Disabilities Act to require an accredited agency to carry out such an assessment. The obligation on the agency to carry out an assessment on the direction of the Disability Support Service should be a condition of accreditation. Specific needs assessments would not themselves be carried out by the Disability Support Service as this could involve a conflict of roles between assessment and its advocacy and information functions.

4.36   The emphasis of the assessment process should be on the direct involvement of the person with a disability, or their family or advocate as appropriate. The process should be conducted only by an accredited agency and should respect the rights and dignity of the person at all times. The assessment process should ensure that:

- the specific needs of the individual are identified as early as possible, so that when they are met, the person will be able to participate in the mainstream of society;

- the needs identified are prioritised and timescaled by the person concerned or their family/advocate and the assessor(s);

- every appropriate agency or service provider of the necessary services is identified.

4.37   The end result of the assessment process should be the Statement of Needs. A copy of this should be given to the person, or their family/advocate. The person with a disability may then access the services/supports directly or they may take it to the Support Co-ordinator at the Disability Resource Centre. A copy of the Statement of Needs which need not identify the individual should be sent to the Disability Support Service to assist in planning and co-ordinating services.

4.38   The prioritisation of needs should reflect the relative importance of each need in enabling the person to exercise his/her rights to participate to the fullest extent of his/her potential in the cultural, social, civil and economic activities of society. Any identified needs which prevent the person doing this must be met and where necessary budgetary provision should be made for them by the appropriate government department.

4.39   People with disabilities or their carers should be able to get an assessment, or access to the Disability Support Service to arrange one, either directly or through a GP or public health official - including area medical officers, community psychiatric nurses, public health nurses, physiotherapists, occupational therapists, etc. It should be stressed, however, that referral by any person other than the person themselves should be done only with the prior knowledge and consent of the individual concerned, their parents and/or advocate as appropriate.

4.40   The resulting Statement of Needs drawn up for each person requiring help should address the full spectrum of services required by that person, including those needs which are not met by existing services. The assessment procedure will assist in identifying and quantifying unmet service needs. To enable the Disability Support Service to co-ordinate the process of identifying and quantifying unmet service needs, it should receive a copy of each statement of needs.

4.41   Monitoring and evaluation of the assessment process will be a function of the National Disability Authority.

Assessment Review

4.42   There should be a process for reviewing the implementation of the assessment of needs process. Review dates should be specified in relation to each assessment, using the following performance indicator measures:

- Is it user driven and user influenced?

- Is it effective?

- Is it accessible?

- Is it responsive to individual needs (in terms of outcomes for individuals)?

- Is the time taken to access the service reasonable?

- Is customer satisfaction level adequate?

Advocacy and Representation

4.43 Advocacy is concerned with getting one's needs, wants, opinions and hopes taken seriously and acted upon. It can take a number of different forms including self-advocacy, citizen's advocacy and patient advocacy. Representation is taken to mean representation by a professional adviser, such as a lawyer.

4.44 Self-advocacy involves the development by people with disabilities of the skills necessary to express their views to the fullest possible extent. Citizen's advocacy refers to the persuasive and supportive activities of trained selected volunteers and co-ordinating staff, who could also be people with disabilities, working on behalf of people with disabilities who are not in a good position to exercise or defend their rights as citizens. Citizens' advocates are unpaid and are independent of service providers. Working on a one-to-one basis, they attempt to foster respect for the rights and dignity of those whose interests they are representing. This may involve helping the person express his or her concerns and aspirations, obtaining day-to-day social, recreational, health and related services and providing other practical and emotional support. Patients' advocates are generally paid and are independent of the institution in which they are based. The range of activities would be similar to that carried out by a citizen's advocate.

4.45 The range and complexity of services available in a modern society through bureaucracies and so on place all citizens at a disadvantage in mastering these complexities. This however, is compounded in the case of people with disabilities and as a result, a special mechanism is needed to restore equality of opportunity for them.

4.46 The Commission believes that advocacy is essential because it allows people to participate more fully in society by expressing their own viewpoints, by participating in management and decision making and by availing of the rights to which they are entitled.

4.47 Proper implementation of many of the Commission's recommendations is dependent on the availability of effective advocacy services. Advocacy services should be independent of service providers.

4.48 Recent years have seen a growth in self-advocacy groups. These groups are predominantly composed of individuals with learning disabilities who come together to discuss their individual and collective concerns at local level, either in the context of a training environment or as people living in their local communities.

4.49   A range of measures are needed to improve the current provision of advocacy and representation:

  •   Education and training in self-advocacy for people with disabilities should form an integral part of the curriculum in schools, training centres, and sheltered work centres, and of work experience. This should be linked to other measures such as representation in management and decision making. Funding for such measures should be included in the budget of all publicly funded education and training schemes.

  •   Self-advocacy should, where appropriate, be supplemented by the provision of citizen's advocacy. Funding and training for such a service should be provided through the Departments of Social Welfare/Health.

  •   In certain situations like training centres, but above all in residential care settings, such as psychiatric hospitals, the provision of independent advocacy services should be mandatory. Legislation for the provision of advocacy should be incorporated into any legislation dealing with particularly vulnerable groups in a residential setting.

  •   Finally, funding should be provided by the Legal Aid Board to ensure that people with disabilities can employ an advocate to access expert legal representation, where necessary.

Appeals and Complaints Procedures

4.50   The provision of adequate complaints procedures currently varies greatly from one area of social services to another. In some areas, statutory rights of appeal already exist. In relation to most payments made by the Department of Social Welfare, for example, a statutory right of appeal exists to the independent Social Welfare Appeals Office. For many other areas of social services, however, no similar right of appeal or formal complaints procedure exists. This lack of any formal right of appeal has been highlighted by the Ombudsman in several annual reports.

4.51   The Commission believes it is essential that individuals should have the right to voice their complaints in relation to the provision of payments and services. It is recommended that a formal complaints procedure be introduced by service providers where such a procedure is not already in place. Such a complaints procedure should be simple, accessible and made known to all users of the services. In the first instance, a complaints procedure should involve a complaint being made to a designated person in the organisation. Such a complaint could be made directly or with the assistance of Support Co-ordinator. In the case of services provided by public organisations, an individual who is dissatisfied with the response to the complaint could make a further complaint under the provisions in the proposed Disabilities Act or through the Office of the Ombudsman. In the case of services provided by non-governmental organisations, an independent office should be established by the umbrella organisation(s) which would have the power to consider complaints concerned. The establishment of a formal complaints procedure should be made a condition of public funding to non-governmental organisations.

Chapter Five

COSTS: BUDGETING FOR EQUALITY

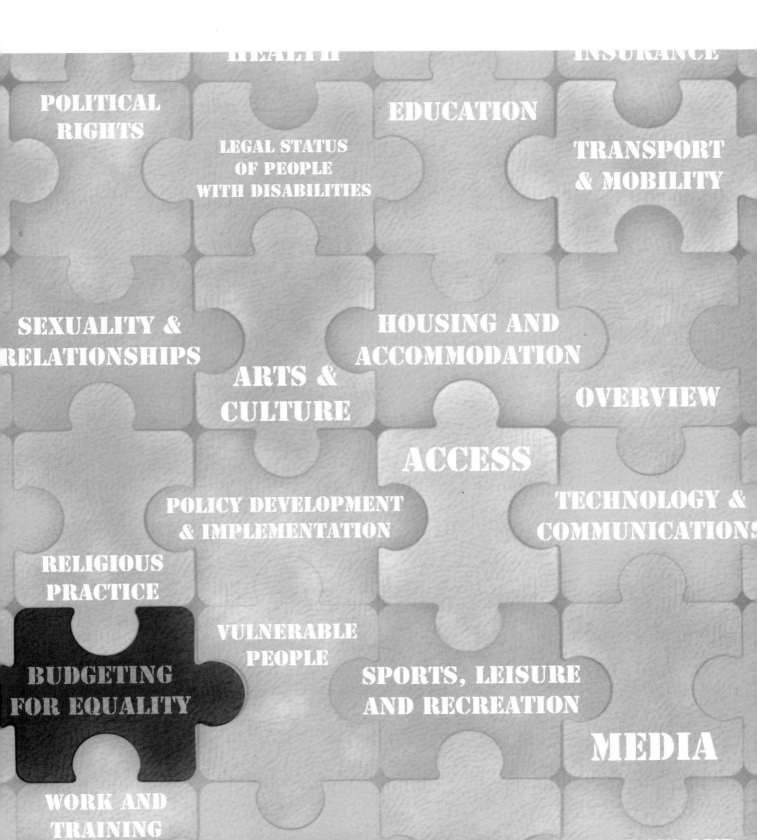

5.1 It is proper that government be concerned with the costs associated with its actions. The terms of reference given to this Commission reflect this concern where we were asked to establish the estimated costs of all recommendations made. A literal interpretation of the terms of reference would require an evaluation of the resource implications of each recommendation. This exercise is not feasible since, as we have noted elsewhere, the required statistical information is not sufficiently detailed. More importantly, however, such an exercise would be inappropriate. While the report contains many recommendations they are in essence the detailed plans which follow from the guiding principles of the Commission's work (1.34). All recommendations can therefore be summarised in one sentence. "People with disabilities must be recognised and treated as having equal status with all other citizens". The question then is whether or not this recommendation is to be accepted. If accepted, costing amounts to budgeting for equality.

5.2 In this chapter we outline the budgeting that will be necessary in order to guarantee equality of status for people with disabilities. It is organised under 7 headings. These are: re-organization of institutions, income support, education, environment, health, enterprise and culture.

The Economic Case for Equality

5.3 The recommendation that persons with disability be granted equal status with all other citizens is a fundamental question of human rights. A society which respects human rights is richer in a way that cannot be measured on any balance sheet. Respect for such rights, however, is a necessary condition for a society to be classified as wealthy. The decision to pursue equality of status for people with disabilities is not a question of economic calculation. Once taken the decision does have economic consequences. To focus entirely on budgeting issues ignores the economic benefits that will accompany the greater inclusion of people with disabilities in society.

5.4 In chapter 6 we note the relationship between poverty and disability. We demonstrate that persons with disability are more likely to live in poverty under the current policy environment. Achieving equality of status will break this link. It will not mean that poverty will be eliminated for persons with disability since the recommendations of this Commission alone cannot eliminate poverty in our land. However, it should bring about a situation where a person with a disability is no more likely to be poor than any other citizen. This change on its own will mean that we have a fairer society. Since equity is a fundamental element of well-being for society this can be classified as an economic improvement.

5.5   The Commission has recommended that policies to achieve equality of status for people with disabilities should involve affirmative action. The operation of affirmative action in the United States has often been the subject of much controversy. The objective of such a policy is to eliminate negative stereotypes. Does it achieve this end? As with any single policy initiative it cannot be seen as a panacea for all problems. US research (Coate and Loury, American Economic Review, 1993) gives credence to the hopes of advocates of preferential policies and the concern of critics. This work suggests that there needs to be a balance between the coercion involved in affirmative action programmes and the incentives given to the targeted group to improve their status. The recommendations of the Commission address this balance. As a consequence, costs for the State will arise in providing funding to individuals while in many cases the role of the State as legislator and not funder is invoked. Success in achieving equality of status depends on the broad implementation of the Commission's proposals. The cost of equality also depends on such a universal adoption of our proposals. In many cases todays costs in one area are tomorrows savings as a consequence of the implementation of recommendations in other areas.

5.6   Economic analysis of equality is generally concerned with redistribution. This, of necessity, involves someone losing in order to bring about a gain for someone else. However, the quest for equality of status in this report should not be viewed simply in this light. In many cases this Commission's recommendations will bring about a reduction in market failures and so will increase efficiency resulting in potential gains for all. The reasons for "market failures" are numerous: failure to take account of third party costs; asymmetry of information; ill-defined property rights. In the case of people with disabilities the reason for the failure of markets to provide for their needs is not as obvious as, say, the reason for market failure in the case of pollution. The reason seems to be related to the relative size of this group in the market and a lack of clarity in the definition of property rights.

Re-Organization of Institutions

5.7   The preceding chapters described the re-organization of institutions that the Commission believes is necessary. Additional costs associated with this change should be minimal once full implementation is achieved. The recommendations are designed to reduce unnecessary duplication and improve efficiency in the delivery of services.

Income Support

5.8   In terms of costing, provision for income support is the most visible cost factor arising from the recommendations of the Commission. Budgetary implications follow from the definition of disability and the details of the recommendations.

5.9   Additional expenditure cannot be avoided in this area. Such expenditure is necessary if we are to achieve equality of status for all citizens is to be achieved. When put in the proper perspective the cost is small amounting to less than £15 per annum per citizen. This is a small amount to pay to advance the cause of equality.

5.10   In chapter 6 this Commission notes that the existing system of income support to persons with disability is unnecessarily complex. This complexity on its own acts as a barrier to recipients involving costs of information and application. It can also involve an affront to dignity since payments often have the appearance of charity rather than entitlement. Reforming the system so as to avoid these unfortunate implications will on its own be of benefit to people with disability.

5.11   Statistics for current schemes make it impossible to be precise in costing the Commission's proposals in relation to income support. This occurs for two reasons. Persons with disability are currently included in broader categories of support, the most obvious being the Disability Benefit. The Commission recommends that this benefit be re-named "Sickness Benefit". As such the benefit falls outside the scope of the Commission's work. However, it is the case that persons with disability currently receiving payment under this scheme will transfer to the new unified pension proposed by the Commission. Second it is to be expected that the number of people eligible for payment could increase once we move away from a strictly medical definition of disability.

5.12   The Commission recommends that income support to persons with disability take three forms.

   •   A unified Disability Pension.

   •   A Costs of Disability Payment.

   •   Revised Carers allowances.

5.13   The reasoning behind these recommendations is outlined throughout Chapter 6.

5.14   The Disability Pension is designed to be a compensation for loss of income due to inability to work to full potential. It would replace the main existing schemes which are: invalidity pension, blind pension and Disability Allowance. It would not involve a means test.

5.15   The Commission would like to see the payment levels reflect the recommendations of the Commission on Social Welfare. However, the costs associated with such an increase relate to broader policy decisions which cannot be attributed to achieving equality of status for persons with disability.

Consequently it is appropriate that costing of the Commission's proposal be related to current levels of payment.

5.16   The Commission attempted to assess the numbers who would be eligible for payment of disability pension. It is not possible to make an exact judgement here. However, a figure of 100,000 of working age permanently unable to work appears reasonable.

5.17   There are currently around 40,000 people receiving the Invalidity Pension and a further 30,000 approximately in receipt of the Disability Allowance. The universality of the Disability Pension should therefore see an increase in recipients of approximately 40 per cent.

5.18   The combined cost of the Invalidity Pension and the Disability Allowance now comes to about £260 million per annum. A 40 per cent increase in numbers might be expected to involve an additional cost of £100 million - assuming similarities in the family structure of new relative to existing recipients. However, this neglects to net out those who switch over from disability benefit to the new disability pension. Half of those currently on disability benefit have been in receipt of this payment for more than two years. This amounts to over 20,000 people. Hence the true increase in expenditure on persons permanently unable to work would be less than 10 per cent. The additional cost would therefore be closer to £20 million. It would arise mainly from extending coverage to those in residential centres and from dropping the means test requirements.

5.19   There would also be a cost associated with payment to those who are under-employed. Here estimates are much more difficult. Assuming that 10 per cent of the population can be classified as having a disability (note that this is a rough figure and its limitations are discussed in Appendix A) a further 200,000 people would be eligible for some support under the disability pension.

5.20   A true costing depends on the distribution of recipients with respect to income. There would be full withdrawal for those on the average industrial wage, for instance. Using data on the distribution of income by households it would be expected that up to 50 per cent of those entitled to benefit would have it fully withdrawn because of income levels. This assumes that payments would actually be made to 50 per cent of those entitled to payment.

5.21   Of those who would receive a payment, it is likely that 60 per cent would be below the income threshold for payment of income tax. Recipients were divided into three groups and average withdrawal rates calculated for each group. These rates are: 25 per cent, 50 per cent and 70 per cent. The last group are also subject to tax on their disability pension.

5.22 Given current rates of pension payment the total cost of a disability pension to those able to work would be £110 million annually. This is an upper bound figure. It is to be expected that those able to work would be less likely to be at the lower end of the income distribution than those permanently unable to work. The above estimate involves a sum of £40 million for those at the lower end of the income distribution.

5.23 The broad thrust of the Commission's recommendations, if implemented, would see greater participation by persons with disability in all areas of life. This would obviously include the labour market. Over time increased participation in education and training should lead to a situation where the job market prospects of those with a disability would improve. It is expected that the cost of income support to those able to participate in work would fall over time. It is important then that this increased cost be seen as a transitional measure. Its level will depend on the speed of implementation of the Commission's other recommendations.

5.24 The Costs of Disability payment is designed to facilitate participation. It is not meant to replace all existing free schemes but rather to bring a unified philosophy to such payments as they apply to persons with disability. There is no way that a specific cost can be assigned to such a payment at this stage since it involves individual assessments. Instead the principle must be accepted and reasonable and appropriate budgeting be made on this basis.

5.25 It is also difficult to estimate the cost of the Commission's proposal for Carers Allowances. The elimination of tax allowances would bring about savings which could be applied towards funding the allowance. However, the Commission's intention is that the principle of a Carers Allowance be accepted. Again, as in the case of the Costs of Disability payment, the implementation requires budgeting that is beyond the scope of the Commission's work.

Education

5.26 Recommendations in the area of education are contained in chapters 11 and 20.

5.27 The recommendations in the area of sports and leisure focus on aspects of access and participation. As such they do not give rise to costs additional to those relating to access. The one cost element, relating to library facilities, can be considered as part of the general cost in relation to education.

5.28 The Commission has made a specific recommendation with regard to funding for education. It recommends that a figure of 1% of the existing education budget (i.e. approximately £20 million at current rates) of additional expenditure be allocated annually to meet the educational needs of students with disabilities.

5.29 It must be stressed that the additional expenditure be seen as an investment. Since greater access to the full range of education services will enable those to more fully achieve their potential, a reduction in dependency should be expected in later life. Therefore today's cost is tomorrows saving in income support payments.

Health

5.30 In this report health has been considered under three headings: general health issues, sexuality and relationships and special needs of vulnerable people. The central recommendations refer to issues of dignity when in receipt of medical treatment. These have implications more for time and mode of delivery rather than cost.

5.31 Costs arise in three main areas: funding to community services, costs of surgical and medical appliances and the capital costs involved in creating a fund to improve facilities for vulnerable groups.

5.32 The Commission has recommended that additional funding be earmarked over a five year period to address shortfalls in community services. However, the re-organization envisaged in the delivery of services could, if introduced rapidly, reduce this cost. This saving could be set against the costs associated with equipment.

5.33 The capital costs associated with building improvements cannot be precisely determined. However, it is arguable that this is not an additional cost. The Commission has highlighted the needs of vulnerable groups and given voice where none was previously heard. In this respect our recommendation is a call for a re-ordering of building priorities in light of past failures. As such, additional budgeting does not automatically follow.

Access and Environment

5.34 Recommendations under this heading are covered in the chapters on access, transport and mobility, housing and political rights.

5.35 Costs may arise in meeting the recommendations under two broad headings. The first relates to conversion of existing buildings and transport facilities and the adoption of new standards for future facilities. The second arises from payments in respect of travel passes and grants towards building improvements.

5.36   The costs under the first heading will be temporary. To the extent that there are additional costs associated with meeting new standards these will be allocated across the whole population and they will bring benefits to the entire population. A bus more accessible to a person with a disability is more accessible for all. At any rate costs in this area arise because they are an adaption to the way in which things are now built. To the extent that all buildings and transport facilities in the future conform to a new standard it can be argued that scale economies should bring cost reductions in meeting standards. Therefore the main costs arise in adapting existing facilities. The Commission's recommendations recognise the need for a reasonable programme here. As a consequence additional costs should be relatively small.

5.37   It is not possible to put a precise cost on the second broad area. In general the additional cost here will be determined only when account is also taken of the recommended Costs of Disability payment. It is important to avoid double counting of costs.

Enterprise and Employment

5.38   This category refers to the participation of persons with disability in work and training and their utilisation of technology.

5.39   The implementation of affirmative action programmes should not be seen as involving cost but rather as a mechanism for overcoming negative stereotypes.

5.40   Costs will arise in the need to provide increased access to adapted equipment and sheltered workplaces. Costs associated with this should be met in large part from earmarking a share of the funds raised through the employment levy.

5.41   Recommendations on access to mobile phones and interpreters will involve additional costs. Again these costs should be taken together with the measurement of the Costs of Disability payment.

5.42   In many areas of access to technology it is to be expected that private firms will be interested in increasing access to persons with disability since this will in turn increase the market for their products. An innovative approach to increasing, access to technology should be adopted whereby government seeks partnership with private firms and thereby minimises its own costs.

Arts Culture and Media

5.43   Cost implications under this heading arise from adaptation of facilities and provision of financial incentives for participation.

5.44   Previous comments on the avoidance of double counting of costs are also relevant here. Adaptation relates to access and again the cost will be broadly borne. To the extent that auditoriums need to be adapted the costs are shared broadly across all users. Bursaries and financial incentives relate in many instances to education broadly defined so that additional costs in this specific area would be small. With regard to putting requirements on the national broadcaster for captioning it could be argued that a portion of the licence fee could be properly earmarked for this purpose. This would result in additional costs being met from advertising revenue and not a claim on the government budget.

Part Three
ECONOMIC RIGHTS

Chapter Six
INCOME & DISABILITY

I live alone. I never go out and so see no one. I am 52 years old and live like a hermit. I get £60 a week.

- excerpt from submission

6.1   If their earning capacity is seriously reduced and they also have to meet the extra costs associated with their condition, people with disabilities are at serious risk of living in poverty. Research carried out by the ESRI shows that households headed by people who are unable to work due to illness or disability are one of the groups in Irish society most likely to live in poverty and to experience basic deprivation.

6.2   As noted already in this report, the absence of detailed statistics about people with disabilities impedes the making of policy. This is particularly true in relation to their incomes and the Commission recommends that further research be carried out into this area. At present we are forced to rely on data which does not correspond to any widely accepted definition of disability.

6.3   Based on data from an 1987 ESRI survey, it is clear that households headed by people who were ill were subject to a higher than average risk of falling under a poverty line as Table 1 shows.

TABLE 1 **RISK OF POVERTY BY LABOUR FORCE STATUS OF HEAD OF HOUSEHOLD**				
Labour Force Status	% in Sample	Poverty Lines		
		40% line	50% line	60% line
Ill but intending to seek work	1.2	30.6	51.2	65.3
Ill and not seeking work	4.8	7.3	25.0	63
All households	100	7.5	17.5	30

Source: Callan et al. Poverty, Income and Welfare in Ireland, ESRI, 1989.

6.4   At the 60% line almost two thirds of all households headed by a person with an illness were below the relative poverty line as compared with 30% of the population as a whole. The ESRI survey found that these households were in the highest risk groups with households headed by an unemployed person or a farmer. These figures only relate to households where the head is ill and do not include households where another member of the household is ill.

These figures broadly correspond with a recently published survey conducted by the Irish Wheelchair Association. Of a sample of 1,000 members of the IWA, 53.5% replied that they had some or a lot of difficulty in managing on their income (14% of the sample did not reply to this question).

In more recent work, Callan, Nolan and Whelan have developed their study of poverty to include a consideration of living standards. Their study showed that, of those households which were below the 60% line and were experiencing "basic deprivation" in terms of their standard of living, 17% were headed by a person who was ill or disabled. Based on this criterion, 42% of households headed by a person who was ill or disabled were living in poverty (compared to 16% of all households). This was a comparatively high proportion topped only by households with an unemployed head (51%).

6.5   Further research needs to be carried out into the income support, both public and private, provided to people with disabilities. Little is currently known about the personal circumstances of those who are in receipt of social welfare payments and there is very limited information available about sources of private income support (e.g. the numbers in receipt of pensions on retirement due to ill health, numbers insured under or in receipt of payments from permanent health insurance). Nor has there been any assessment of existing payments to establish the degree to which payments reflect needs. All these issues need to be addressed in order to establish a comprehensive system of income support.

6.6   However, the Commission would not like to see lack of research being used as an excuse to delay essential reforms. The recommendations which are set out in this chapter are based on the personal and professional experience of the members of the Commission, on existing research and studies and, perhaps most importantly, on several hundred submissions from people with disabilities themselves which clearly indicate the need for urgent reform.

6.7   People with disabilities need income support and assistance with costs relating to their disability for two reasons. Firstly, many of them are not in employment and, therefore, do not have an income from work. Secondly, disability gives rise to extra costs in areas such as equipment, care, travel, telephone, fuel, food, clothing and laundry, hospital and medical expenses, home treatment (e.g. physiotherapy) and home services (e.g. home help). These two needs raise distinct issues and the Commission has addressed them separately.

6.8   On the basis of the available research and of the submissions made to the Commission, we believe that income support for people with disabilities is currently highly inadequate. The provision of adequate income support is essential, both to ensure that people with disabilities do not live in poverty and to allow them to participate fully in society.

At national level, there is no coherent policy of income support for people with disabilities. There is no unified system: income support is fragmented and lacking in co-ordination.

Income support payments are currently administered either by the Department of Social Welfare or by the Department of Health, through the regional health boards. They are accompanied by a bewildering array of free schemes and grants and allowances aimed at augmenting income or addressing specific problems faced by people with disabilities, such as mobility difficulties. They have developed in a piecemeal fashion over time, and the system of payments is neither coherent nor comprehensive. In addition, the division of responsibilities between the two departments owes more to historical accident than to rational planning.

6.9   Existing payments are related either to income or to costs. They can be broadly categorised into eight groups:

- **Disability benefit and invalidity pension.**
  These are contributory payments (i.e. based on payment of social insurance contributions) administered by the Department of Social Welfare. Disability benefit applies to people whose employment has been interrupted due to short or long term illness: invalidity pension is paid as a result of a long term disability.

- **Occupational injuries benefits.**
  Also administered by the Department of Social Welfare, these payments are for employees who have suffered injury from an occupational accident or disease arising from their work.

- **Blind Pensions.**
  Administered by the Department of Social Welfare, this includes a means tested payment to persons aged 18 or over who are so blind that he or she cannot perform any work for which eyesight is essential or cannot continue his or her ordinary occupation. There is also a blind welfare allowance administered by the Department of Health. This is a weekly means tested payment whose statutory basis is unclear. It may be paid to a person who is already receiving the blind pension or the disabled persons maintenance allowance.

- **Department of Health payments.**
  These include the rehabilitation allowance, infectious diseases maintenance allowance, blind welfare allowance, mobility allowance for people unable to walk and motorised transport grant and also include the Disabled Persons Maintenance Allowance until its transfer to the Department of Social Welfare on 2nd October, 1996.

- **Payments to carers.**
  There are two main payments in respect of caring: the means tested carers' allowance administered by the Department of Social Welfare and the domiciliary care allowance, a payment in respect of children with disabilities who require constant care, administered by the Department of Health.

- **Free Schemes.**
  These schemes include "free" travel, electricity, gas, TV licence, phone,

fuel, butter vouchers and come under the Department of Social Welfare. They are not confined to people with disabilities.

- **Supplementary Welfare Allowance.**
  This is also a general social welfare scheme and is not aimed specifically at people with disabilities. It includes weekly additional payments in respect of housing, diet and exceptional heating costs and once off payments in respect of exceptional needs.

- **Income tax allowances and tax concessions.**
  In addition to these provisions provided by the State a person with a disability may receive support from a former employer (occupational pension); a private insurance company (permanent health or critical illness insurance); or the legal system (compensation).

6.10 The Commission has identified several serious weaknesses in the current provision of income support:

- The level of allowances do not make provision for the costs of disability, which can be very high for many people.

- Information on entitlements and regulations is poor.

- Each allowance and scheme has a separate set of assessment processes, and people with disabilities are faced with a bewildering array of forms and examinations. The medical model of assessment is a serious problem.

- Health boards differ widely in their application of eligibility and means testing criteria.

- The absence of an appeals system in relation to allowances and schemes operated through health boards.

- The withdrawal of allowances when people spend time in hospital creates hardship.

- The non-payment of allowances to people in residential care, which creates unacceptable levels of dependency.

- The disincentive to participate in education, training or work which arises because of the lack of flexibility in the income support systems for people with disabilities.

6.11 To address these deficiencies, a comprehensive system of income support for people with disabilities should be established which would apply national standards to payments. A person with a disability must have a right to the disability payment once they meet the qualification conditions. The system must be flexible and capable of being tailored to meet the needs of the individual.

6.12   There is a need to establish two types of payments:

- a payment to compensate for loss of income due to an incapacity for full-time work, or to work to full potential, to be called a "Disability Pension".

- a graduated payment to meet the additional everyday costs associated with disability. This payment would be irrespective of whether the person with a disability is at work or not. It should be called the "Costs of Disability Payment".

6.13   At present, the three main payments in the income support area are the contributory invalidity pension, the means-tested blind pension both administered by the Department of Social Welfare and the means-tested Disabled Persons Maintenance Allowance (DPMA) which was administered by the Health Boards up to 2nd October, 1996. From that date, responsibility for the scheme was transferred to the Department of Social Welfare and the scheme has been re-named Disability Allowance. Whilst the Commission welcomes the transfer of this scheme to the agency responsible for mainstream income maintenance payments, the system of payments for people affected by long-term incapacity for work remain unnecessarily complex.

6.14   The current disability benefit payment relates generally to illness rather than disability: it should be renamed "Sickness Benefit". As it relates to the total labour force and not just people with disabilities, this payment is outside the scope of this report. However, an enquiry needs to be carried out to see if any people with disabilities are included for two years or more. If so, they should be given the choice of transferring to the new Disability Pension.

6.15   The principal of "rights not charity" requires that all disability payments should be provided for in legislation which makes clear that there is a legal right to payment.

Disability Pension

6.16   The Commission recommends that a unified scheme called the Disability Pension should be established to provide support for people with disabilities who are incapable of full-time work in the long term due to disability. The Disability Pension would be administered by the Department of Social Welfare and would replace the three main existing schemes.

6.17   The Disability Pension should be a pension payable to all people with disabilities, including those who live full-time or part-time in residential settings, who meet the qualifying conditions. This payment would be a step towards achieving equal citizenship for all people with disabilities.

6.18   The disability pension should not be means-tested, as the qualifying conditions can protect against misuse.

6.19   The disability pension should be a weekly pension. The initial rate of payment should be the same as the current rate for invalidity pension, including payments for dependants. The rates of payment recommended by the Commission on Social Welfare should be achieved as a matter of priority in relation to all income replacement payments.

6.20   Incentives to undertake employment should be openly available to persons in receipt of disability pension taking particular account of the extent to which a person is allowed work without losing entitlement and the extent to which the pension is reduced on the basis of such income.

6.21   Qualifying Conditions:
A person must be aged 16 to 66 with a disability or illness resulting in their not being able to undertake work which would otherwise be suitable for a person of their age, experience and qualifications. They must have either a minimum number of PRSI contributions and medical certification or, in the absence of these contributions, medical certification that they have been substantially disabled and are likely to be permanently incapacitated.

Additional Costs Of Disability

6.22   Disability gives rise to extra costs. The National Rehabilitation Board has carried out an illustrative survey of 30 people with disabilities in urban areas and is currently carrying out a further survey on 30 people in a rural area. Initial results indicate that most participants had additional disability related costs. These included general living costs, food, heating, clothes, laundry services, equipment, aids and furniture and adaptations to their homes. While the small numbers involved mean that the case studies cannot be used to estimate average additional income needs for all people with disabilities, they do clearly indicate that people with disabilities have significant additional costs associated with their disability.

6.23   At present, there is no comprehensive payment to meet these significant extra costs faced by people with disabilities. There are, however, a range of payments and benefits-in-kind which, in practice, go some way towards meeting these costs. These benefits are not comprehensive and in many cases are paid on a discretionary basis.

6.24   The additional costs of disability can be classified according to area of needs as follows:

- Equipment

- Mobility and Communication (travel and telephone)

- Living Costs (fuel, food, clothing etc.)

- Medical

- Care and Assistance (including personal assistants)

6.25 On the basis of the aforementioned surveys and the available information, the State should, as a matter of principle, acknowledge its role of supporting people with disabilities and their families in meeting the additional costs arising from disability.

6.26 We recommend that the Department of Health and Social Services introduce a variable Costs of Disability Payment where services are not or cannot be provided. This payment should be available to all people with disabilities irrespective of their age and employment status. This payment should not be taxable.

6.27 We recommend the implementation of a nationwide assessment procedure based on needs, and the establishment of an independent appeal system in relation to such assessments.

6.28 To facilitate the above, a system to co-ordinate the mix of services and payments at an appropriate level is required. This co-ordination role would involve assessing needs and co-ordinating the provision of payments and services - as outlined in Chapter 4 of this report.

6.29 Where possible, existing schemes should be used to meet the additional needs of disability. There is at least one existing scheme in each area of need identified above. These could be built upon, thereby reducing the overall cost of the new payment. Only where this is not possible should there be eligibility for a Costs of Disability Payment.

6.30 In addition to the above two payments mentioned, a separate payments system for carers is required.

Payments For Carers

6.31 There are two main payments to carers at present. The domiciliary care allowance is paid in respect of the care of children between the ages of 2 and 16 with severe disabilities: it is administered by the Health Boards on behalf of the Department of Health. The carers' allowance is an income replacement payment for carers administered by the Department of Social Welfare. There are also a range of tax allowances which are broadly in the area of caring for a person with a disability. These include the "incapacitated child allowance", the "dependent relative allowance", the "blind person's allowance" and the "allowance for the care of an incapacitated individual".

6.32   We recommend that the existing domiciliary care allowance should continue but its administration should be transferred to the Department of Social Welfare.

6.33   The carers' allowance, however, needs major overhaul. A large majority of carers are women but the restrictive nature of the present criteria means that many carers do not qualify for the allowance. This results in exploitation of many carers and is a major issue which needs to be addressed by the state immediately. The definition of "carer" is too restrictive and should be reviewed.

6.34   We recommend the payment of a Carers Allowance to all carers. Where appropriate, the person being cared for should be consulted about the decision to grant or terminate a payment.

6.35   Qualifying Conditions:
Persons caring for all people who require full-time care and attention should be eligible for this payment.

Where a person qualifies for the domiciliary care allowance, he or she will automatically qualify for the carer's allowance when the individual being cared for reaches age 16 unless they go into a full-time residential setting.

Carers of a person in a five day residential setting should also be paid on a pro-rata basis, i.e. weekend or holiday payment.

Persons caring for more than one person with a disability should receive a pro-rata payment, i.e. double, treble etc.

The carer should not be disqualified if he or she is engaged in any additional work outside their home. A certain amount of earnings should be disregarded for the purpose of the means test.

In some other EU countries (e.g. France), carers are awarded fully-paid contributions which entitle them to social welfare benefits with the cost being met by the State. This approach should be followed in this country.

6.36   The rates of payment recommended by the Commission on Social Welfare should be achieved as a matter of priority in relation to all income replacement payments.

6.37 Subject to the introduction of this new carers allowance the existing tax allowances should be phased out for new claimants. The costs of these allowances should be put towards the cost of the new payment.

6.38 The means test should be related to the carer's means only and should not include that of his/her spouse or partner.

6.39 This payment should not be taxable.

National Anti-Poverty Strategy

6.40 The Commission notes that the Government is currently engaged in a consultative process towards establishing a National Anti-Poverty Strategy. The Commission welcomes this initiative and recommends that specific regard be given within any Anti-Poverty Strategy to combating the disproportionate impact of poverty on people with disabilities.

A Strategy for Equality Report of the Commission on the Status of People with Disabilities

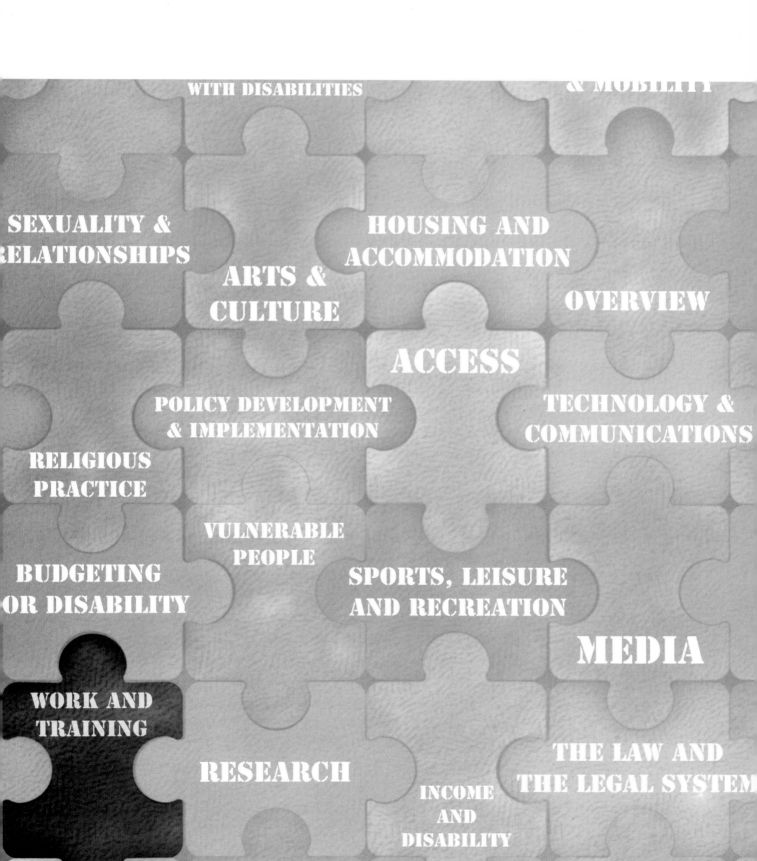

Where are the jobs? I have never had paid work, and feel sometimes bitter that I have nothing to show for myself. Even though I don't consider myself to be old, the years are slipping away in terms of finding a job, like so-called normal people. I have hopes and dreams about the future, and don't see why I, or any person with a disability, should have to settle for anything less. I feel if nothing is done that I will still be doing courses to fill in time in ten years' time.

- excerpt from submission

7.1   Employment and training are important routes for people with disabilities to achieve economic and social independence. Unfortunately, they are among the many areas in which people with disabilities are at a disadvantage compared to the rest of society. Their abilities and their potential contribution to the economic and social development of Ireland have yet to be positively recognised. The removal of barriers which prevented the full participation of women in the Irish workforce provides a practical example of how, on the basis of equality, people with disabilities can achieve greater participation within the world of work.

7.2   Reliable statistics on the numbers of people with disabilities within the workforce are not available. The evidence which does exist suggests that the unemployment rate among them is significantly higher than in the labour market as a whole and that employment, where it is available, is often poorly paid and of a low-status. Surveys by organisations concerned with disability suggest unemployment levels of 70% upwards.

7.3   There are clear links between disability and poverty, a connection which is aggravated by high unemployment. Both unemployment and poverty are likely to have a disproportionate effect on people with disabilities compared with other sectors of the population. A fundamental change in existing employment policies is needed to reduce the exclusion experienced by people with disabilities and to reduce the impact of poverty on the individual and members of their families.

7.4   The rapid increase in long-term unemployment since 1980 has created additional barriers for people with disabilities. Labour Force Surveys show that the unemployment rate for those under 25 who left school with no qualifications is significantly higher than for others. People with disabilities are generally likely to be particularly disadvantaged in this regard.

7.5   The report of the Task Force on Long-Term Unemployment (December 1995) recognised the need for positive discrimination measures in favour of those at a particular disadvantage in the labour market. A number of such measures, such as the Employment Support Scheme, have proved their cost-effectiveness in getting people off long-term state supports and into open employment. Notwithstanding substantial savings to the Exchequer in payments such as disability allowances, the resources allocated to such measures are currently insufficient to allow them to be used to full effect.

7.6   The Commission welcomes the government's commitment to the early introduction of legislation to outlaw discrimination in employment and training on the grounds of disability and recommends that appropriate legislation, which should take account of the experience of similar existing legislation in other jurisdictions, be introduced as a matter of immediate priority.

7.7   It also supports the recommendations of the National Economic and Social Forum's report on "Equality Proofing Issues" which promotes equality for people with disabilities. It recommends that the Minister for Equality and Law Reform should bring proposals to Government within six months aimed at securing agreement to a policy of "disability proofing".

7.8   The Commission believes there should be increased expenditure on creating sustainable employment for people with disabilities. The current Government Pilot Programme on Employment of People with Disabilities (PEP) is one example of such investment. This programme should be evaluated as a matter of urgency and, subject to positive results, be renewed and expanded.

7.9   Consideration should be given to allocating a greater proportion of EU financial support to direct employment measures, including the creation of new jobs in personal services for people with disabilities, worker co-operatives, and the development of job-seeking skills. An appropriate proportion of the 1% employment levy should be allocated to the development and provision of work opportunities for people with disabilities.

7.10   Many workers with disabilities acquired their disability while in work. A UK survey has shown that, of 1.5m economically active people with disabilities, about 70% became disabled while in work. As a basic measure towards the prevention of avoidable disabilities, the provisions of the Safety Health and Welfare at Work Act should be properly resourced and enforced and monitored to ensure that the Act is not used in a manner which impedes the employment of people with disabilities. Consideration should be given to the introduction of a system of disability/rehabilitation leave to enable people who acquire a disability while in employment to avail of medical and/or rehabilitation programmes outside the scope of existing leave arrangements, in order to facilitate their retention in employment and reduce the levels of avoidable unemployment.

7.11   The Commission also notes the continuing incidence of disabilities arising from farm accidents and recommends that State and representative organisations in the agriculture sector should develop additional safety awareness programmes and policies at national and local levels.

Employment

7.12   Overall government responsibility for vocational training and employment of people with disabilities should be assigned to the Department of Enterprise and Employment. It should produce a strategy paper on the employment and training of people with disabilities within six months of responsibility being assigned.

7.13   The Department of Enterprise and Employment should arrange for the collection, collation and publication of comprehensive labour market statistics in respect of people with disabilities from an early date.

7.14   Some people with disabilities have secure open employment or, in a number of cases, self-employment, with little if any formal assistance. Many have obtained employment through vocational training and job placement services specifically for people with disabilities. Further assistance is clearly required, however, if the number of people with disabilities at work is to be increased. Indeed, the Government has already acknowledged that further measures are needed if the situation is to improve.

7.15   The most direct Government measure to assist people with disabilities in getting jobs has been the three per cent quota of public service jobs reserved for them. Although introduced in 1977, the quota was only achieved for the first time in the civil service within the past three years. It has not yet been achieved in the wider public service.

7.16   The Government, in *A Programme for Renewal*, committed itself to fully implementing the quota system in the public service and to giving serious consideration to its statutory extension throughout the economy. The Commission endorses the Government's commitment to the full implementation of the quota within the public sector and recommends that this objective should be fully attained within three years. It further recommends stricter monitoring of quota compliance within both the civil service and all State bodies and annual publication of the situation in each government department/State body. Recruitment of a person with disabilities under the public sector quota scheme should not be regarded as being in breach of any recruitment embargo which may exist.

It is disappointing that many of the agencies which exist to provide services to people with disabilities and which receive substantial Exchequer funding give a poor example in employing people with disabilities. It is difficult to understand how such organisations hope to persuade others to employ people with disabilities when their own record in this regard is poor.

7.17   All Exchequer-supported organisations which have been established to provide services to people with disabilities should attain an eight per cent quota within four years.

7.18   People with disabilities participating in, advising or providing consultancy services to the State, State agencies, county enterprise boards and so on should be properly remunerated for their contributions.

7.19 As already noted, the Government promised to consider a wider quota system for the whole economy. There are many arguments for and against employment quotas and their extension to the economy as a whole. The Commission has heard evidence that a number of private sector organisations have voluntarily decided to initiate moves to employ a greater proportion of people with disabilities in their workforce and to encourage other private sector employers to do the same. While the Commission has yet to be convinced that such initiatives will be widely followed, it welcomes what it hopes will be a new commitment to greater equity in private sector recruitment.

7.20 In the light of this, the Commission does not recommend the enforcement of a mandatory quota in the private sector for people with disabilities at this time but recommends that the position be reviewed after three years. That will allow private sector employers adequate time to take voluntary action to include people with disabilities within the workforce and ensure equality of employment opportunities and policies. Should less than three per cent employment be achieved within that period, however, the Commission recommends the implementation and enforcement of a mandatory quota in this sector.

7.21 Employers are represented on the National Advisory Committee on Training and Employment and, together with representatives of trade unions and other key interest groups, have contributed to the development of a number of initiatives to promote employment for people with disabilities. One such initiative, the Positive to Disability Symbol, was awarded for the first time in 1996 to a number of organisations which operate positive policies in relation to the recruitment and employment of people with disabilities.

In awarding contracts of business, the state and its agencies should, subject to compliance with EU or national regulations, give positive consideration to suppliers of goods or services who comply with the employment quota or the Positive to Disability Programme.

7.22 The Commission considers that there is a need to better inform employers, social partners and state agencies in areas such as disability awareness, access auditing, disability equality training and disability prevention training. Such areas have the potential of creating new employment opportunities for people with disabilities.

7.23 The Employment Support Scheme, mentioned earlier, provides wage subsidies in respect of people with disabilities. Employers may also be assisted, where it is necessary to adapt a workplace or equipment, under the National Rehabilitation

Board's Workplace/Equipment Adaptation Grant Scheme. In 1995, grants under the scheme assisted the recruitment or retention in employment of 82 people with disabilities. However, the scope of the scheme is limited by inadequate funding.

The Commission recommends that additional resources be made available to enhance these measures and to develop further initiatives. The Employment Support Scheme is a beneficial investment by the state in promoting employment and the Commission recommends that it be funded to achieve a minimum target of 500 jobs a year for people with disabilities over the next three years. It also recommends that the Equipment Adaptation Scheme be expanded to allow payments to people seeking employment and that a minimum target of 500 unemployed people with disabilities receiving such assistance a year be achieved over the next three years.

7.24   The importance to employers of non-financial supports should not be under-estimated. The availability of advice, information and support, when needed, can make an important difference in employers' decisions on recruitment and the retention of people in employment, and such supports should be provided.

Disability awareness training for managers, employees and trade union representatives, should be developed and undertaken in partnership with employer and worker representatives. People with disabilities should be involved in the development and delivery of such training: the state should provide funding to facilitate the training of people with disabilities as awareness trainers.

7.25   The Commission commends the actions of IBEC and ICTU in forming consultative committees to advise on disability issues. Such committees provide a basis for additional actions and policies by the social partners and the Commission recommends that they develop their mechanisms to include people with disabilities within their membership and policy strategies.

7.26   The Commission notes the positive policies of Social Partners at European level. The Commission supports the framework of actions by Social Partners in the Declaration of European Businesses against Exclusion and the HELIOS II programme concerning the economic integration of people with disabilities.

7.27   National and regional structures of co-operation between employers, trade unions, organisations of people with disabilities, State agencies and the voluntary sector should be established to explore, promote and implement policies which increase or create employment opportunities for people with disabilities. Social partners in national, sectoral or industrial agreements should implement an equality clause which promotes the recruitment of people with disabilities and which supports measures which promote the retention in employment of workers who acquire a disability. National economic agreements should contain clear and measurable objectives towards promoting employment of people with disabilities, who should be clearly consulted in such processes.

7.28   The Commission is impressed at the potential of people with disabilities being self-employed and indeed of creating new employment opportunities for unemployed persons. Clear potential exists within the services, community and co-operative sectors. The Department of Enterprise and Employment, in conjunction with the Co-operative Development Unit of FÁS, should establish a pilot programme of worker co-operative employment by people with disabilities with a target of 100 jobs a year being achieved over the next three years.

7.29   The Commission comments later in this report on the current dynamic taking place in the areas of arts, culture and the media. These expanding sectors of the economy provide new opportunities for the employment of people with disabilities and these opportunities should be grasped. The Department of Enterprise and Employment, in conjunction with the Department of Arts, Culture and Gaeltacht, should initiate programmes to promote and identify employment opportunities for people with disabilities within these areas.

7.30   Various alternative forms of employment between the extremes of competitive open employment and sheltered work settings have been developed to help meet particular needs. One such alternative, commonly called Supported Employment, continues to develop. It involves a number of key elements, notably:

- integration: a person with severe disabilities must be a regular employee of the business and work with co-workers who do not have disabilities,

- paid work: work performed is paid for,

- individualised services: all aspects of the supported employment should be tailored to the needs and capabilities of the person concerned,

- ongoing supports: comprehensive supports such as transport, money and time management, advocacy and strategies for managing social and communications issues must be available for each person who needs them, for as long as required.

7.31   There are many people with disabilities, however, who may not have the capacity to work in open employment and for whom some form of sheltered employment may be the best option. There is an acute shortage of sheltered work places, which are virtually restricted to those who have completed training programmes in centres linked to existing sheltered work places.

The Commission is aware that the NRB National Advisory Committee on Training and Employment (NACTE) is reviewing the medium and longer-term needs, but recommends that government funding should be provided in the 1997 Budget to ensure the continuation of existing under-funded sheltered workplaces and the addition of 500 places.

7.32   The Department of Enterprise and Employment should establish a resource to advise and assist agencies, communities or individuals to develop new employment opportunities, including sheltered workshops. Support should include help with market research, product development, marketing, financial management, and so on.

7.33   Sheltered employment is not generally covered by employment protection legislation and there are no officially approved standards for the establishment and operation of such schemes. Pay is usually given through informal arrangements in the form of a supplement to the individual's Disability Allowance: these arrangements do not involve formal employment relationships and lack the normal protection which such relationships provide.

   The status and rights of people with a disability in sheltered work settings should be defined and appropriately protected. Standards should be introduced for the establishment and operation of sheltered workshops.

7.34   Consideration should be given to the introduction of measures to promote the use of goods and services from sheltered workshops among organisations in receipt of state funding and public contracts.

7.35   All public employment services should be fully accessible to people with disabilities. Occupational guidance should continue to be available to all people with disabilities who seek it.

7.36   People with disabilities should be eligible, without restriction as to period of unemployment, to participate in all government employment measures directed at those who are unemployed. This includes schemes such as Community Employment, Workplace, Jobstart as well as programmes of County Enterprise Boards, Area Partnerships, Leader and other initiatives .

Training

7.37   The acquisition of relevant skills, through education and training, is essential in order to compete for jobs, particularly in a situation of continuing high unemployment. Training opportunities for people with disabilities must be at least as good - in terms of their availability, relevance to job needs, standards reached and recognition by employers - as those for other people.

7.38   Much of the training for people with disabilities is provided by voluntary or non-governmental organisations and regional health authorities in specialised training centres and largely with financial support from the European Social Fund.

7.39   There have been a number of important measures, particularly in recent years, to help ensure that the quality of training meets specified standards at least comparable to those obtaining in more mainstream training centres. For example,

- A National Accreditation Committee was established in 1996 to oversee the implementation of the approved Standard of Vocational Training;

- From 1992 to 1995, 240 instructors in specialised centres were awarded the Certificate in Training (Special Needs);

- At the end of 1995, 55% of all courses in specialised centres were leading to nationally recognised certificates: it is planned to have all courses certified by 1999;

- £33.58m of European Regional Development Funding has been allocated over the period 1994 to 1999 to improve and update training centre premises and equipment.

7.40   Notwithstanding the excellent training being provided in many specialised centres, the fact remains that such training is largely segregated in nature. It is separate in both policy and in terms of governmental responsibility from mainstream training.

This is not to suggest that integrated mainstream training of itself is the best option for all people with disabilities. Many mainstream centres are not sufficiently accessible to cater for all disabilities. Specialist instruction and other skills are not available, and curricula, equipment, etc. may not be entirely appropriate. There is no doubt, however, that mainstream training offers a wider choice of courses than can currently be offered through specialised centres, as well as the practical ambience of integration.

7.41   Equality of training opportunity, which does not exist at present for all people with disabilities, requires that the present policies and systems be fundamentally reviewed and revised.

7.42   People with disabilities participating in training should be paid an appropriate training allowance and retain their secondary benefits. Matching funding for European Social Fund supported training should not be dependent on attracting persons who are availing of disability-related income.

7.43   An immediate review of mainstream vocational training programmes should be undertaken with a view to maximising their accessibility to people with disabilities.

7.44   The range of training choices for people with disabilities should be extended by inviting appropriate training providers outside the specialist agencies to offer relevant and suitable programmes. Such providers must be properly accredited and could include educational establishments, employers, private training organisations as well as public mainstream agencies.

7.45   New, innovative and more flexible models of training should be encouraged. There should be a greater concentration on job placement activity.

7.46   Priority might be given to training which integrates people with and without disabilities.

7.47   Training in training centres, whether specialised or mainstream, is not the only or necessarily the best method of acquiring skills, knowledge and attitudes for employment. Many employers have both the competence and facilities to provide suitable training; work experience should play an important part in equipping people for work. The Commission supports additional actions by employers in these areas and notes the development of examples such as "Job Coach" programmes in other EU states which are of direct benefit to the employer and person with disabilities.

7.48   Distance/open learning and new technology provide potential for many different approaches. There is considerable scope for innovation and more flexible forms of training.

7.49   For many people with disabilities, training in areas such as life skills, social skills, representational skills, self-advocacy and assertiveness are, and should continue to be, integral parts of vocational training. Training should continue to be available for those who wish to work in sheltered or supported work settings.

7.50   Specialist agencies should be encouraged to offer mainstream and integrated programmes.

A Strategy for Equality Report of the Commission on the Status of People with Disabilities

Chapter Eight
INSURANCE

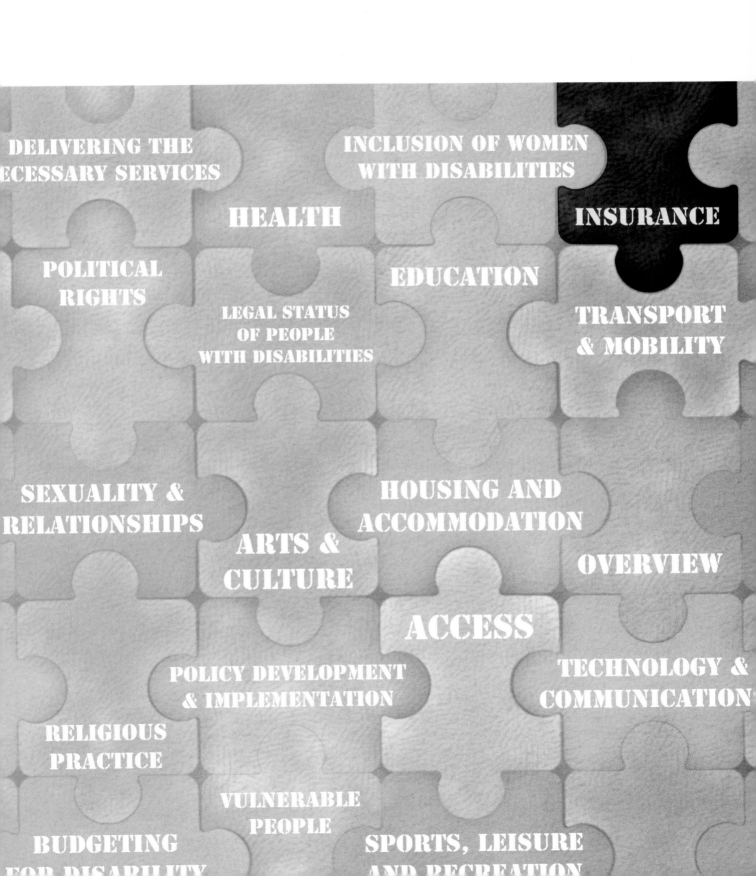

DELIVERING THE
ECESSARY SERVICES

INCLUSION OF WOMEN
WITH DISABILITIES

HEALTH

INSURANCE

POLITICAL
RIGHTS

EDUCATION

LEGAL STATUS
OF PEOPLE
WITH DISABILITIES

TRANSPORT
& MOBILITY

SEXUALITY &
RELATIONSHIPS

HOUSING AND
ACCOMMODATION

ARTS &
CULTURE

OVERVIEW

ACCESS

POLICY DEVELOPMENT
& IMPLEMENTATION

TECHNOLOGY &
COMMUNICATION

RELIGIOUS
PRACTICE

VULNERABLE
PEOPLE

BUDGETING
FOR DISABILITY

SPORTS, LEISURE
AND RECREATION

8.1 Insurance is another area in which people with disabilities are disadvantaged and discriminated against. In particular, drivers with disabilities find it extremely difficult to get motor insurance, even when they have a long number of years with no claims bonuses.

8.2 Insurance companies claim that they do not discriminate against drivers with disabilities. Where drivers do get insurance, however, it appears to be common practice among insurance companies to apply extra loading to them. We have found no proof, actuarial or otherwise, that drivers with disabilities are in general associated with greater risks.

8.3 The Ombudsman's office should investigate, and publish its report, before the end of July, 1997 on any loading by insurance companies of drivers with disabilities. Powers should be given to the Ombudsman's office to examine companies' actuarial figures and records.

8.4 Legislation should be introduced by the Department of Enterprise and Employment to prevent insurance companies from refusing quotations to drivers with disabilities.

8.5 Although the greatest cause of concern related to motor insurance, there were also complaints about loadings on life insurance policies as well as difficulties in obtaining permanent health insurance cover, a product supplied by the life insurance market. Also of concern was the failure of the VHI to provide certain facilities.

8.6 In addition, there are problems with people with disabilities being refused entry into institutions or public places because they were seen as an "insurance risk". In one case, refusal was to third level education. The inability of employers to obtain affordable insurance for employees is also a problem.

Recommendations

8.7 To address these problems, the Commission recommends that the Department of Equality and Law Reform should introduce anti-discrimination legislation to ensure the following:

(i) Any insurer may not discriminate against any person or group of people with a disability on the basis of their disability, when quoting for or issuing insurance cover, provided, however, that cover for specific disabilities and diseases may be excluded or provided subject to a higher charge, and benefits with respect to specific disabilities and diseases may be limited in amount, if the party providing insurance cover can establish the permissibility of such an exclusion, higher charge, or limitation pursuant to the requirements at (b) of this section.

(ii)   Any insurer may not discriminate against any individual, company or body when quoting for or issuing insurance cover for any event involving people with disabilities, provided, however, that cover may be excluded or provided subject to a higher charge, if the party providing insurance cover can establish the permissibility of such an exclusion, higher charge, or limitation pursuant to the requirements at (b) of this section.

(iii) Any insurer may not discriminate against any individual, company or body when quoting for or issuing motor insurance, provided, however, that cover for specific disabilities and diseases may be excluded or provided subject to a higher charge, and benefits with respect to specific disabilities and diseases may be limited in amount, if the party providing insurance cover can establish the permissibility of such an exclusion, higher charge, or limitation pursuant to the requirements at (b) of this section.

(b)   For purposes of establishing the permissibility of any exclusion or limitation, the party providing insurance must establish by clear and convincing evidence that the exclusion, higher charge, or limitation: (1) is not based on stereotype or prejudice; (2) is supported by sound and current actuarial data; and (3) is necessary to the realisation of a fair and reasonable rate of return on investment by the party providing insurance.

8.8   In the above recommendation the following definitions should apply:

Insurer: Any person or body providing insurance cover whether in the business of insurance or otherwise.

Insurance Cover: Insurance cover shall be deemed to include both insurance cover and any benefit or payment arrangements which constitute the practical equivalent thereof.

Disability: Disability shall be deemed to include a person's actual disability, history of disability, perceived disability and association with a person who has an actual disability, has a history of disability or is perceived to have a disability.

Discrimination: Discrimination shall include, without limitation, any refusal to deal on the same basis as the person providing insurance ordinarily and customarily deals with those seeking to obtain insurance cover; the imposition of any application conditions or requirements in excess of those that the person providing insurance ordinarily and customarily imposes on those seeking to obtain insurance cover; the charging of premiums in an amount exceeding that which the person providing insurance/benefits less than those ordinarily and customarily provided pursuant to cover of that kind and type.

Part Four
SOCIAL AND CIVIL RIGHTS

Chapter Nine
ACCESS

All my school go to a cinema once a month. I'd love to go there but they told me that the place in which the films are shown is upstairs. Please try and stop things from being held upstairs or downstairs.

- excerpt from submission

9.1   Access is the gateway to full participation in society for people with disabilities. In its broadest sense, it does not just mean access to buildings or the external environment of streets, parks and beaches. It also means access to rights like the right to travel freely, the right to health care, the right to education, the right to housing, the right to personal social services, the right to communications, the right to benefit equally from the Information Society, and the right to express their sexuality. In short, it means full and equal access to all the rights, responsibilities and benefits of society.

9.2   This chapter is concerned with access to the built and external environments, which for most people with disabilities, is a pre-requisite condition necessary to enable their access and participation in any or all of the other aspects of social and civil society.

9.3   The frustration and anger caused to people with disabilities by the inaccessibility of buildings was all too evident in the submissions to the Commission. Added to buildings themselves was the lack of consideration and awareness displayed by managers. Either singly or together, they create a sense of exclusion which can take a person with a disability to the edge of despair and confirm them in their isolation and marginalisation from society.

9.4   Numerous references were also made to other barriers, needlessly placed in the way of the full participation of people with disabilities. For instance, wheelchair users find it impossible to go to beaches even though that could be rectified by simple and inexpensive arrangements. The absence of a bleeping system on traffic lights makes life so difficult for people who are blind.

9.5   The introduction in 1991 of the Building Regulations with a section on access for people with disabilities - Part M (Access for Disabled People) which referred only to new buildings and significant extensions to older buildings raised the hopes and expectations of many people. Unfortunately, those hopes have given way to a weary resignation. Despite strong pressure, the pace of change has been agonisingly slow.

9.6   One of the main reasons for the state of resignation is clear from reading the regulations. Their approach to the question of access is not aimed at establishing an enabling environment for everyone but of making special provision for special cases. For example, requirement M1 reads: "Reasonable provision shall be made to enable disabled people to have safe and independent access to a building and to those parts of a building to which it is appropriate to have access". Implicit in that is the suggestion that it might be "reasonable" to deny people with disabilities access to certain parts of buildings.

9.7   Although the regulations cover safe and independent use of buildings by people with impaired vision or hearing, the wording of requirements suggests that the approach to access is still rooted primarily in access for people with impaired mobility.

9.8   Furthermore, there is no consideration of the benefits of improved accessibility for everybody and there are inconsistencies between Part M and other parts of the regulations dealing with fire (Part B) and stairways, ramps and guards (Part K).

9.9   The approach taken by the Building Regulations generally results in designers and others interpreting the cited minimum requirements as being optimum or even maximum requirements. They also reinforce the idea that just a few accessible features in a building will do rather than making the building as a whole accessible.

9.10   Such deficiencies are compounded by the lack of definition of terms such as "reasonable", "practicable" and "appropriate". The absence of clear definitions leads to vagueness in their application, especially when there are no clearly-defined rights of redress.

9.11   The other main disappointment with the Building Regulations is the apparent lack of enforcement of Part M. Local authorities are responsible for ensuring compliance with the regulations, although the legislation is worded in such a way that building inspection per se is not mandatory. This works to the detriment of people with disabilities since good, workable access is still considered by many designers and building owners to be less essential than other aspects of the regulations.

9.12   Mandatory access to existing buildings and to the external environment has been achieved elsewhere only through anti-discrimination legislation. The same mechanism has been used to ensure the provision of information in non-print formats and of sign interpretation. Even with anti-discrimination legislation, however, a supporting structure of technical and non-technical information and back-up is essential to ensure that "accessibility" is not confined to the minimalist approach of building codes.

9.13   The success of legislation on access elsewhere rests on the accuracy with which such terms as "reasonable accommodation" and "undue burden" are defined. In the absence of clear criteria on this issue in Ireland "reasonable" has been interpreted to mean "reasonable in terms of cost" (i.e. cheap) as opposed to reasonable compared to an entity's income or assets as in the USA.

9.14   Definitions and understandings of what is "reasonable" vary according to cultural circumstances. Accessible features can be considered as an expensive, troublesome add-on which responds to the demands of a very few people, or as a facilitative approach to design which ensures that all users can gain maximum benefit. While goodwill abounds in Ireland, the evidence points to a scenario nearer to the former than the latter.

9.15　A more creative way of looking at this issue is to study a particular place and to see if a solution is possible to problems of access. If it is, then it is practicable. If the solution does not work, it is not reasonable: if the solution does work, it is reasonable. So long as it works for preferably 99% (if not, in some circumstances 95%) of all users, then it is both reasonable and practicable. In this way "practicable" defines "reasonable" and not the other way round. This uncompromising approach clearly puts people with disabilities, rather than designers, at the centre of the process. It removes the element of emotion or sympathy from the equation, replacing it with scientific rationality. This approach is implicit in the regulations accompanying the Americans with Disabilities Act.

9.16　Attitudinal changes cannot be achieved by legislation alone. The key notion of accessible design offering benefits to everyone is beginning, slowly, to take hold, largely because of two linked considerations: demographics and economics.

9.17　While these factors may in time prove compelling, education is necessary to shift the predominant culture away from "special needs" and towards concepts of equal, active citizenship and the universal right of access. Such education is needed for designers, building owners and managers and the public in general.

9.18　In making recommendations to deal with the deficiencies outlined in this chapter, the Commission believes that people with disabilities should be involved at all key stages of the process. They should be involved especially in a national committee, resourced by the Department of the Environment and set up to develop policy and practice and monitor progress in relation to the universal right of access to the built and external environments. The committee should include representatives of user groups, providers, regulators, and appropriate Government departments and agencies.

9.19　The Commission recommends that the Department of the Environment should ensure that the universal right of access for all citizens becomes the over-arching principle which guides all relevant legislation, policy and practice in Ireland. The planning laws, fire regulations, health, safety and welfare legislation and all other legislation and guidelines which refer to any aspect of the built and/or external environments should also be reviewed by the Department from this perspective.

9.20 The Commission recommends that the Building Regulations, 1991 should be reviewed in the Department of the Environment to:

- eliminate inconsistencies from the Technical Guidance Documents which work to the detriment of people with disabilities.

- ensure that each local authority establishes an efficient building control department with responsibility for implementing the Building Regulations (and the Road Traffic Acts) fully and immediately.

- make building inspections mandatory.

- ensure that Part M is enforced vigorously.

9.21 The Department of the Environment should bring forward legislation to introduce access certificates, along the lines of existing fire certificates, specifying that buildings are safe and appropriate for use.

9.22 The Disabilities Bill to be introduced by the Department of Equality and Law Reform should ensure that all premises in public ownership or open to the public in any way (including employees, customers etc.) and the services and facilities they contain should become accessible to all citizens over a short timescale. The legislation should require pro-activity on the part of the public and private entities in achieving compliance.

9.23 The Department of Justice should also propose amendments to all legislation pertaining to the granting of licences to premises open to the public - including licences to places of entertainment and public assembly, public houses and restaurants - to require the District Court to have regard to the adequacy of access by people with disabilities.

9.24 The Department of Equality and Law Reform should introduce Equal Status legislation concerning access to goods, facilities and services as soon as possible, ensuring that the legislation and any accompanying regulations and/or guidelines define what is reasonable and what constitutes undue difficulty in such a way as to minimise derogations which mitigate against the universal right of access.

9.25 Given the importance of changing professional and public attitudes, the Department of the Environment should introduce a public awareness campaign to educate all citizens about the universal right of access. Professional bodies of architects and designers such as the Royal Institute of Architects in Ireland (RIAI), the Society of Designers in Ireland (SDI) and the Institute for Design and Disability (IDD) have already done some work to promote accessibility.

9.26 The Commission recommends that the RIAI and SDI should ensure that the universal right of access becomes a key criterion in all their courses, competitions and activities. Schools of architecture and other bodies involved in designer education should demonstrate practical commitment to the universal right of access as a teaching principle. Education and professional formation courses for architects and other designers should include examined studio projects involving universal (barrier-free) design.

9.27 FÁS should give consideration to extending its training for building control personnel to other interested participants, particularly facilitating people with disabilities to become involved. Training on access issues, starting from the principle of the universal right of access of all citizens, should be included on all vocational training courses, including in-service and continuing training, for design and building management professionals, such as planners, architects, engineers, fire/safety officers, interior designers, graphic designers, building managers and all allied service providers.

9.28 NRB is the sole agency in Ireland which can grant the International Symbol of Access to a premises. The use and usefulness of the International Symbol of Access is currently being reviewed by NRB.

The Commission recommends that the Department of the Environment should seek authorisation from Rehabilitation International to award the Symbol and that the Department draw up, in consultation with appropriate bodies, clear criteria and conditions governing the award of the Symbol. The scheme should then be relaunched, with all previous recipients invited to re-apply.

9.29 State funding mechanisms, including the National Lottery, should introduce accessibility to all citizens as a key criterion for the projects they fund.

9.30 However limited the benefits of the existing Building Regulations, the absence of any legally binding regulations regarding the external environment is worse. Standards vary enormously from place to place. Among the many barriers facing people with disabilities, especially those with mobility and sight impairments, are the conditions of pavements and the haphazard placing of street furniture and shop displays on them.

9.31 The existence of regulations would contribute significantly to the development of standards for roads, pavements, parkways, etc. in order to ensure equal participation for people with disabilities. The Department of the Environment should introduce legislation to regulate and enforce standards in these areas. It should also introduce legislation to regulate and enforce standards in signage to ensure consistency in symbol language, readability etc.

9.32   The prohibition of parking on pavements should be rigorously enforced and planning permission should be required for placement of street furniture. Local authorities should ensure that all pavements are dished and have tactile paving by the year 2000. Where pedestrian zones are created using cobblestones, a smooth path should also be provided. Wheelchair users should be entitled to use bicycle lanes.

9.33   Each local authority should employ an access officer to co-ordinate and promote access activities in their areas.

9.34   There has been a rapid development of local access groups, which are coalitions of people with disabilities, designers, interested local authority staff and people working in the field of disability. They are involved in checking out access for people with disabilities to the built environment. Most also advise building owners and contractors and provide advice on accessible parking, the dishing of footpaths and other aspects of the external environment.

9.35   The Commission recommends that the formation of an umbrella organisation for local access groups should be facilitated. Local access officers should support groups with training, technical information, advice on campaigning and group development.

9.36   In addition, local authorities should provide funding for local access groups and consult with access groups throughout the construction of new developments in the built and external environments.

9.37   The Department of the Environment should fund local authorities to improve accessibility in their areas on foot of agreed community based action plans.

Chapter Ten
HEALTH

DELIVERING THE
NECESSARY SERVICES

INCLUSION OF WOMEN
WITH DISABILITIES

HEALTH

INSURANCE

POLITICAL
RIGHTS

EDUCATION

LEGAL STATUS
OF PEOPLE
WITH DISABILITIES

TRANSPORT
& MOBILITY

SEXUALITY &
RELATIONSHIPS

HOUSING AND
ACCOMMODATION

ARTS &
CULTURE

OVERVIEW

ACCESS

POLICY DEVELOPMENT
& IMPLEMENTATION

TECHNOLOGY &
COMMUNICATIONS

RELIGIOUS
PRACTICE

VULNERABLE
PEOPLE

BUDGETING
FOR DISABILITY

SPORTS, LEISURE
AND RECREATION

When Peter was a baby and up until five years of age we were advised to put him in residential care, predicting that "he would ruin our life". This was a cause of distress when we needed support.

- excerpt from submission

10.1 Health is a state of complete physical, mental, emotional and social well-being and not merely an absence of disease or infirmity. Like the rest of the population, people with disabilities aspire to live in the best possible state of health and wish to have access to a full range of quality health services. Up to now, the needs of people with disabilities have almost always been met on a medical basis; thus many services which are not medical in nature, e.g., training and employment, have inappropriately been provided under the aegis of the Department of Health.

10.2 Health and personal social services have evolved over the years in response to a multiplicity of needs and pressures. This has resulted in services which are in need of a much greater degree of co-ordination. Consumer experience indicates that disability awareness training for health professionals of every discipline would be desirable. Submissions to the Commission also remark on a bias in the health services towards a cure rather than a care model.

10.3 Submissions to the Commission and statements at listening meetings showed that people with disabilities, parents and carers have serious concerns as to the quality of some existing services and about the lack of some fundamental services. Problems experienced with services include:

- inaccessibility of hospitals, health centres and doctors' surgeries;

- the concentration of vital services in Dublin;

- the unpredictable availability and underfunding of community services such as home helps and respite care;

- a widespread lack of disability awareness;

- the lack of consumer control of services;

- lack of clearly defined complaints procedures.

10.4 In formulating its recommendations, the Commission sought to build on proposals set out in the health strategy document Shaping a Healthier Future. The Commission broadly agrees with the objectives, principles and philosophy of the strategy, and looks forward to a real commitment from the Department of Health and health authorities to its implementation over the next few years.

Hospital Services

10.5 A visit or stay in a hospital/health facility can be a traumatic experience for many people with disabilities and their carers. Many hospitals, clinics, Health Board offices and other health facilities are not accessible or user friendly to people with disabilities. For example, many have steps but no ramps, narrow doors, unsuitable toilet facilities, no provision for communicating in Braille, or through sign language, and outside, high kerbs and lack of suitable car parking. Hospitals and other settings in which services are provided should be accessible both externally and internally.

10.6 Long periods of waiting in outpatient departments can cause discomfort and distress for some people with certain disabilities. Some of the special hospital and residential care facilities are located in buildings or provide accommodation which is inappropriate and below an acceptable standard.

10.7 In many instances children, adults and carers have to travel long distances, often at their own expense, for assessment or treatment. This is due to the concentration of services in the larger centres of population, particularly in Dublin. In this context the Commission welcomes the commitment in the Department of Health strategy document "Shaping a Healthier Future" to the development of regional services.

10.8 Relatives of people with disabilities who are attending a specialist service which is a long distance from their home should receive support in making regular visits to them. This is especially important in relation to children with disabilities. Such support may include free travel, crèche facilities etc. Ambulances for both routine and emergency admissions must be equipped to transport all persons including those in electric wheelchairs.

10.9 When a diagnosis, the impact of which is disabling is being given to a person, doctors should be required to advise the individual, or their family as appropriate, of the Disability Support Service (see Chapter 4) and the location of the nearest Resource Centre. A hospital based key worker should be allocated to each person who can facilitate communications between hospital staff, family and the person with a disability. This key worker would also be responsible for making arrangements to inform all relevant community services prior to the person's discharge.

10.10 Close liaison is required between hospital maternity units and all community services for children with disabilities. The key worker mentioned above should ensure that on discharge, parents of a child with a disability are allocated a key worker in their local Health Board to facilitate the effective delivery of services.

10.11 Staff in casualty departments must receive disability awareness training as a matter of urgency and the Department of Health should issue guidelines to casualty departments as soon as possible setting standards for the appropriate treatment of people with disabilities. All hospital staff at all levels should receive disability awareness training which addresses basic customer service and basic skills in dealing with people with disabilities.

10.12   In relation to use of scarce resources in the Health Services Persons with a disability offer opportunities for major health and social gain, which is now one of the key organising principles for the service. The Commission, therefore, recommends that special service programmes are organised for persons in this group which provide rapid and convenient access to relevant services designed to improve the overall quality and independence of their lives. In doing so, the service should reach out in a pro-active way to ensure that such a person is never inadvertently excluded because of his or her disability.

Community Care Services

10.13   The Department of Health has had a policy of providing a wide range of services in the community instead of in large institutions since publishing its health strategy Shaping a Healthier Future in 1994. Unfortunately, the shift to community-based services has not been smooth and community care services have developed in an unplanned and uncoordinated fashion. Some vital health and social services are excellent in some areas and totally absent in others. These vital services include personal care, home help and home care attendant services; psychological, occupational and psychiatric support services; occupational therapy, physiotherapy, and speech therapy; social work services.

10.14   Certain groups of people with disabilities have particular difficulty gaining access to health and personal social services. They include:

- people with brain damage as a result of accidents or other causes;

- people with rare syndromes;

- people with dual or multiple disabilities

- people with more significant disabilities and behavioural problems, who are sometimes treated as a lesser priority.

10.15   New services will have to be developed for people with disabilities in a co-ordinated and innovative way with service providers working together in partnership arrangements. For example, it is clear that few resources have been invested in the development of services for people with physical and sensory disabilities and that there may be insufficient funds to meet the huge range of service needs of this group over the next few years.

10.16   All surgical and medical appliances should be supplied free of charge to holders of the Long Term Illness Card. Health Act procedures for the supply of technical aids should be redefined ensuring that there is an adequate definition for technical aids and equipment and standard procedures for assessing requirements. The provision in the Act which allows refunds for medical and surgical appliances should be implemented. Research into the development of technical aids and equipment should be encouraged by government, and people with disabilities should be involved in the design of such research. Additional funding is required to ensure that there is a comprehensive supply of technical aids, as well as rapid, efficient assessment procedures. Money should also be provided by the Department of Health for the next five years for repair services for technical aids.

10.17   Day activity centres should be further developed nationwide on a permanent basis with appropriately trained staff and access to all modern therapies, including music, art, drama and alternative therapies like aromatherapy and reflexology etc.

10.18   Due regard should be taken in account of the particular needs of people with mental health/emotional difficulties and/or behavioural difficulties, as many of them have been excluded from a lot of the existing day activity centres and thus continue to experience social and recreational exclusion.

10.19   Three services are of vital importance to people with disabilities:

•   the home help scheme;

•   residential respite care;

•   personal assistance

10.20   The present role of home help assistants should be extended to provide more comprehensive care, including personal care as well as household duties and care at unsociable hours, where that is needed. Home help assistants should receive a basic training which includes disability awareness training as well as education about proper personal care assistance. Schemes such as the Home Care Attendance Scheme are to be welcomed. This Scheme is flexible and available at short notice to people with disabilities.

10.21   Respite care is a crucial element in community support services for people with disabilities. In recent years there has been a considerable expansion of this service for people with learning disabilities in the Mental Handicap area and there needs to be a similar expansion for those with a physical/sensory disability. The service should be flexible, including a range of options including home support, organised holidays and residential care. Sufficient funding should be provided to ensure a suitable service in terms of quality and frequency to all those who need it. Services should not be developed using inappropriate health/hospital buildings, which would continue the isolation of those least powerful in society. The Department of Health should develop minimum standards for respite care facilities and ensure that all new and existing units comply with those standards.

10.22 Personal assistance services should be provided for people with significant physical disabilities. A personal assistant, a concept coming from the Independent Living Movement, is someone employed directly by a person with a disability to assist him/her in participating in everyday life at home, school, work, or leisure activities. They are trained for their role through formal and informal training in which people with disabilities are fully involved. They facilitate Independent Living, which concerns empowering people with disabilities to live as they want, with the same choices as people without disabilities, using mainstream services and taking control over their own lives.

The Commission welcomes recent developments in peer counselling and peer support amongst people with disabilities. For example, there are now 5 trained deaf counsellors for deaf people. The Commission recommends that further ongoing support and development of these services should be given by the Departments of Health and Social Welfare.

10.23 Additional revenue funding should be provided over a five-year period to address current shortfalls in services for people with disabilities including

- day services

- therapy services such as occupational therapy, speech therapy, and physiotherapy

- respite care

- personal assistance services for people with significant disabilities

- peer counselling and peer support

- Counselling including genetic counselling

- residential care

10.24 GPs surgeries should be adapted where necessary to make them accessible to people with disabilities. The cost of such adaptation could be met from the general practice development fund and the indicative drug target scheme. The practice of having specialist outpatient clinics in general practice settings should be promoted and expanded.

10.25 The Commission recommends the development throughout the country of units specialising in continuing therapeutic care for people who have been discharged from medical rehabilitation centres (e.g., for paraplegia due to road traffic accident). Such units would be staffed by teams consisting of physiotherapists, occupational therapists, nurses and social workers, who would have ongoing supervision from the relevant specialised centre from which a patient had returned. In the central unit they would have regular refresher courses, training in new techniques, and opportunity to familiarise themselves with the individual treatment needs of any patient destined to return to their area. Other examples of people who would benefit greatly from such an approach would be the post-operative patient with a heart-lung transplant who now needs home care and special physiotherapy, the haemophiliac patient needing special regulation of their clotting factors and physiotherapy for the knee, the person suffering from juvenile diabetes etc.

Health Service Attitudes

10.26 The Commission heard and received complaints about the manner in which some health service personnel treat and communicate with people with disabilities, their parents and carers. This experience indicates the need for disability awareness training. The training of health care staff should therefore include a comprehensive disability awareness module designed in consultation with the Council for the Status of People with Disabilities.

Disability awareness training should be provided for all doctors at both undergraduate and postgraduate levels. And, as stated earlier, staff in casualty departments must receive disability awareness training as a matter of urgency. All hospital staff at all levels should receive disability awareness training which addresses basic customer service and basic skills in dealing with people with disabilities.

10.27 National standards should be set by the Department of Health for services provided to persons with a disability in the community. These should apply to medical, nursing, and paramedical staff.

A review of selection criteria for health care training should be undertaken with an increased emphasis on choosing candidates with interpersonal skills. This should involve assessing attitudes and personality via an interview prior to selection.

A postgraduate course for medical and paramedical personnel should be devised to improve their communications with people with disabilities. Such communications training will need constant revision using continuing medical education techniques developed by various medical bodies. A large number of health care staff have graduated without any training in communication skills or disability awareness whatsoever, as such courses are only recent additions to university curricula.

10.28 General practitioners and other community care personnel should receive up-dated training in screening and detection of persons at risk.

10.29 Genetic counselling services should be available nationwide as a matter of urgency.

Consumer Choice And Legal Rights

10.30 People with disabilities, their parents and carers complained about the lack of consumer participation in the planning and evaluation of health and social services and many felt that there should be structures to facilitate feedback from people using the services. In some cases, e.g., where clients cannot speak for themselves, parents were fearful of demanding a better quality service, in case the service they were getting was withdrawn.

Ways of maximising choice of service should be examined. For example, people with disabilities or their carers could be given control, either direct or indirect, of part or all of their allocation of resources for the purchase of services.

10.31 Case conferences concerning a person with a disability should include the person themselves and their family, as appropriate, as well as professionals from community and hospital services.

10.32 Medical and paramedical education should actively address patients' rights. The right to hear one's diagnosis in a sensitive and humane manner should be recognised. Medical personnel should be obliged to inform patients of all significant effects of therapy, including pharmaceutical preparations, surgical and investigative procedures, electroconvulsive shock therapy, psychological interventions and so on.

10.33 All persons, having been fully informed of their rights, can refuse to undergo treatment. This right of refusal must be respected by professionals and such a refusal should not interfere with the right of people to receive any other form of recommended treatment to which they give informed consent.

The Department of Health should issue a code of practice to deal with situations where it is legally possible to institute treatment without consent. Legal safeguards should exist to prevent abuse of people receiving such treatment.

10.34 Patients must give full and free consent before participating with doctors/nurses in medical tutorials, examinations or case conferences.

10.35 No person should be overlooked for treatment or have treatment delayed or curtailed because of a disability.

10.36 Effective complaint procedures should be developed and operated by each Health Board. Rights advisers must be employed in every psychiatric hospital and there should be a Patient Advocate, not employed by the Department of Health, in every hospital.

10.37 Operational policies, including complaints procedures, in psychiatric facilities are reviewed by the Inspectorate of Mental Hospitals in the course of its annual statutory inspection of those facilities. Under the new legislation, the powers and duties of the Inspectorate of Mental Hospitals under the Mental Treatment Act, 1945 will be vested in a Commission for Mental Health Services.

10.38   In reviewing the legality and appropriateness of detention the Mental Health Review Board should ensure that patients' clinical conditions are such as to warrant detention.

10.39   The families of people who are mentally ill or experience emotional difficulties should be provided with counselling and education by the Health Boards.

10.40   A sign language interpreter service should be available to facilitate deaf persons in accessing health services.

Organisation

10.41   Each Health Board should review existing levels of services with reference to the principles of equity, accountability and quality of service and draw up five year plans to provide comprehensive community-based services for people with disabilities. These plans must be submitted to the Minister for Health by July 1, 1997, for approval.

10.42   The policy report for mental health services, Planning for the Future, and for mental handicap services, Needs and Abilities, should be reviewed urgently. The Commission welcomes the imminent publication of the report of the Review Group on Physical and Sensory Disability.

10.43   The government should implement forthwith its policy to appoint advisory committees to each health authority in line with the recommendation of the national health strategy. Such committees should be comprised of consumer groups including people with disabilities and should have access to senior management levels.

10.44   As set out in Shaping a Healthier Future, complaints procedures should be developed and there should be a statutory obligation on each health authority to provide feedback on consumer opinions to the Minister for Health.

10.45   The Commission recommends that each Health Board takes a consistent approach to the changes expected of them as a result of the Health Strategy, to ensure an equitable service nationwide.

Chapter Eleven
EDUCATION

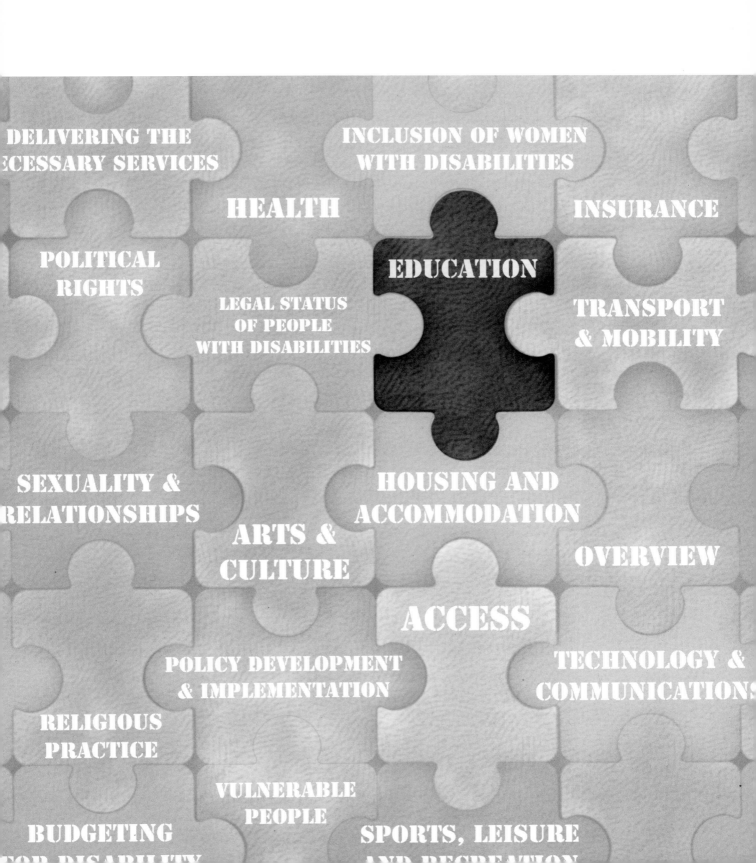

If I accepted defeat in my efforts to have my daughter educated with her peers she would follow so many other children from the west of Ireland... there seems to be unlimited money to send my child away from home but none to enable her to stay at home with her family and friends.

- excerpt from submission

Introduction

11.1   Education is just not schooling. Education is a process of sharing, developing, building, strengthening, encouraging and recognising the abilities of people. Education is achieved through many ways, the person is central to all. Education shares and respects diversity. Its aim is to enhance and enable the person to achieve his or her own goals. Terms used within this chapter reflect the existing terminology used within the current Irish education system.

11.2   If one is to measure the status of people with disabilities by their rate of participation and success in education, equality is still a long way off. Participation by people with disabilities in education at all levels is significantly below that of the population in general.

11.3   Children and adults with disabilities must come in from the margins and education must be made equally available for everyone. If sufficient resources and planning are applied now not only will the quality of life for people with disabilities improve, but their economic dependence on the state will be reduced in the long run.

11.4   The number of people with disabilities in education is estimated to be at least 4% of the school-going population. Approximately 8,000 pupils with disabilities are enrolled in 114 Special Schools and some 3,800 pupils with various disabilities are in special classes in primary schools. There are also about 8,000 pupils with "specific disabilities" in ordinary classes in primary schools. A further 2,300 pupils are enrolled in 48 special classes at post-primary level: another 100 pupils with disabilities are enrolled in the five designated post-primary schools.

The most recent figures for those attending third-level education indicate that there are approximately 1,000 students with disabilities. Unfortunately, no comprehensive figures are available for the numbers of children with disabilities in pre-school or the number of adults with disabilities attending local adult education centres.

It is estimated that up to another 2.5% of the population in mainstream education are people with disabilities. Thus, this chapter is concerned specifically with a minimum of 4% of all pupils and students who have special education needs in both special and mainstream schools, in third level colleges and in adult education centres of learning. However, we recognise that due to the poor quality of existing statistics the proportion could be higher.

11.5   One of the greatest areas of concern to the Commission is the lack of co-ordination between three Departments, Education, Health and Justice. Primary responsibility for the education of children, young people and adults must lie with the Department of Education, which should consult and co-ordinate activities with other Departments. It is imperative that the Department of Education should be the accountable authority in relation to all educational matters of concern to adults and children with disabilities and their families.

11.6   It has been the policy and practice of the Department of Education for some years now to educate as many children with disabilities as possible in mainstream schools. We see the present position as a base from which it will be possible to move quickly towards an inclusive education system.

11.7   In seeking to move forward towards equality and inclusiveness, the Commission has identified several barriers to the full participation of children and adults in education:

- Lack of legislation establishing the right to an appropriate education. Until there is an Education Act the manner in which the state provides for the educational needs of children and adults with disabilities will be decided in an ad hoc manner and entitlements will remain unclear.

- Lack of information: a substantial number of submissions to the Commission indicated problems in finding information on educational options and entitlements. This poses major difficulties for parents and students in making decisions about education.

- Lack of resources: a high proportion of children and adults with disabilities have particular needs which must be met in order to enable them to participate in education on an equal footing. Not all the accommodations required cost money but the lack of adequate funds to meet the needs of people with disabilities, whether in mainstream or in specialist schools, is the single greatest barrier to their educational participation.

- Poor attitudes: the lack of awareness about disability issues and the negative stereotyping of people with disabilities still create barriers for people with disabilities.

- Lack of educational needs assessments: many parents encounter difficulties in having an appropriate educational plan drawn up for their son or daughter.

- Lack of appropriate curricula to respond to individual needs: this is evidenced by the great number of adults with disabilities who, despite going through the school system,continue to have numeracy and literacy difficulties.

11.8   The Commission hopes to address all of these barriers. Its proposals for an equality strategy in education are based on a set of principles which potentially form the basis of an education charter of rights.

The Commission on the Status of People with Disabilities asserts the following principles in regard to the education of every citizen with a disability. The Commission further asserts that the rights explicit and implicit in these principles should be incorporated in all education policy, and should be enshrined in any legislation.

- Every child is educable. All children, including those with disabilities, have a right to a free and appropriate education in the least restrictive environment. Appropriate education for all children with disabilities should be provided in mainstream schools, except where it is clear that the child involved will not benefit through being placed in a mainstream environment, or that other children would be unduly and unfairly disadvantaged.

- Every individual has an equal right to educational provision, which will enable him or her to participate in all aspects of economic, social, cultural and political life, to the fullest extent of his or her potential.

- The unique needs of the individual person must be the paramount consideration when decisions are being made concerning the appropriate provision of education for that person. In so far as is practical a continuum of services must be available to meet those needs close to the person's home and family.

- It is the responsibility of the State to provide sufficient resources to ensure that pre-school children, children of school-going age and adults with disabilities have an education appropriate to their needs in the best possible environment.

- Parents have primacy in the decision-making process as soon as their child with a disability has been identified as having particular educational needs. They [and the child whenever appropriate] must be entitled to make an Informed choice on the educational placement of their child.

- There shall be an accessible appeals procedure on educational enrolment recommendations. This will have due regard for the rights of the child, the rights of the parents and the educational rights of other children.

- All schools have a responsibility to serve children with disabilities in the least restrictive environment. Each school plan must strive to make schools inclusive institutions. To facilitate inclusive education, due recognition must be given to the rights and needs of teachers for resources, initial education, and continuing professional development.

- Flexibility and formal linkages should be built into educational provision at local level. It must be a statutory duty of all existing or new management structures to secure access to high quality and appropriate education for all children and adults with disabilities.

- Priority should be given to the needs of people with disabilities, within the broad framework of educational provision, and this should be reflected in the allocation of resources.

Education Act

11.9 The rights explicit and implicit in the above principles should be incorporated in all education policy and enshrined in the forthcoming Education Act. The Act must accord to all people with disabilities, irrespective of the degree of their disability, the right to an education appropriate to their needs and abilities.

11.10 An inclusive Education Act should enshrine and stimulate further progress towards inclusion while increasing support to specialist schools. It should facilitate co-ordination and linkages between mainstream and specialist schools and between specialist vocational training centres and centres offering adult education opportunities.

11.11 The Act should also set out clearly the entitlements of students and the rights of parents. The Commission strongly recommends that its Education Charter of Rights should be incorporated into the legislation.

11.12 All people with disabilities should be offered an appropriate education in the environment of their choice. The concept of an "appropriate" education needs to be clearly defined in legislation. In this regard, the Commission favours the definition of "appropriate" which is contained in the American Individuals with Disabilities Education Act (IDEA). It states that for a programme to be "appropriate" it must be based on and responsive to the child's individualized educational needs as identified in the evaluation process. The IDEA requires that a written Individual Education Programme (IEP) is developed for the adult or child with a disability.

11.13 Legislation must create a strong presumption that students will be placed in the least restrictive environment. The onus of proof in demonstrating the inappropriateness of a placement in a mainstream school should be placed on the school authorities. It should be rebutted only by demonstrating objective impossibility, or that such placement would not be in the best interests of the child, or that placement would unduly hinder the education rights of other children.

11.14 Legal provision is also required for individual assessments of need and the development of an individual education plan which would give effect to the student's educational requirements. This legal provision should take the form of a statutory instrument and should contain provision for enforcement. The individual plan should assess the resources required to meet the students' needs and make recommendations for placement (see Chapter 4). Assessments should be carried out by an independent agency, ideally under the auspices of the proposed Regional Education Boards, and should be holistic in nature. Education plans should be reviewed annually and revised in the light of a child's changing and developing needs.

The legal rights, roles and responsibilities of parents must be clearly outlined in relation to any assessment or decision-making process and should reflect the constitutional rights of parents in the matter of their child's education.

11.15   A second opinion should be available in relation to decisions about placements and an appeal procedure should be available to an independent body by either the parent, pupil or school authority. Schools and educational establishments should be required to make every reasonable accommodation to meet the educational needs of a student, in line with the choice of the student, or where appropriate, the parents. The right to refuse entry must be allowed only in very exceptional circumstances: refusal should not be possible solely on the grounds of resources.

11 16   The National Disability Authority, in collaboration with the Department of Education, would be the appropriate body to monitor and enforce the disability provisions of the Education Act.

11.17   Although the overall formulation of education policy is ultimately the prerogative of the Government, specifically that of the Minister for Education, local policy issues should, as far as possible, be decided locally, within the overall policy framework. The proposed Regional Education Boards will create greater opportunities for local planning and greater opportunities for parents and students with disabilities to influence the shape of local services.

11.18   In particular, the Regional Education Boards must have a statutory duty to ensure that every child with special educational needs is provided with an appropriate education. They should be required to provide:

- assessment facilities

- access to independent appeals procedures in relation to placement recommendations;

- consultation with parents and children in the planning of local services;

- information to parents, people with disabilities, the Disability Support Service and the public about all aspects of services in the area.

11.19   Legal provision for the participation of parents of children with disabilities in the assessment and placement of their child has already been proposed. But that is only the starting point for parental involvement. Parents must be acknowledged as full and equal partners throughout the educational process and be provided with guidance and support, full information about their child's progress, and be allowed to contribute meaningfully to it.

11.20 Furthermore, consultation with people with disabilities and their representative organisations must be a key feature of future policy formation. A permanent committee on the educational needs of children with disabilities should be established. Its membership should include parent representatives, student representatives, representatives of the Departments of Education, Health, Justice, Equality and Law Reform, the Disability Support Service, Health Boards and Regional Education Boards (when established), teacher and management representatives, specialist providers, and representatives of psychological and other support services.

11.21 It should have direct links with the Co-ordinating Group of Secretaries and the Council for the Status of People with Disabilities. It will be essential that parents and students are fully represented and do not have minority status within the Committee.

Community Education Plans

11.22 The Education Act should require the Department of Education - and the Regional Education Boards when established - to draw up Community Education Plans to meet the needs of students with disabilities on a regional basis. The Act should also impose a legal obligation on the Department of Education through the Regional Education Boards to assess the education needs of all people with disabilities who request an assessment, including those who live in residential settings.

11.23 The core provisions of the Community Education Plans should be contained in the Education Act and should include:

- Speech and occupational therapy;

- Physical education;

- Support and counselling for parents;

- Psychological support;

- Technical aids and supports;

- Communications support;

- School transport, including an escort where necessary;

- Classroom assistants;

- Resource and remedial teaching;

- Personal assistants;

The plans should be drawn up in consultation with the Council for the Status of People with Disabilities and organisations of people with disabilities.

11.24 The Education Act should require the Department of Education (and Regional Education Boards) to take into account the needs identified in the assessment procedures in drawing up the Community Education Plans. The Department should also be statutorily required to take into account the needs identified in deciding both the level of funding and the type of services for which funding is provided.

Support Services

11.25 The lack of support services is one of the greatest barriers to the equal participation of people with disabilities in education. Such services range from information, advice and guidance to psychologists and specialist teachers. They also cover technical and mechanical appliances and equipment; transport; therapies, including speech therapy, physiotherapy and occupational therapy.

11.26 There are difficulties at present in relation to the availability and organisation of these support services. The school psychological service is one such: it should be increased significantly in strength and its role and operation needs to be broadened.

11.27 The gaps in the provision of therapies have been highlighted in several reports, as well as in the submissions received by the Commission. The provision of those supports has to be a matter of right rather than choice as access to them is essential to enable a child to achieve his or her educational potential.

11.28 It is the view of the Commission that essential supports should be provided in a coherent and co-ordinated basis within each local area. Specialist support personnel should be brought together into cohesive local teams. They would provide information and support to local schools and teachers' centres as well as students and parents and assist in drawing up school plans for the inclusion of students with disabilities. There should be strong links and networking at local level between the Teams and the local Disability Support Service.

11.29 Education support services should be available to all children with disabilities and their families from the earliest possible point, namely the point of diagnosis of disability. The measures required to meet an individual's needs could be identified at the stage of the individual Needs Assessments outlined in Chapter 4.

11.30 The current lack of clarity, regarding who provides what support services results in hardship, delay and serious frustration for children, adults, parents and teachers. The Commission recommends that the provision of support services should be the subject of joint action between the Health Boards and the educational authorities. A technical aids and appliances' fund should be set up at local level, funded jointly by educational and health budgets, from which the necessary appliances would be purchased, without the need to decide whether a particular appliance is an educational or a medical appliance. This distinction is often impossible to make in practice and quite irrelevant from the point of view of the child's/student's well-being and educational development.

11.31 Support teaching services - remedial, resource and visiting teachers - should be extended to cover all children with disabilities in both special and mainstream schools, especially in their early years when support and guidance is essential. Due recognition of the contribution of these teachers and appropriate time-tabling is recommended to allow them fulfil their roles. The Commission recommends that more specialist support teachers should be employed, especially for schools and students who do not get such a service at all.

11.32 The absence of accessible school transport and sufficient numbers of bus escorts to travel with children represents a further barrier to participation in mainstream education for many students. It is not an acceptable reason for denying a child the right to attend a local school. Where local school transport is not an option for a child with a disability, alternative supports must be provided.

11.33 The present review of the school transport service offers an opportunity to examine imaginative possibilities for the provision of an integrated local transport service which would provide accessible transport services in a local community. (see Chapter 13: Transport and Mobility)

   Transport or alternative support should also be available to students who wish to advance to further education or third level education.

Curriculum and Assessment

11.34 There is a fundamental need to develop programmes which accommodate different rates of learning and different learning needs within the mainstream classroom. To accommodate students with disabilities in mainstream schools, curricula should allow for flexibility, additions and adaptations. Where necessary, students with disabilities in mainstream settings should have specially adapted teaching methods, materials, curricula and examination regulations.

11.35   The National Council for Curriculum and Assessment should establish curriculum development projects for pupils at primary and post primary levels. This work should be done in consultation with the agencies providing special education services who have done excellent work on developing curricula to include students with disabilities. Special emphasis should be placed on education for creativity, appropriate testing and examination procedures, and upon adequate and appropriate extracurricular activities.

11.36   Curriculum flexibility is particularly important in second level education where the academic focus and the high level of emphasis on language skills can create difficulties for many students with disabilities. There is evidence of a high number of early school leavers, especially among students with learning disabilities who have attempted to "fit" into mainstream classrooms. New models utilising specialist classes, special and mainstream schools and the sharing of school facilities are urgently needed so that all students are enabled to achieve a recognised educational qualification.

11.37   The curricular needs of all pupils in specialist settings should be reviewed, based on ages, abilities, needs and aspirations.

11.38   Special national schools should be reclassified as primary and post-primary schools to recognise the fact that students attend such schools up to the age of eighteen years. Post primary special schools should attract all of the facilities, improved teacher ratios, posts of responsibility, and additional capitation that applies to mainstream post primary schools.

11.39   In relation to assessment, greater flexibility is required from the state, individual schools and examining bodies in their approach to, and methods of, examining students with disabilities. A fair and appropriate system of examination testing and of assessment should be provided for the student with a disability. All examinations should be offered in a place and manner appropriate and accessible to people with disabilities.

Oral examinations should be available for those who have difficulty with writing or visual text. The Department of Education should provide a suitably qualified interpreter for those who require one in oral examinations.

Special arrangements, for which pupils with specific learning disabilities are eligible, should be available to all pupils with disabilities without distinction. Adolescents who experience mental health difficulties should be reasonably accommodated to sit their exams when they are fit and able.

11.40   A system of standards must be applied to all specialist schools. The option of access to mainstream certification must be available to those in specialist education settings.

11.41 A greater emphasis should be placed upon forming links between vocational training centres and all local post primary schools. This is especially important for students whose abilities are more skill based than academically based.

Pre-schools

11.42 It should be the responsibility of the Department of Education to provide high quality, appropriate pre-school services to children with disabilities. Teaching personnel should have a background and training which equips them to respond to the particular needs of young children with disabilities. Every encouragement and practical support, including financial support, should be given to community playgroups and pre-school groups who wish to include young children with disabilities in their services.

Special Schools

11.43 The number of pupils in special schools is estimated at 0.9% of the total primary and post-primary school-going population. The special and mainstream systems have tended to operate in almost total isolation from each other for historical reasons. This duality needs to be addressed so that they come together into the regular educational system.

11.44 The Commission recognises that the unsupported inclusion of students with disabilities in mainstream schools can discriminate against them, even where integration is ideal in principle. This is true for example in the case of children and adults who are deaf and whose first language is sign. It is important to respect the needs of the deaf child and their absolute right to a specialist education whether in a specialist school or a designated setting attached to a mainstream school. Similarly, adults who wish to have access to further education options through sign language should be enabled to have such educational options met at local level.

11.45 In order to remove the duality of the special and mainstream systems, a series of actions will be needed:

- it should be feasible for a student to be enrolled in more than one school at any time;

- closer curriculum linkages with joint planning between specialist and mainstream schools for individual students;

- bridging the huge gulf between teachers in the separate systems;

- practical supports for closer linkages, such as flexible transport arrangements;

- a funding strategy in which funding is linked to the student rather than to any school.

It is the Commission's view that innovatory or pilot programmes should be initiated in a number of local areas in the short term to achieve the necessary linkages, outlined above.

11.46   The development of the network of supports proposed in this report and in the report of the Special Education Review Committee (1993) will take some time to put in place. For these reasons, there is a need for a systematic plan to develop a clear specialist role for special schools in the longer term. That role will involve catering for children with very special needs who cannot be accommodated within the mainstream system. Work done in the specialist schools should be developmental, innovative and capable of dissemination to the wider educational community in order to facilitate greater levels of inclusion.

11.47   To facilitate these specialist roles the schools concerned should have a core multi-disciplinary staff, which is free of the constraints imposed on staffing ratios by changing student numbers. It should be in the nature of the specialist role of these schools that numbers should fluctuate as students move between them and the mainstream as individual needs change and develop. All specialist schools should be required to have in place a policy and a programme to support their students in linking into the wider community in all possible ways.

Designated Schools

11.48   Designated schools are mainstream post-primary schools which are supported and funded by the Department of Education to meet the needs of pupils with specific disabilities. The number of designated schools at present is small, five in total.

11.49   The Special Education Review Committee has proposed the extension of the designated school concept to primary education. The Commission has several concerns about this proposal. There is a real worry among people with disabilities and parents that the availability of a designated school in an area would act as a disincentive to other local schools to make proper provision for students with disabilities, even in cases where such provision might only require the addition of physical access facilities.

The availability of a designated school must not be seen as justification for not spending resources to provide accessible transport or support services. The child's right to the least restrictive placement, and the parental right of choice cannot be frustrated on the grounds that a cheaper option exists.

The main benefit of a designated school might be to locate facilities there for children with rare disabilities, who would otherwise have to leave their local area in order to receive an education. The Commission recommends that an in-depth evaluation of the concept of designated school should be carried out before any further developments in this area occur. We further urge that local parents be consulted fully if consideration is being given to the development of a designated school in an area.

Third Level

11.50   The Commission supports the general recommendation of the Report of the Committee on Access and Participation of Students with Disabilities in Higher Education that "there should be full integration of persons with disability in the higher education system, and that appropriate funding provisions should be put in place to support this policy".

11.51   The Department of Education should fund pre-university and college education courses such as the Pre-University College Course at Roslyn College which prepares people with disabilities for university and third-level colleges. While such preparation may be achieved within secondary schools in the long-term, there is currently a substantial need for this service.

11.52   The Commission commends the work presently being undertaken by TCD and UCD around the specific inclusion of adults with learning disabilities on a university campus. The development of research into the educational needs of people with learning disabilities, the development of appropriate curricula and teaching methods, and greater access over time by people with learning disabilities to different levels of education appropriate to their needs is essential.

Teacher Training

11.53   All initial and continuing teacher education programmes should include modules on meeting the needs of pupils with disabilities. Elements on disability awareness and appropriate curriculum design should be included. Sign language or braille should be taught as part of all teacher training courses.

11.54   The specialist education element should be taught within the general context of child development and educational psychology. Specialist modules should incorporate obligatory components on the identification, assessment and teaching of pupils with disabilities and special educational needs. Emphasis should also be placed upon working with and including parents, special needs classroom assistants and visiting teachers, as well as on the principles of guidance and counselling.

11.55 More advanced courses and more alternative methods leading to qualifications in aspects of specialist education are required.

11.56 Induction programmes should be organised for any teacher, visiting teacher or special needs assistant who is taking up for the first time a post with defined responsibility for the teaching or care of children with special educational needs, whatever the stage of his or her career.

11.57 All in-service courses supported by the Department of Education should have an input on disability awareness, as is the case with gender equality. In addition to in-service courses, booster courses and one-day conferences should be held regularly in order to give teachers the opportunity to update their skills and to access best practice.

11.58 In-service education and training for guidance counsellors should be provided to ensure that they are aware of all of the options, including specialist training and further education facilities, that are accessible and available to young people with disabilities leaving school.

11.59 Physical education teachers should be encouraged to develop alternative strategies and games that are inclusive of all the children enrolled in their school.

11.60 More opportunities should be created for people with disabilities to become teachers in both specialist and mainstream schools.

11.61 Entry procedures to teacher training courses for deaf candidates should use subject suitability as the criterion. Ability in the area of sign language and an aptitude for teaching should be central to selection for training. The teacher training course should meet the educational needs of deaf teachers and their students.

Funding

11.62 Meeting the needs of people with disabilities can, and must be regarded as an investment, and not as a burden on society. There is no doubt that the improvements needed in order to bring about equality and full participation will require additional expenditure. We recommend that a figure of 1% of the existing education budget (i.e. approximately £20 million at current rates) of additional expenditure be allocated annually to meet the educational needs of pupils/students with disabilities. Given the very high levels of educational disadvantage experienced by this group, and the commitment of government to the targeting of disadvantage, such an increase is justifiable and, indeed, essential in terms of social justice.

11.63 Funding should be linked to the student and should follow the student as he or she moves to appropriate educational settings. In the Commission's view, it is not appropriate to link funding levels, teacher allocations or staff student ratios to diagnostic disability categories. The level of funding or other supports must relate to need, rather than to diagnostic categories, since there is no necessary link between these two concepts.

11.64 School managements should be encouraged to move towards inclusiveness by a range of incentives and supports which would enable them to develop programmes and support structures for inclusion. Support should not be provided in the form of non-specific grants: it should be given for specific planned reforms, development of materials, appropriate in-career programmes, and physical adjustments to buildings. School managements who make good progress towards being an inclusive school should be awarded a "Positive to Disability" symbol of excellence, analogous to the scheme for employers referred to in Chapter 7: Work and Training.

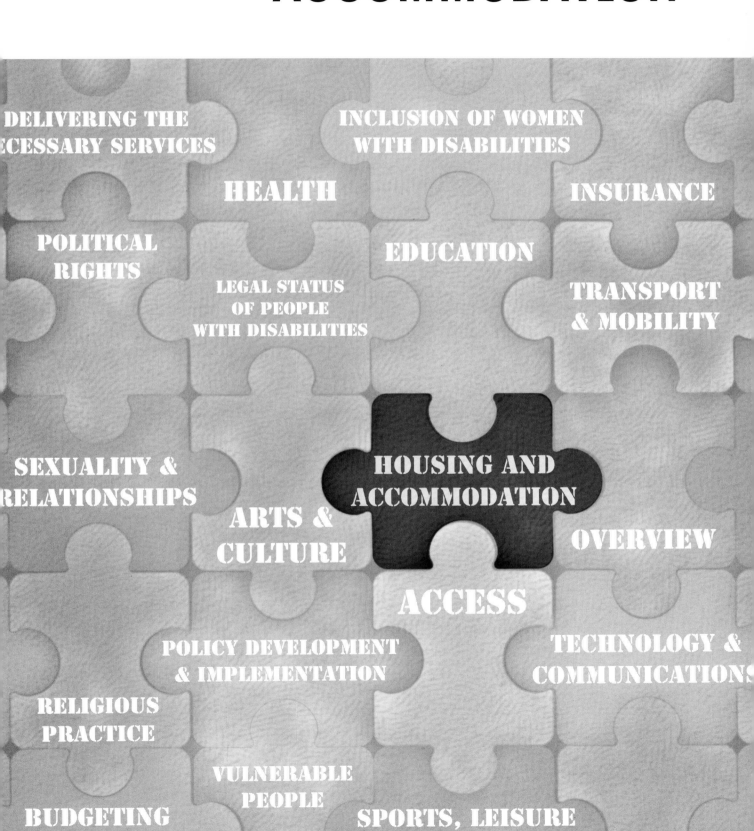

Chapter Twelve
HOUSING AND ACCOMMODATION

DELIVERING THE
NECESSARY SERVICES

INCLUSION OF WOMEN
WITH DISABILITIES

HEALTH

INSURANCE

POLITICAL
RIGHTS

EDUCATION

LEGAL STATUS
OF PEOPLE
WITH DISABILITIES

TRANSPORT
& MOBILITY

SEXUALITY &
RELATIONSHIPS

HOUSING AND
ACCOMMODATION

ARTS &
CULTURE

OVERVIEW

ACCESS

POLICY DEVELOPMENT
& IMPLEMENTATION

TECHNOLOGY &
COMMUNICATIONS

RELIGIOUS
PRACTICE

VULNERABLE
PEOPLE

BUDGETING
FOR DISABILITY

SPORTS, LEISURE
AND RECREATION

Our son lives in a private rented basement flat for which the rent is 33 pounds a week plus the cost of light and heat. His flat is substandard but is the best that he can afford. He has no security of tenure and is unable to put down roots. In short, his flat is a place where he exists rather than a place where he can feel at home.

- excerpt from submission

12.1   Housing provides much more than shelter in modern society: it is the base from which people participate in society and can reflect as well as dictate their level of participation. Yet there is no formal or constitutional right to housing. The primary responsibility for providing housing rests with the individual: those who can afford to do so are expected to house themselves, if necessary with the aid of grants and other incentives. State provision of housing is confined to the social housing arena. In practice, however, virtually all housing receives a significant degree of state assistance in one form or another.

12.2   Treating people with disabilities the same as other citizens in relation to housing creates major barriers for them: in reality, it means they have less freedom of choice than other people, are often heavily dependent on family members, and are sometimes left in situations of acute social isolation. It has also led to the removal of people with disabilities from their local communities and their inappropriate placement in expensive institutions.

12.3   The links between disability and low incomes and the added costs of suitable accommodation mean that people with disabilities are at a disadvantage when it comes to housing and, in particular, to home ownership. As in other areas, equal status for people with disabilities requires that they have the means to exercise their right to equality in housing. The rights to personal autonomy, to a similar range of choices as everyone else, and to participate in the life of the local and national community clearly require the removal of existing barriers, positive provisions and a redistribution of resources in housing.

12.4   If housing is to provide the base from which people with disabilities participate in society, then policies must address not only the question of the physical fabric of buildings and the serviceability of the wider environment but also the services, supports and income required to facilitate independent living.

12.5   The concept of Independent Living (already referred to in Chapter 10: Health) is fundamental to this approach and, in the Commission's view, should underpin policy on housing. Independent Living is the ability to decide and to choose what a person wants, where to live and how, what to do and how to set about doing it. It also involves establishing and taking control of the total management of a person's everyday life and affairs. The philosophy behind it is generally defined as living like everyone else, having the right to self-determination, to exert control over one's life, to have opportunities to make decisions, to take responsibility, and to pursue activities of one's own choosing, regardless of disability.

12.6   It is also important to clarify, in relation to accommodation, the distinction between residential care and residential accommodation. The Commission uses the term residential care to apply to accommodation and services for people who require constant supervision and care in order to live with any degree of independence. Residential accommodation is used in relation to accommodation for people who can live independently and who choose to live in residential centres or who live in residential centres because of a lack of other housing and personal assistance options and who may, at some point in the future, move to some other community housing/living option.

12.7   In setting about removing the barriers facing people with disabilities in relation to housing and accommodation, a number of factors have to be taken into account:

- the complexity of housing: there are a variety of different housing sectors with 90 different housing authorities in Ireland. There is also the interdependence of accommodation, the wider physical environment, social and health services and income support systems to be considered.

- inequities in the housing system: virtually every household in Ireland is subsidised but the subsidies are heavily biased towards owner occupation and many are regressive. This effectively discriminates against those outside the system or on its margins and is particularly pernicious in the case of people with disabilities because of the link between disability and low income.

- absence of formal policy: this results in people with disabilities being treated differently in different local housing authority areas and across disability groupings.

- supply and demand sides of market: the housing requirements of many people with disabilities are different to the 'norm' for which housing is designed. This has received little formal recognition in housing policy and where it is addressed it tends to be at the level of individual demand rather than supply. There are no guidelines, for instance, about the construction of a quota of houses specifically designed to wheelchair-accessible standard in the private or social housing sectors.

- designated housing: there is no tradition of housing authorities providing 'special housing' for people with disabilities as part of their building programmes. Where there is a specific housing provision for people with disabilities it tends to be provided by the voluntary/non profit and co-operative housing sector.

12.8   There are also specific housing problems faced by individuals or groups of people with disabilities. For instance, people previously in receipt of the Disabled Persons Maintenance Allowance are not entitled to any income maintenance payment once they go into long term residential accommodation. This leads to huge anomalies with other people in the same place entitled to insurance related benefits such as invalidity pension or blind pension. Those not entitled to insurance related benefits receive no statutory allowance, make no contribution to their maintenance, and are dependent on a small "pocket money" allowance given at the discretion of the local Health Boards.

12.9   A number of submissions to the Commission also drew attention to the risks of homelessness faced by people with psychiatric disabilities who often face serious accommodation problems after being discharged from hospitals. Single people tend not to be given priority in housing allocations: a review by the Irish Wheelchair Association found that it was generally difficult for young single people with physical disabilities and on low incomes to be housed by local authorities.

12.10   As a first step towards creating housing equity for people with disabilities, the Department of the Environment should formulate and publicise in accessible form a policy on housing for people with disabilities. This would provide information for planners, consumers and housing suppliers about the situation and requirements of people with disabilities and the options available.

12.11   As part of its policy formulation, the Department of the Environment should collate information about the demand for, and the take up of, housing for people with disabilities. It should commission the ESRI to undertake further analysis of the 1996 assessment of housing needs to establish the requirements of people with disabilities and the reasons for the low level of assessed need to date. All future national assessments of housing needs by local authorities should explicitly address the housing requirements of those living long term in residential centres.

12.12   In addition, ongoing information on access features and the suitability of housing for people with disabilities should be made available by those involved in supplying housing whether in the commercial or non-profit sectors. People with disabilities should be invited to contribute to the reviews underway in the Department of the Environment on the various measures introduced under A Plan for Social Housing.

12.13   Data should also be collected on the role of the increasingly important non-profit and voluntary housing sector in meeting the requirements of people with disabilities and on the relative merits of the various models of support housing which are now operational.

12.14   To enable this sector to make a greater contribution, the Commission recommends that adjustments be made in the capital assistance available and that a properly defined scheme of funding for support housing services be put in place. Funding from the Voluntary Capital Assistance Scheme should only be granted to housing agencies which are building to the standards of Lifetime Adaptable Housing.

12.15 The Commission strongly recommends the adoption of a policy of building Lifetime Adaptable Housing as the norm in all housing sectors. Such a policy is of crucial importance in facilitating independence and choice for people with disabilities.

12.16 Lifetime Adaptable Housing is about convenience and safety and has two major characteristics - accessibility and adaptability. The concept is based on the principle that homes should be accessible to all (children, elderly people and people with disabilities) and easily adapted to satisfy changing requirements, such as a temporary or permanent disability, throughout a lifetime. A number of features are included at the construction stage so that homes can be adapted easily later on, if necessary. The main features are:

- no steps at entrances

- wider doors and corridors

- low level light switches

- downstairs toilet

- easy opening doors and windows

- good living space throughout

- accessible bathrooms

- easy to operate taps and fittings.

This new policy should be implemented through the assimilation of Part M of the Building Regulations into all other parts of the Regulations. An education and awareness programme should be put in place to promote understanding of the concept among developers, designers and builders.

12.17 Standards for Lifetime Adaptable Housing should be phased in with the immediate adoption of those aspects of adaptability which are relatively easy to apply and are based on a greater awareness of design requirements. The next phase, the application of more adequate space standards for full Lifetime Adaptable Housing, should be provided for in legislation and operational within three years.

12.18 Section 23 type incentives should be adjusted to allow a higher rate of allowances (between 10% and 20%) for units which meet the Lifetime Adaptable Housing specifications. It is also recommended that the financial incentives to seaside resorts should require a specified proportion of all eligible dwellings to be built in accordance with the new standards.

12.19 In order to improve existing houses, the Commission recommends that the Disabled Person's Grant should be modified to cover up to 95% of approved costs. The grant should be extended to the occupants of new houses and to those renting in the voluntary/non-profit housing sector who have security of tenure.

12.20 There should also be greater uniformity in the implementation of the grant by housing authorities. Information about the grant and its appeals procedures needs to be made available more widely.

12.21 The Commission also believes that local housing authorities throughout the country should be proactive in building up a supply of suitable housing. Schemes now available under A Plan for Social Housing should be utilised in a strategic manner.

12.22 The problems of people with disabilities on low incomes in securing housing have been noted earlier. The Commission recommends that three new schemes be put in place to improve their prospects of home ownership and to help offset the additional costs of suitable housing. Each of the proposals builds on an existing scheme.

- A new grant to incorporate the Disabled Person's Grant and the first time purchaser's grant should be introduced where a first home is being purchased by a person with a disability and where additional housing costs are likely to be incurred.

- The Shared Ownership System should be widened to allow house purchasers with a disability on low incomes to receive the enhanced first time purchaser's grant.

- A financing arrangement should be developed to allow approved voluntary and non-profit housing bodies to provide an equity sharing tenure based on a 50% ownership by people with disabilities on limited incomes.

People in Residential Centres

12.23 No statistics on the numbers of people with physical and sensory disabilities inappropriately placed in institutions have been compiled since the early 1980's. The Commission recommends that such statistics should be compiled immediately and published before December, 1997. A plan of action to ensure

that those inappropriately placed be moved to a more appropriate setting should then be put in place and no person with a physical or sensory disability should be inappropriately placed in these institutions in the future.

12.24   There is a critical lack of proper planning to meet the residential needs of people with disabilities, some of whom can live independently, but many of whom cannot. A range of successful accommodation options already exists in very limited numbers which encourage a full and active lifestyle. These and other new and innovative options should be encouraged. For many people with disabilities, now on long waiting lists, they could represent a further choice of accommodation for the future.

12.25   Many parents of people with disabilities, some very elderly, live in great stress because of the size of the waiting lists and the uncertainty of their child ever having an alternative option to living at home. Respite care places relieve some of the problems for parents but the future residential needs of their child are a constant source of preoccupation and worry. This is particularly the case in relation to children and young adults.

12.26   Several years ago several of the agencies providing services for people with disabilities bought single houses in residential estates. Some of these worked well but others had problems, including vandalism in some cases. Staff and residents in these houses frequently felt isolated and alone.

In order to overcome such problems, housing options for people with disabilities should include a mix of different arrangements. Single houses, houses capable of accommodating four or five people; bungalow units clustered together; a group of three or four town houses with a communal garden - all of these options must be included. They should be situated close to amenities and retail outlets in order to maximise independence and they must have the appropriate support staff.

12.27   Consideration has to be given, too, to the special accommodation needs of people with disabilities and their partners.

12.28   The Commission recommends that a review be undertaken of people with disabilities in residential centres to establish accurately their numbers, locations and living conditions. Similarly, there should be a review of the people on waiting lists for residential centres to see if these lists could be reduced substantially by the provision of other services. The information obtained from these reviews would also help the planning of housing and accommodation options for the future.

12.29   Action should be taken to ensure that the rights of people living in residential centres are protected. The following are particularly recommended:

•   All residential establishments should publish an operational policy.

- A Bill or Charter of Rights (see below) should set parameters for the operational policy.

- An Independent Ombudsman should oversee residential centres, resolve grievances and ensure that proper consideration is given to the views and concerns of residents.

12.30 Residents should be actively encouraged to participate in the running of residential centres and a target set of 50% representation by them or their advocates on management boards within five years. Residents should be trained in preparation for management roles and in the skills necessary to live independently. Disability equality training should be provided for residents, staff and management.

12.31 Income supports should be provided in a way which promotes autonomy and choice with payments made directly to individuals rather than to institutions. Payments should be clearly defined as between accommodation, personal assistance, and care elements.

12.32 People living in residential centres should have access to an Independent Living Fund which should be established to allow the employment of personal assistants and to train people with disabilities in the management of personal assistants. The Disability Support Service should also assist residents to obtain the best value and the most appropriate mix of services.

12.33 A Charter Of Rights for residents of residential centres should contain the following essential elements:

- Specific provisions setting out the detailed services provided by the institution.

- Quality standards of services to which the person is entitled.

- The right to information and the manner in which that will be provided.

- The manner in which records will be maintained and the right of access to records.

- The right of access to complaint procedures and the manner in which the complaint procedures will operate.

- The right to an independent appeal.

- The right to advocacy and representation.

- The right to participate in management and monitoring, and

- A system of review and amendment of the Charter taking into account the views of service users.

12.34   It is essential that a system of overseeing and monitoring of standards in residential accommodation should be set in place by the Departments of Health and Environment (to be reviewed by the National Disability Authority) if these recommendations are to be implemented in practice as well as in theory.

Chapter Thirteen
TRANSPORT AND MOBILITY

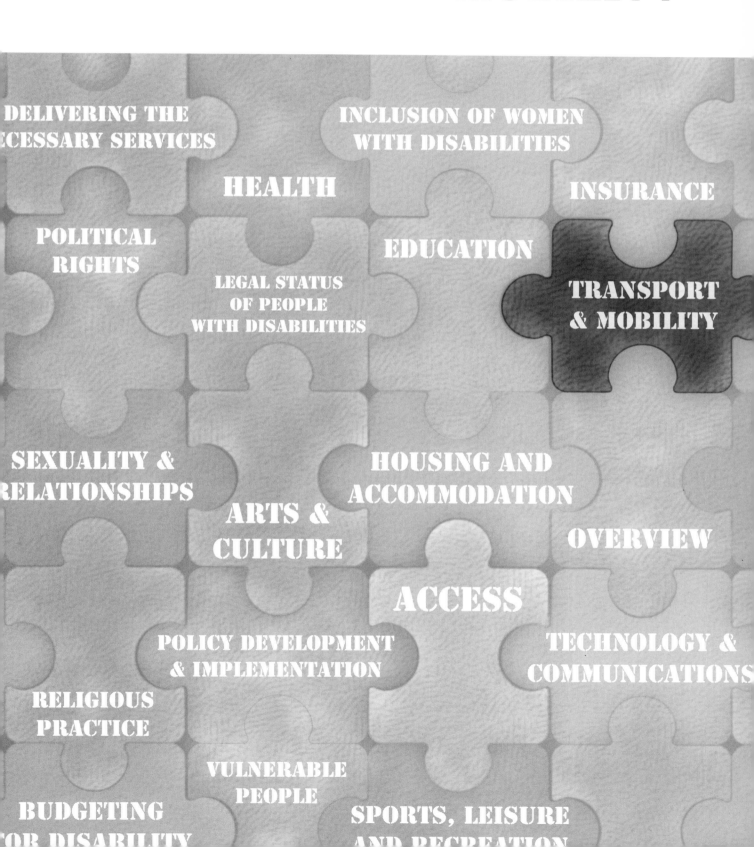

I looked forward to being of the right age to obtain free public transport. My wife and I could see parts of Ireland we didn't know. Not only were the buses and trains inaccessible but to obtain my pass I would have had to climb a flight of stairs in my wheelchair to get the necessary documents.

- excerpt from submission

13.1   Providing forms of transport that would be more accessible is not just an issue of interest to people with disabilities. It would benefit a wide range of other people as well, including people with prams or buggies, elderly and young people and people laden down with shopping. Unfortunately, Ireland has lagged behind other countries in making its transport system more accessible for everybody, with especially harsh consequences for people with disabilities.

13.2.   Transport companies have introduced modifications to some of their vehicles but frequently claim that the costs are prohibitive and the changes would benefit only a small number of people. However, the costs of suitable rolling stock are decreasing as more and more countries require transport operators to make their systems accessible to all customers. The European Union is drafting proposals for common rules on the construction of minibuses, buses and coaches and Transport Commissioner Neil Kinnock recently published a Green Paper on public transport which stresses the need for more accessible systems. Furthermore, accessible transport offers operators the prospect of increasing revenue through increased numbers of passengers once systems are recognised to be available to all potential users. In overall policy terms, accessible transport will allow more people with disabilities to continue living in their own homes and communities, creating savings in other areas such as health and social services.

13.3.   Unfortunately, the experience of people with disabilities has been largely negative. There is a long catalogue of difficulties facing them when they attempt to use all forms of transport. As well as problems with vehicles, they include those caused by the absence of video, audio and braille information about accessible services and timetables. Such problems combine to dissuade people with disabilities from attempting greater use of public transport.

13.4   Many journeys on public transport require the use of different services which means that any break in the chain makes the whole journey impossible for people with disabilities. In order to address this and other problems, a co-ordinated approach is required to all forms of transport and the information services that accompany them.

13.5   The Commission therefore recommends that all new and used rail rolling stock and road vehicles ordered for public transport (including those ordered by private operators) from January 1st, 1997 must be accessible to all users. The Government should take measures to ensure that no licences will be issued for the transportation of people unless these vehicles meet the accessibility criteria. In addition, at least 80% of all transport and transport services purchased by Health Boards from 1st January 1997 for transporting clients must be wheelchair accessible.

13.6   On the information front, the Department of Transport Energy and Communications should provide an information centre about the accessibility of all services. It should be available through a freephone number, on Aertel teletext and in alternative media to print. All terminals and stations should also provide visual, audio and, ideally, braille information on arrivals and departures as well as the accessibility of specific services. A clear map of stations or terminals and their facilities should be sited at their entrances and at ticket offices. The buildings, of course, should all be made fully accessible.

13.7   Ease of access also depends on the attitudes of the community as well as those of transport staff. The Council for the Status of People with Disability should develop a public awareness programme as well as staff training programmes on customer care. This training must, where possible, be conducted by people with a disability.

13.8   The Commission also recommends that a National Mobility Training and Advice Centre should be established immediately. It should offer advice on mobility aids for all categories of people with a disability as well as training and orientation for people with disabilities themselves. Local training could be sub-contracted out to non governmental organisations but minimum standards must be set by the National Disability Authority. Such training should include the use of public transport and the rules of the road to prepare a person with a disability for using whatever aid they require.

13.9   The Commission welcomes the appointment of a person with a disability to the board of CIE and hopes this will set a precedent for other state and semi-state boards. In relation to transport, consultation with people with disabilities and their representative organisations is essential at all stages in the planning and delivery of services. Community Action Plans should include a local structure for the planning and implementation of accessible transport services. This structure should be based on the local structures of the Council for the Status of People with a Disability and include representatives of the Council, the National Disability Authority and transport companies.

Authority and transport companies.

13.10   The free travel pass scheme, administered by the Department of Social Welfare, is available to some people with a disability. Whilst it covers a spouse it does not automatically cover a companion and can restrict the days and times of travel. Parents of children with disabilities who hold the free travel pass may have to pay. For children living far from the special schools they attend this can often mean travelling 6 to 12 hours per week unsupervised. This is not acceptable.

13.11   Many people with disabilities need a companion to travel with them. The Department of Social Welfare should introduce a standard Disabled Persons

Public Transport Travel Pass which should automatically cover a companion and should not restrict days and times a person can travel on public transport.

13.12   The Commission also recommends an immediate increase in the present Mobility Allowance to bring it up to a minimum of £40 per week and that it should be index linked.

Rail Transport

13.13   An accessible rail network depends primarily on the design of the rolling stock (train carriages) and on the surrounding infrastructure. Stations have proved to be as inaccessible as rolling stock, making it frequently impossible for people with disabilities to get to the correct platform or to board or alight from trains.

13.14   Iarnrod Eireann has stated that any new rolling stock it purchases will be accessible to all. Meanwhile, it provides one wheelchair space in the dining car on mainline trains. That is a less than adequate interim solution: not all services have a dining car and those that do have no provision for a second passenger in a wheelchair. It is also impossible to manoeuvre or park a wheelchair and toilets are totally inaccessible on mainline trains.

The newer rolling stock on the suburban DART and Arrow services is wheelchair friendly but these systems are inaccessible to some other people with disabilities. DART and Arrow feeder buses are inaccessible to wheelchair users, thereby breaking the transport chain for many potential users of suburban rail.

13.15   Stations throughout the rail system are a major problem with overhead bridges, wide gaps between platforms and trains, and, more recently, the addition of security gates at some stations. On the DART system, only 15 of the 35 stations are accessible from both sides of the tracks. Some people with disabilities have keys to locked gates but others have to rely on station workers to allow them in. On the Arrow system, most stations are unmanned and a communication device is out of reach of wheelchair users.

To make the DART system fully accessible would cost an estimated 2 to 3 million pounds but there are no plans to implement that.

13.16   Iarnrod Eireann has undertaken to make the planned new Light Rail Transport system fully accessible.

13.17   There is also a serious lack of information available on trains and within stations. Without onboard visual aids, people with hearing impairments have no way of knowing what station the train is approaching while people with visual impairments have no way of knowing unless announcements are made.

People with learning disabilities also have great difficulty travelling alone on trains.

13.18 The general recommendations already made about rolling stock and making all stations, terminals and information accessible to people with disabilities will help to alleviate these problems. Accessibility should apply to all facilities in stations and terminals, including buffets, left luggage, Fast Track services, telephones and toilets.

Buses

13.19 Buses are the most widely used form of public transport, so their accessibility is particularly important for people with disabilities. In many rural areas, in particular, they are the only regular form of transport available.

13.20 Irish bus companies say they are in favour of accessibility but claim that accessible buses cost more to buy, incur extra running and maintenance costs, and create longer delays at stops. Finding accessible bus models to suit Irish conditions should prove possible, however, given technological advances and the experiences of other countries such as Finland. In the US making existing buses accessible was found to be not as expensive as transport companies claimed before the Americans with Disabilities Act was passed in 1990.

13.21 The Commission recommends that every CIE, Bus Eireann and Dublin Bus depot should have at least one accessible bus by June 1, 1997. The Department of Transport Energy and Communications should subsidise the additional cost of such vehicles: thereafter, the bus companies should bear the cost of replacement vehicles. The Commission also recommends that Ireland should ensure that the forthcoming EU directive on buses and coaches requires them to be accessible to all citizens.

13.22 A pilot accessible bus service (the Omnilink) began in Dublin in May 1995 with five City Imp size buses. Each has a remote controlled ramp, a kneeling facility, two wheelchair bays (also suitable for prams and buggies) and seating for other passengers. It has not been successful, however: the service was not properly advertised and, consequently, was under-utilised. Only one of the buses is in operation and the other four are in storage.

13.23 The Commission recommends that the Department of Transport, Energy and Communications and Dublin Bus provide the necessary funding to ensure a viable Omnilink pilot project by advertising and running it properly. Each should provide £250,000 towards the cost and the results of the pilot should be published.

13.24 Among the other problems people with disabilities have with buses are shelters without seating and, for people with visual impairments, the difficulties of ascertaining whether a bus is coming and whether it is the one they want. The Commission recommends that a limited amount of seating be included in the design of bus shelters. In addition, there should be discussions with the Council for the Status of People with Disability about providing destination and timetable information in braille in shelters. Consideration should also be given to erecting bus shelters in rural areas.

13.25 Many of the buses used as school transports are old and an adaptation programme should be started in 1997 to make them accessible to all students. EU funds should be sought for the programme which should be completed in five years.

13.26 School buses which sometimes carry up to 70 children of disparate ages are not supervised unless this is done voluntarily by parents. An inadequate number of buses for special schools - which usually carry at most 10 to 12 children - have escorts. The procedure for employing escorts is an ad hoc one and, with the dangers of abuse allegations, should be examined closely. Proper and adequate training must be given to escorts.

13.27 Research should be carried out into the possibility of using school buses outside times when they are required for transporting students. They could be used to take people with disability and others to day care centres, day activity centres, shops and so on. This research should examine the improvements in the quality of life that the use of these buses could bring to many individuals. The results should be published.

13.28 "Special" transport is provided by some organisations catering for people with disabilities but is usually limited to their own activities. This transport provides a useful function although it obviously cannot fulfil the role of making people with disabilities full and equal participants in all aspects of life. It must also be recognised that the name of an organisation on the side of a bus or coach along with the word 'ambulance' can and does identify people with a disability as different, underpin the view of disability as a medical condition and carry a stigma.

13.29 Where possible, all transport which caters for people with disabilities should have an escort on the bus as well as the driver. Both the escorts and drivers should be properly trained and have Garda clearance before they are employed.

13.30 There are a number of other options for providing transport services for people with disabilities which could be examined. These include:

- Vantastic; set up in Dublin in 1995, this involves two accessible vans and eight trained drivers and can be booked for regular or one-off trips. However, the scheme has been dogged by financial difficulties.

- Service Routes; bus services open to everyone but specially adapted for people with mobility impairments. Using smaller than average vehicles, the routes usually go into housing estates and up narrow roads. They could be of particular benefit to rural areas where the basic problem with public transport is its unavailability. Service routes could be set up as joint ventures between private operators and voluntary or statutory groups.

- Post Buses; these collect and deliver mail and carry passengers, using vehicles like estate cars, Land Rovers and mini-buses. They run on a published route and to a timetable and could also provide a valuable service for people in rural areas and people with disabilities if accessible vehicles were used.

- Social Car Schemes; they provide volunteer drivers (who receive a petrol allowance) for people with disabilities, usually for short trips. One such scheme was successfully run around Letterfrack in North West Connemara.

Cars

13.31   The private car provides optimum mobility for many people with a disability who see it as the key to their quality of life. Where they cannot drive, a car in the household aids their mobility and freedom. In rural areas a car is often the only method of transport which a person with a disability can use.

13.32   Technology has enabled more and more people with disabilities to drive adapted cars. But there is no fully equipped centre in Ireland with information on the latest technology for vehicle adaptation and driver assessment. The Council for the Status of People with a Disability should investigate the feasibility of setting up, in conjunction with the Northern Ireland authorities, a Driver Assessment Centre to make available to people throughout Ireland the latest technology in these areas.

13.33   There are some generous concessions for drivers with disabilities although they do not compensate them in full for the extra costs they incur. The present VAT and VRT rebates on cars for drivers with disabilities should be retained and the maximum rebate increased from the present limit of £7,500 and linked to the Consumer Price Index.

13.34   The medical criteria governing eligibility for drivers' concessions should be examined in consultation with the Council on the Status of People with a Disability and the National Disability Authority. This examination should review the present regulations and bring forward proposals for future regulations. The

Disabled Drivers Medical Board of Appeal, currently administered by the National Rehabilitation Board, should be continued.

13.35 The present disabled drivers badge should be replaced by one that is acceptable within the E.U. It should be issued to the driver concerned and should be transferable when they are travelling in a car other than their own.

13.36 The Department of Social Welfare should replace the present motorised transport grants operated by the Health Boards with a new first-time grant for motorists with disabilities. This should be:

- payable to first time purchasers who qualify under the criteria governing eligibility for drivers with disabilities;

- sufficient to cover 75% of the net cost of a standard new car (after rebates);

- restrict any means test to the driver only.

13.37 The vast majority of people with disabilities who do not drive do not receive concessions as passengers although, as already noted, having a car in a household is essential to many people with disabilities. Present VAT and VRT rebates on cars for passengers with disabilities should be retained at the present limit of £12,500 and linked to the Consumer Price Index.

13.38 The Commission welcomes the 1996 Finance Act amendment of the rule "that an adaptation of a car/van for the use of a disabled passenger must amount to 20% of its cost" to 10% of the original cost of the car and recommends that the percentage be reduced to zero over the next three years. Those not eligible under the criteria above should be entitled to a rebate of duty on 200 gallons of petrol/diesel in a calendar year on journeys on which they are a passenger, provided they are registered with the Council for the Status of People with a Disability.

13.39 As with drivers with disabilities, the medical criteria governing eligibility for concessions to passengers should be examined in consultation with the Council for the Status of People with a Disability and the National Disability Authority. A badge for passengers with a disability should be introduced for people who qualify under any of the above schemes and should be transferable to any car in which they are a passenger.

13.40 The problems faced by people with disabilities in getting motor insurance have already been covered in the chapter on insurance (Chapter 8).

13.41 To get maximum benefits from a car both drivers and passengers with disabilities need to park close to their destination. The lack of designated parking spaces, and the abuse of those that do exist, frequently thwart them. At present it is up to each local authority or private developer whether they provide designated parking spaces and there is a wide disparity in practices.

13.42   The Department of the Environment should produce before the end of 1997 a three year plan for the introduction of country-wide regulations on street and local authority parking spaces for people with a disability. They should cover the dimensions, number and siting of spaces and should exempt holders of the new badges for drivers and passengers with disabilities from payment of parking fees. Local authorities should provide a ratio of 1:25 of on street parking spaces for drivers/passengers with disabilities by the end of 1998. Penalties for improper use of these parking spaces should be severe and strictly enforced. All regulations introduced by the Department of the Environment should be compulsory on all local authorities.

13.43   Private car parks (as in multi storey car parks and shopping centres) also provide a limited number of car parking spaces for drivers with disabilities. However, these are most often abused by members of the general public who are not aware of the necessity of having these spaces.

13.44   The Commission recommends that planning laws should specify that a minimum of 1:50 parking spaces be set aside for drivers/passengers with disabilities in private developments. Management of these developments should ensure the correct use of these parking spaces.

Taxis and Hackneys

13.45   In some ways taxis and hackneys are the ideal form of transport; they operate door-to-door, can be summoned by telephone or fax, and can be used by most members of society. However, they have two major disadvantages; cost and the lack of wheelchair accessibility.

13.46   The majority of wheelchair users welcomed the arrival of 90 wheelchair accessible taxis in Dublin and the decision of Dublin Corporation that new licenses require wheelchair accessibility. This development has not been reflected in other cities and towns nor in rural areas with hackney services.

13.47   The Commission recommends that all local authorities should take cognisance of the needs of people with disabilities when issuing new licences and that taxi drivers should not be licensed without taking a training programme in the care of passengers with disabilities.

Air

13.48 By and large airports cater reasonably well for passengers with disabilities. Aer Rianta has been to the fore in projecting a positive attitude to accessibility and runs disability awareness training programmes. Parking and set-down spaces at Irish airports are readily available for people with disabilities. Within the airports, stand-by wheelchairs and buggies allow people with mobility impairments to cover long distances. Visual and audio information is available.

13.49 The introduction of airbridges and lifts have made boarding aircraft easier for everyone. However, airbridges are only available at Shannon and Dublin Airports. A lifting device on the catering truck is used in Cork Airport and there are plans to introduce a similar device at Dublin Airport at gates which do not have airbridges.

13.50 Aircraft, however, remain problematic. Carriers argue that in order to remain competitive they must seek maximum passenger loads and this leads to narrow aisles and miniature toilets. The Commission recommends that all aircraft have an onboard chair available to allow people with disabilities to access the facilities. All safety announcements on board planes are made by voice and some thought must be given by airlines to including people with a hearing impairment in these procedures.

13.51 Many people with disabilities have had major problems with one Irish carrier which restricts the number of passengers with disabilities on each flight. This causes problems for people leaving from rural airports where the number of flights per day is limited.

13.52 Some carriers also require that passengers with disabilities and their doctors fill in a medical form. Some of the questions to be answered on this form - which is also used for people suffering serious illnesses - are insulting to people with disabilities. We welcome the discussions that have taken place between Aer Lingus and the Commission in an effort to resolve this problem and hope that these discussions will continue with the Council for the Status of People with Disabilities.

13.53 The Commission recommends that the completion of a medical form should not be requested of people with disabilities by airlines unless a person is undergoing medical treatment. It also suggests that Irish airlines propose to IATA that separate forms be used for people with disabilities and for people suffering illnesses to ensure that only the information required for ensuring a smooth passage for people with disabilities is requested.

Sea Travel

13.54 Because of our island situation, ferry accessibility is very important, both for Irish people with disabilities travelling abroad and for the growing number of tourists with disabilities from Britain and the Continent. The ferry terminal at Rosslare is fully accessible and similar standards should apply to all other ferry terminals.

13.55 Most of the existing large ferries between Ireland and Britain and the Continent are only accessible with difficulty for people with mobility impairments. There is usually a small lift from the car deck and a cabin suitable for a wheelchair user. However, the ferries may not be accessible to people with sensory disabilities as there seems to be a lack of braille and all announcements are made by voice.

13.56 Internal ferries such as Tarbert-Killimer and others are inaccessible to wheelchair users and others unless they stay in cars.

13.57 The Commission recommends that only ferries which are accessible to all should be licensed to carry passengers.

Chapter Fourteen
TECHNOLOGY AND COMMUNICATIONS

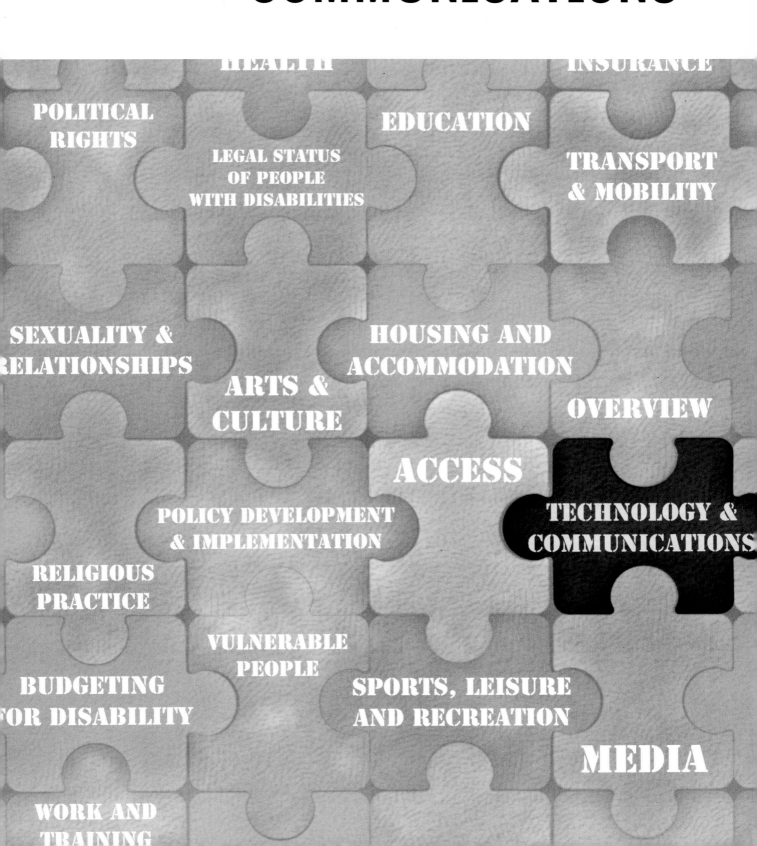

Technology can bring about major improvements in the quality of life for people with disabilities. Its introduction into the lives of people with disabilities needs to be carefully planned and delivered in a coherent and consistent manner so that all relevant avenues of technology are made accessible and readily available.

- excerpt from submission

14.1   Independence is a very important aspiration for most people. In the context of people with disabilities, it could be defined as requiring dignified self-determination with or without the assistance of others.

14.2   Technology and telecommunications can play a major role in helping people with disabilities to secure equal status in most areas of life and society. It can help people with hearing impairments to communicate; visually impaired people to 'read' and use computers; physically impaired people to live independently, work and to get about. However, it can also create barriers with the increased sophistication of everyday services such as banking and buying tickets. Too much technological adeptness may also be required of people: those with mobility impairments, for example, may be asked to use wheelchairs bristling with technology that are not always easy to learn or use.

14.3   General-purpose items of technology in everyday use should be usable by everybody, including people with disabilities, but often they are not. For example, there is a whole range of household consumer products like washing machines, cookers, and microwave ovens which use digital displays which communicate nothing to people with visual impairments. To include the kind of speech technology frequently used in children's toys in them when they are manufactured would literally cost pennies.

14.4   The main classes of technical aids listed by the International Standard Organisation (ISO 1992) indicate the wide range of equipment, devices and adaptations available as assistive technology. They range from simple, low-tech items like adapted clothing to high-tech robotics and include aids for:

- Orthoses/prostheses (for spine or limbs; orthopaedic footwear)

- Personal mobility (wheelchairs; turning and lifting aids; orientation aids)

- Communication, information, signalling (optical aids, hearing aids, writing aids. computers, alarm systems, telephone, face-to-face systems)

- Handling (for operating things; environmental control systems; hand, finger or reach aids; aids for carrying or transporting; robots)

- Housekeeping (aids for preparing meals, dish washing, eating/drinking, cleaning)

- Home adaptation (adapted furniture; aids for opening/closing doors, windows, curtains; lifts; safety equipment)

- Environment improvement (climate control)

- Personal care and protection (aids for using toilets and for washing/bathing; adapted clothing, shoes)

- Recreation (toys and games, exercise and sports facilities, gardening equipment)

- Therapy (dialysis, medicine dosing, testing/analysis, stimulation, sore prevention)

14.5 The present system of delivering assistive technology to people with disabilities is totally inadequate and frequently unjust. It does not meet the requirements of the UN Standard Rules; it is based on legislation that is vague and open to different interpretations; it contains many anomalies between groups of disabilities and regions of the country.

14.6 Responsibility for providing assistive technology rests primarily with Health Boards, supported by voluntary bodies. This automatically places it within an inappropriate medical and charity context rather than basing it on rights and a holistic approach. There is little or no accountability and no procedures for appealing decisions. Services, when available, can often be very slow.

14.7 The Commission recommends that the Department of Social Welfare and the Department of Transport Energy and Communications should introduce legislation to ensure access to assistive technology and telecommunications, in line with the UN Standard Rules. Access to this technology should include financial access.

14.8 A single existing agency should be responsible for all assistive technology and for disseminating information about new technological developments. Services should continue to be provided by a mixture of state and voluntary organisations but voluntary sector services must be properly funded and regulated.

14.9 This agency should also provide an adequate assessment service of the most appropriate technical aids for people with disabilities (see Chapter 4). It should examine an individual's needs and the available options and make recommendations. In doing so it should look at:

- The diversity of the user's needs

- The local support and availability for the aids

- The finance available

- The stability and nature of the person's disability

- The person's technical ability.

14.10 Many user's needs are simple. They may only require, for example, a non-conventional telephone which can be bought from a telephone shop. But user's needs are often more complex than they appear at first and careful consideration is required in recommending equipment that is affordable, available, adaptable and user friendly. The assessment must be holistic: if a user's disability is of a changing nature, it is vital that whatever is recommended is adjustable to changing needs.

14.11   The overall agency should set up nominated assessment centres and support them with appropriate funding for equipment, staff and training. There should also be a county network of 'feeder' or 'outreach' centres to provide primary assessments and training. All assessment must be based on a person centred approach.

Telecommunications

14.12   Various telecommunications applications also fall within the definitions of assistive technology. These include applications for carrying out services at a distance such as care (telecare), transactions (teleshopping), learning (distance education) and work (teleworking). Interactive communication (by the ordinary voice telephone or services like text telephony) and access to mass media (text captions on television programmes) can also help to meet needs for social contact and information.

14.13   However, telecommunication can also create new barriers through isolating people. In some cases, it may provide the preferred or only option but in other cases there may be a preference for more traditional and social ways of doing things. It is important that telecommunication does not substitute for face-to-face social contact, visits to shops or participation in mainstream employment and education.

14.14   The Commission recommends that the Department of Transport Energy and Communications should ensure that all companies licensed to provide telephone services should provide text telephone, a relay service and other special or adapted equipment required by people with disabilities. These services should not cost more than conventional telephones. All new public payphones should be accessible to everybody, including people in wheelchairs.

14.15   Drivers with disabilities who qualify for concessions should also qualify automatically for free mobile phone rental and a number of call units to cover any emergencies when they are travelling alone.

14.16   The Commission also recommends that RTE and other television stations with national licences should expand the number of hours and the range of programmes which are sub-titled. There should be a minimum of 50% of all programming hours captioned by 1998 and this should increase to all programming as soon as possible afterwards.

Communications

14.17   The ability to communicate is a fundamental human quality. For many people with disabilities it is a right which does not exist on a daily basis. Facilities are extremely limited for those whose first language is sign language and for those who do not communicate orally.

14.18   Interpreting support is clearly needed in public services such as hospitals, garda stations, courts and schools. Most information and public documents are available only in written text, with major consequences for people with sight impairments. Reader Services must be made available to people who need them and on conditions that are not so stringent that they exclude a large number of people.

14.19   People who are deaf and deaf/blind have communication skills which require some patience and training to understand. Such training is not available at present and should be provided in an approved centre. Interpreters should also be trained and available to people with speech impediments. Training for interpreters should be provided as a matter of priority, based on similar centres in the UK such as at Durham University.

14.20   There is also a need to recognise sign language which is not currently recognised in Ireland although it is at European level.

Chapter Fifteen
THE LAW AND
THE LEGAL SYSTEM

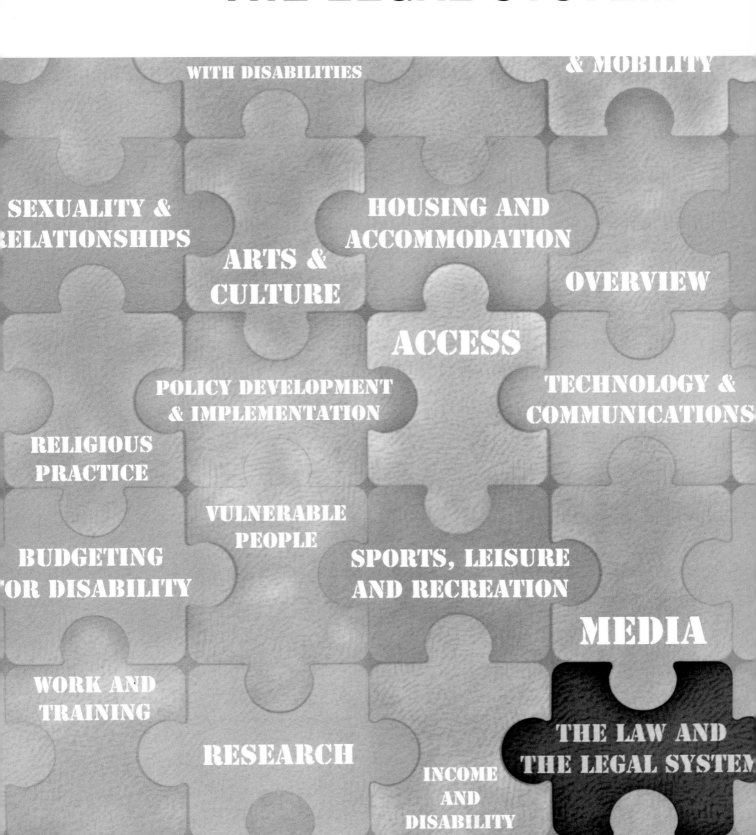

I had the unfortunate experience of representing a tenant in X Courthouse. The man was confined to a wheelchair, the consequence of which was that he had to be manhandled by members of the Garda Síochana up one steep flight of stairs, then up three steps and then down another four steps and then up a further five to reach the court room which is in the newly refurbished county council offices.

- excerpt from submission

15.1   Access to the legal system is a matter of fundamental importance in a democratic society and is recognised as such in the Irish Constitution, the European Convention on Human Rights and in international law. However, there are many barriers standing in the way of full access to the law and the legal system for people with disabilities in Ireland. These include the familiar ones of access to buildings and to information as well as specific procedures and practices of the legal system.

15.2   A range of measures are needed to ensure the right of access to the law and the legal system for all Irish citizens. These should include an action programme by the Department of Justice to make all courts fully accessible to people with disabilities, consultation with the legal professional bodies in relation to access for people with disabilities to legal advice and to training as lawyers, and a general raising of awareness amongst the legal professions towards disability issues.

15.3   Legislation, including statutes and Ministerial and other regulations, are generally only available in standard written form which means that they are inaccessible to many people who have visual disabilities. The Commission believes that all public documents should be provided in a range of appropriate formats, including large print, braille and computer disc.

15.4   Legal documents such as court summonses are also available in printed form only. These are frequently difficult to read and understand even for people who do not have any visual or learning disability. All legal documents should be as clear and easy to understand as possible. In addition, an information leaflet should be enclosed with documents in relation to court proceedings, which would give specific advice in relation to access to the court for people with disabilities and other relevant information. Court staff should be aware of disability issues and should be able to deal with inquiries from people with disabilities.

15.5   Issues surrounding the provision of legal services to people with disabilities should be pursued by the Council for the Status of People with Disabilities and the Law Society.

15.6   The Legal Aid Board should examine all its offices and make them fully accessible to people with disabilities. It should also assess the accessibility of its services in relation to people with visual and hearing disabilities in order to ensure that appropriate facilities (such as sign language translation) are fully available.

15.7   It is clear from submissions to the Commission that many courts are extremely inaccessible for people with mobility disabilities, inhibiting the right of access for such people whether they be members of the public, plaintiffs, defendants, witnesses, jury members, court staff, lawyers or judges. The

Department of Justice should make all court buildings accessible over a period of five years. Information in relation to the accessibility of court buildings (accessible parking, entrances, toilets, facilities for people with hearing disabilities, etc.) should be provided for all people with disabilities using the court system.

15.8 Having gained access to the courts themselves, two further issues arise for people with disabilities giving evidence. The first is in relation to people who require interpretation such as those who have a hearing disability. The Garda Commissioner has recently decided to employ sign language interpreters in all cases where their services are required. This is a very positive development but it does not apply to the civil courts. Provision should be made for a similar scheme in relation to all services provided by the Legal Aid Board, including court appearances. Similar provisions should be made for people with speech disabilities who require interpretation facilities.

15.9 The second issue which arises in this regard is in relation to the giving of evidence by people with general learning difficulties or intellectual disabilities. At present, the general common law rule is that all persons capable of understanding the nature of the oath and capable of rational testimony are able to give evidence. This can create difficulties for people with intellectual disabilities in that they may not be capable of understanding the nature of the oath or, alternatively, the court may consider that they are not capable of rational testimony.

15.10 The Law Reform Commission has proposed that the oath should be abolished and replaced by an affirmation. In relation to people with learning disabilities, it has also proposed that a test of competence to give evidence should be introduced and that such persons should not be required to affirm. However, this does not apply in relation to the civil law where the old rules still apply. It is particularly important that all efforts should be made to ensure that people with intellectual disabilities are facilitated in giving evidence in court. In particular, the court needs to be sensitive to the particular needs and abilities of such people. Consideration should be given to extending the changes in criminal law to all types of case.

15.11 Some people with disabilities are specifically excluded from serving on juries under the Juries Act 1976. The First Schedule to that Act, which sets out a list of persons ineligible to serve on a jury, includes two types of people with disabilities:

- people who have insufficient capacity to read, deafness or other permanent infirmity, and

- people who suffer or have suffered from mental illness or mental disability and, on account of that condition, are either

(i)   resident in a hospital or other similar institution

or

(ii)   regularly attend for treatment by a medical practitioner.

15.12   These provisions should be repealed from the Juries Act 1976. In reviewing the accessibility of courts, the Department of Justice should make sure that they are fully accessible to allow people with disabilities to act as jurors.

15.13   The criminal law in relation to persons with mental incapacity is based on legislation going back to the 19th century and is in urgent need of reform. An inter-departmental committee reported on the issue in the late 1970s but its proposals have never been implemented. At present, the law in this area is under somewhat piecemeal review, with the Department of Health considering some aspects and the Department of Justice reviewing others. In the light of developments in this area since the late 1970s, there is a need for a new public review of mental incapacity and the criminal law to be carried out by the Law Reform Commission or by an inter-departmental committee.

15.14   People with disabilities who wish to qualify as lawyers find themselves up against the physical barriers in the two professional schools for lawyers, the Law Society in the case of solicitors and the Kings Inns in the case of barristers. Neither of these premises are easily accessible for persons with mobility disabilities. Further difficulties may face them in relation to books and training materials. In addition, neither body appears to incorporate any element of disability awareness training or specific training on aspects of law likely to be relevant to people with disabilities.

15.15   The Council for the Status of People with Disabilities should enter into discussion with both the Law Society, the Bar Council and the Kings Inns in relation to the provision of legal services to people with disabilities. These discussions should also cover access by people with disabilities to their professional training courses.

15.16   Unlike the position in relation to jurors, there is no specific legal provision to disqualify persons with disabilities of any kind from becoming members of the judiciary. In order to be appointed as a judge, however, it is first necessary to have been a practising lawyer. The difficulties many people with disabilities face in entering the legal profession thus prevent full access for people with disabilities to judicial appointments.

Crime

15.17 Research from others countries - there is little available in Ireland - suggests that people with disabilities are more likely than other people to be the victims of both general crime - including theft and break-ins in the persons home - and physical and sexual abuse. Research in London found that harassment and abuse was, in several cases, specifically related to the person's disability. There is clearly a need for urgent research in this area in Ireland: it should be funded by the Departments of Justice and Health.

15.18 In the Irish context, the Commission believes it is essential that more research into the specific problems faced by people with disabilities in relation to abuse is required and that the relevant authorities should draw up policies and guidelines in this area drawing on best practice.

15.19 In the light of other countries' research findings, the relevant public bodies (including the Departments of Justice and Health, Health Boards, Gardai) must review existing policies in order to ensure that adequate protection and support is provided for people with disabilities. Such a review should draw on the lessons learned in the UK and on proposals put forward there by the National Society for the Prevention of Cruelty to Children and by the National Rehabilitation Board in Ireland.

15.20 Disability awareness training should be provided to all Gardai and others working in this area as part of their general training. All police stations should be fully accessible to people with disabilities and Gardai and other personnel who are able to communicate in sign language should be available.

The Criminal Justice System: Children

15.21 A significant proportion of children who come in contact with the Juvenile Justice System are described as having general learning disabilities. However, they often suffer from a range of disadvantages and it is difficult to distinguish the effects of learning disabilities from the other disadvantages. Accordingly, it is suggested that the most appropriate way to develop policies in relation to such children is to see them as children with a range of disadvantages (including general learning disabilities) rather than highlighting their disability.

15.22 The Commission recommends:

- That the Child Care Act by fully implemented as a matter of priority so as to ensure that a system of child welfare services is in place to prevent, where possible, children coming in contact with the juvenile justice system.

- The urgent reform of the juvenile justice system so as to put in place a child centred system of juvenile justice. This need was emphasised in the report of the Task Force on Child Care Service published in 1981. A juvenile justice bill has been promised for over 10 years and the current government programme includes a commitment to enact a bill to update the law dealing with young offenders and to extend the juvenile liaison scheme.

- Appropriate services should be provided for all children and young people with disabilities who become involved in the juvenile justice system, including education, training and accommodation.

- In the development and implementation of policies in this area, disability issues should be fully incorporated at all stages.

The Criminal Justice System: Adults

15.23   There is a lack of information in relation to the extent to which people with disabilities are to be found in the criminal justice system. It seems likely that people with disabilities make up at least the same proportion of the prison population as they do of the general population. Some particular aspects of disability may be over represented in the prison population. Unfortunately, disability has not been considered in any great detail in the studies which have been carried out to date.

15.24   The issue of people with disabilities in the prison system should be the subject of further long-term research by the Council for the Status of People with Disabilities. Such research should be funded by the Department of Justice and should investigate the extent to which people with different types of disability are to be found in the prison population and the extent to which the current prison system meets their specific needs. It should propose long term proposals for reform in the light of its findings.

15.25   The Department of Justice should review the accessibility of prisons for people with disabilities. All new prison buildings should comply with the building regulations in this regard.

15.26   The Department of Justice should ensure that all educational and training courses and materials provided are appropriate to the needs of people with disabilities. Prisoners with learning disabilities should be identified; special programmes, with the emphasis on remedial education, should be set up; and continuous assessment carried out in all cases with a view to suitable placement following release.

15.27   All prison staff should receive disability awareness training.

Chapter Sixteen
POLITICAL RIGHTS

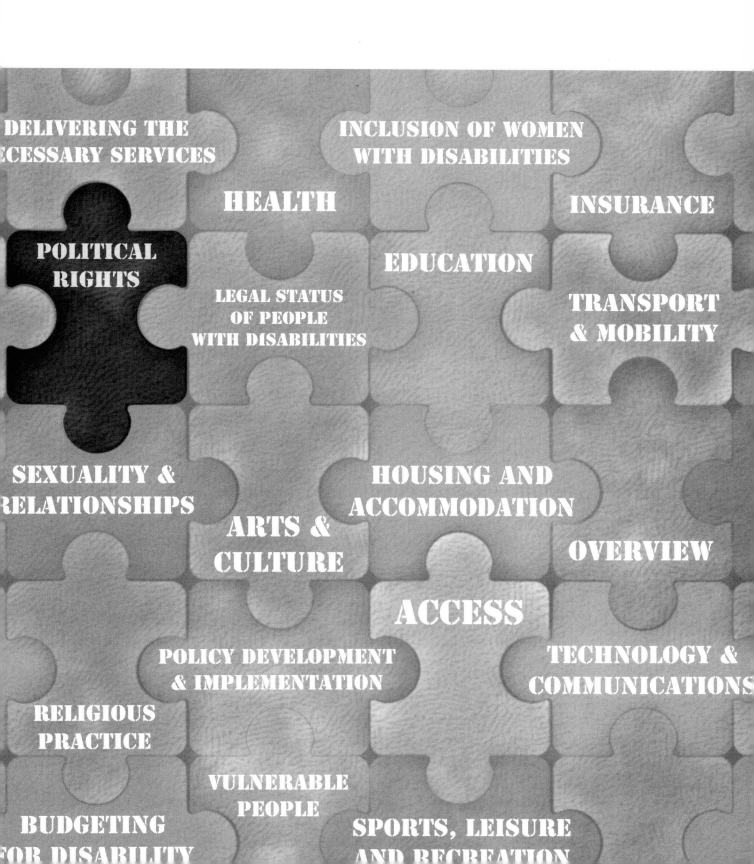

DELIVERING THE NECESSARY SERVICES

INCLUSION OF WOMEN WITH DISABILITIES

HEALTH

INSURANCE

POLITICAL RIGHTS

EDUCATION

LEGAL STATUS OF PEOPLE WITH DISABILITIES

TRANSPORT & MOBILITY

SEXUALITY & RELATIONSHIPS

HOUSING AND ACCOMMODATION

ARTS & CULTURE

OVERVIEW

ACCESS

POLICY DEVELOPMENT & IMPLEMENTATION

TECHNOLOGY & COMMUNICATIONS

RELIGIOUS PRACTICE

VULNERABLE PEOPLE

BUDGETING FOR DISABILITY

SPORTS, LEISURE AND RECREATION

The real problem does not relate to legislation or policy but to the implementation of these. The level of service is poor because people with disabilities are in a minority and have no worthwhile voice

- excerpt from submission

16.1 Many people with disabilities are unable to exercise their right to vote because polling stations are often inaccessible and because polling procedures, like cards and ballot papers, are not disability friendly. People with disabilities do not have a right to a postal vote.

16.2 A working party recommended in 1983 that a list of eligible postal voters (including people with disabilities) should be compiled each year alongside the electoral register. This recommendation was not accepted on the grounds that postal voting was open to abuse. No evidence was presented to the Commission that there is such a risk of abuse from postal voting by people with disabilities.

16.3 The Electoral Act 1992 provides for a very limited form of voting for people with disabilities. Those who are unable to vote in person at their polling station because of physical illness or physical disability can have their names recorded on a "special voters" list. A presiding officer together with a Garda calls to people on the 'special' list with the ballot paper which must be completed there and then. The legislation also provides that a person whose name is not on the special voters list who satisfies the returning officer that he or she is unable by reason of physical illness or physical disability to vote at the appropriate polling station may be allowed to vote at a more accessible polling station.

16.4 In view of the obvious inadequacies of the present arrangements, the Commissions recommends that all polling stations, booths and procedures should be made accessible for people with disabilities.

16.5 The Department of the Environment should provide a special budgetary allocation in order to ensure that this recommendation will be brought into effect as a matter of priority. A senior officer in the Department should review all voting procedures in consultation with people with disabilities and make sure that all necessary changes are introduced. This would include the printing of photographs of the candidates on ballot papers in order to assist people in voting; the design of polling booths; and the production of voting papers appropriate to the needs of people with disabilities (e.g. in braille).

16.6 People with disabilities who are unable to attend at a polling station should be entitled to be registered on a postal voting register and should be entitled to a postal vote.

16.7 People with disabilities are under represented amongst candidates for election and elected politicians at both local and national levels. Political parties have not taken sufficient positive action to encourage people with disabilities to stand for election and the Commission recommends that all parties should establish affirmative action programmes to encourage people with disabilities to participate fully in local, national and European politics.

Chapter Seventeen
THE INCLUSION OF WOMEN WITH DISABILITIES

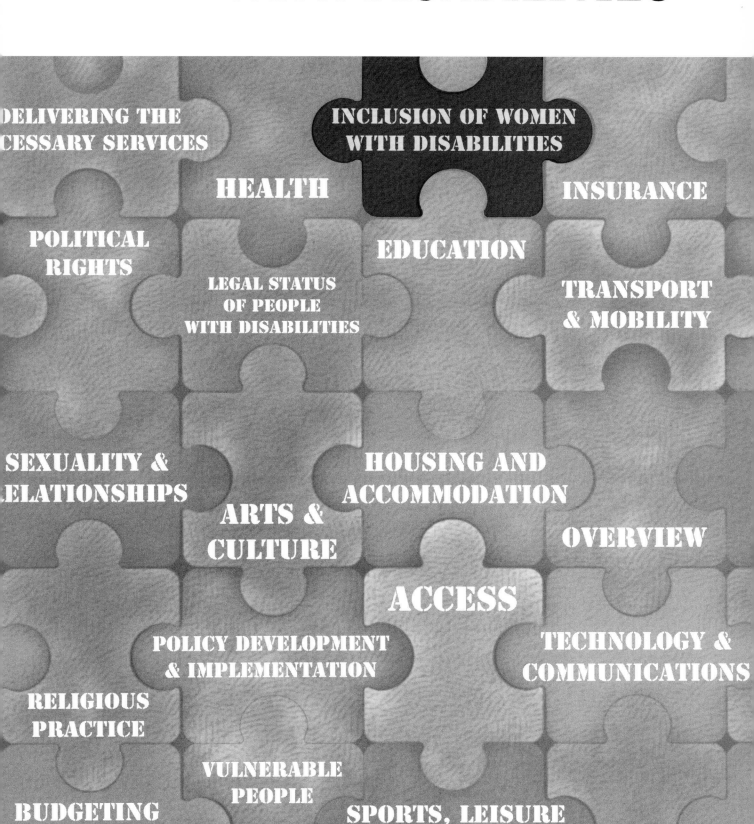

DELIVERING THE
NECESSARY SERVICES

INCLUSION OF WOMEN
WITH DISABILITIES

HEALTH

INSURANCE

POLITICAL
RIGHTS

EDUCATION

LEGAL STATUS
OF PEOPLE
WITH DISABILITIES

TRANSPORT
& MOBILITY

SEXUALITY &
RELATIONSHIPS

HOUSING AND
ACCOMMODATION

ARTS &
CULTURE

OVERVIEW

ACCESS

POLICY DEVELOPMENT
& IMPLEMENTATION

TECHNOLOGY &
COMMUNICATIONS

RELIGIOUS
PRACTICE

VULNERABLE
PEOPLE

BUDGETING
OR DISABILITY

SPORTS, LEISURE
AND RECREATION

It is time for Irish society...to do something practical to enable women with disabilities to contribute their valuable talents and perspectives to the nation as a whole.

- excerpt from submission

17.1 During its work, the Commission has been aware of the history and struggle by women for equality in all areas of life. The leadership given by women in highlighting equality issues, often against a hostile environment, has provided a true example of how change can be achieved and how people should be valued as being individuals. Women are equal and contribute to the full spectrum of life and development in Ireland.

17.2 Disability equality is no less important than gender equality. If we take the national population figures for the male and female percentages, we could say that at least 5% (150,000) of the population are women with disabilities. Certain facts also need to stated:

- Disability is a gender issue, because traditional and outdated attitudes in Ireland have resulted in women, as people with disabilities and or as family members, being expected to make do with less or being asked to undertake under-valued or under-resourced responsibilities.

- A woman with disabilities encounters "double disadvantage" both as a person with a disability, and then as a woman with a disability.

- The "caring" role attributed, in the main, to women has allowed and facilitated the State to escape its responsibilities in relation to disability issues.

- Women with disabilities have largely been excluded from the women's movement and the general public issues or debates concerning family life and sexuality.

- Government has not provided adequate access for the participation and fair representation of disabled women at local, national and international levels.

- Women with disabilities are still not included in the decision-making processes, policy making and political structures of government.

- Women with disabilities must be recognised as potential leaders in the communities.

- Women with disabilities are under-represented in the decision-making structures of voluntary organisations, even those which provide support for people with conditions which affect more women than men.

17.3 The Commission believes that no woman's experience of disability should render her powerless in relation to the basic rights of all women, e.g., the right to vote, the right to have a partner, the right to be a wife, the right to be a mother, the right to be a homemaker, to be a community leader, the right to work and, most importantly, the right to economic independence.

17.4   The Commission recommends that the National Women's Council address the impact of disability on gender equality. Specific action and research should be undertaken to combat the reality of the double exclusion experienced by women with disabilities.

17.5   Women with disabilities must be consulted in developing policies for them and they should be sufficiently resourced to maintain their status within the family and within the local community.

17.6   In order to ensure that women with disabilities are enabled to participate at all levels of society it will be necessary to:

- provide structures and spaces in which women with disabilities can meet together to discuss matters of common concern and to find ways of improving their situation;

- ensure that policy makers and others are informed and aware of the issues arising from women's experiences of disability, based on the social understanding of disability rather than relying on the medical and individualistic model of disability;

- Disability Equality and Awareness Training will be necessary to enable non-disabled women to learn, understand and reflect upon their own attitudes to disability. Such training should be facilitated by women with disabilities;

- All women's groups when they are developing projects at local level should consider the accessibility of such projects to women with disabilities through consultation with local women with disabilities;

- An equality proofing mechanism should be developed so that the impact of a particular project or proposal on women with disabilities is always considered.

Chapter Eighteen
SEXUALITY AND RELATIONSHIPS

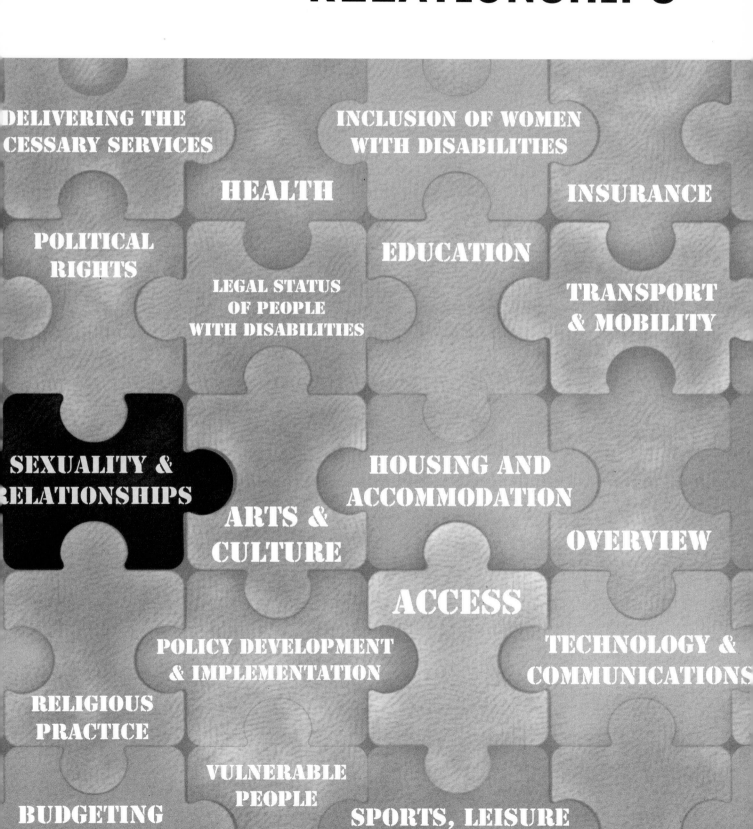

DELIVERING THE NECESSARY SERVICES

INCLUSION OF WOMEN WITH DISABILITIES

HEALTH

INSURANCE

POLITICAL RIGHTS

EDUCATION

LEGAL STATUS OF PEOPLE WITH DISABILITIES

TRANSPORT & MOBILITY

SEXUALITY & RELATIONSHIPS

HOUSING AND ACCOMMODATION

ARTS & CULTURE

OVERVIEW

ACCESS

POLICY DEVELOPMENT & IMPLEMENTATION

TECHNOLOGY & COMMUNICATIONS

RELIGIOUS PRACTICE

VULNERABLE PEOPLE

BUDGETING FOR DISABILITY

SPORTS, LEISURE AND RECREATION

Not one doctor in the whole year my husband was under treatment asked him anything at all about his sexual relationship and how that was altered since he was paralysed - not one. It was completely ignored. Is that usual or normal? A healthy 44 year old with two kids?

- excerpt from submission.

18.1   The right of people with disabilities to the same degree of fulfilment through relationships and sexuality as anyone else must be included in any list of equal rights. This has widespread implications for the providers of services in housing/accommodation, education, training and counselling.

18.2   Sexuality is still a topic surrounded by sensitivities and is not as straightforward an issue to address as others in this report. But it is an area in which extraneous factors impact strongly on people with disabilities, preventing them from enjoying this aspect of themselves to the full. Without a change in general conditions and attitudes, there is little chance of real equality in relation to sexual matters.

18.3   People with disabilities are denied their sexuality primarily by the stigma which surrounds and pervades disability. In a society in which the cult of the "body beautiful" reigns one becomes less sexually acceptable the further one is from the stereotypes of beauty. For many people with disabilities this is a further burden on top of low economic and social status.

18.4   Men and women with disabilities experience this phenomenon in slightly different ways. Men with disabilities may fail to meet the standards of sexual acceptability on the grounds of economic and social status with stereotypical beauty requirements coming in second place. For women, economic and social status may take second place to the demands for physical beauty. Gay men with disabilities, however, have problems being accepted in a community which holds the "body beautiful" in high regard and are doubly discriminated against by a society which stigmatises gays and lesbians as well as people with disabilities.

18.5   A further stigmatising factor is the fear of what will happen if people with disabilities have children. There are fears that offspring will be disabled and questions raised as to whether disabled people are "fit" or "able" to parent. It may well be that these fears are in fact the prime source of all the prejudices that people with disabilities experience in relation to their sexuality.

18.6   The result of such prejudice is the "desexualising" of people with a disability - the refusal to acknowledge their sexuality. There are various ways in which this occurs, including:

•   Treating a person with a disability like a child: many people with a disability are treated like children, not only by the general public but also by professionals and family members.

•   Treating a person with a disability as genderless: some people argue that a "disabled" toilet is a denial of the fact that disabled people are men or women first while others argue that unisex toilets allow access to individuals whose assistants are of the opposite gender.

- Treating a person as though their appearance is unimportant: not only is the appearance of people with disabilities often considered unimportant but sometimes they are dressed, by others, in clothes more appropriate for children.

- Treating a person as if their body is not sexual: people with a physical disability who are handled more than most report that the experience of being handled without the appropriate respect leaves them feeling as if their bodies have no value or sexual worth.

- Leaving people naked in hospitals for long periods as medical and paramedical staff work around them: the invisibility of sexuality in the health services is an indicator that it is low on their agenda despite its relevance to people's lives.

18.7   These practices may arise from an unconsciously determined need, on the part of caring personnel, to suppress the sexuality of people with disabilities. It is this need which must be tackled if those with disabilities are to enjoy equality in sexual matters.

18.8   Approaches to sex which promote any activity which both partners find pleasurable, comfortable and safe would benefit many people with disabilities. An inherent aspect of this type of approach would be an encouragement of communication between partners, as an ability to express one's sexual needs and pleasures is an essential aspect of healthy sexual relationships. Sexual aids or devices may be essential or desirable to achieving an enjoyable sexual life. However, they are difficult to procure.

18.9   The Commission recommends that the Department of Health should develop policies (including delivery structures) in conjunction with the Council on the Status of People with Disabilities in relation to the sexual rights of people with disabilities. These policies should cover the following areas:

- the right to privacy and dignity,

- the right to accessible information and guidance,

- the right to counselling as appropriate,

- the right to their bodily integrity and how this can be protected, in accordance with their ability to protect themselves,

- the right to information on family planning, contraceptive services, sex therapy services, sexual equipment, and on the prevention and investigation of sexual abuse.

18.10   Given the almost total lack of research to date in this area, the Commission believes that consultations with people with disabilities should be undertaken immediately to establish priority areas for research. These consultations should be carried out by the Health Research Board under the auspices of the National Disability Authority and funded by the Department of Health.

18.11   To address the issues raised above, the Commission also recommends that disability and sexuality awareness be included in the professional and academic training of all those who work with people with disabilities whether they are paid staff or volunteers.

Relationships

18.12   People with disabilities sometimes find that their able-bodied peers are not interested in developing intimate relationships once they are aware of a disability. Not only does the stigma associated with disability reduce the sexual value of the people affected but people without disabilities fear that association with them would reflect on their own sexual and social status. Myths of dependence also create a fear that becoming involved with a person with a disability would result in all sorts of caring responsibilities.

18.13   Most damaging in this process, however, is the way it can result in people with a disability feeling that they are not sexual, not attractive, or not worthy. Sadly, this also results in people with disabilities rejecting each other and valuing relationships with other partners more highly. It also means that people with disabilities are more vulnerable to abusive relationships, feeling either that they deserve no better, or would be unable to attract a more respectful relationship.

18.14   Disability can also cause enormous strains on relationships within families. The birth of a child with a disability requires parents to cope with their own very confused emotions as well as the reactions of others. Without support and counselling it may be difficult for them to come to terms with all their feelings: if unresolved, such contradictory feelings start to impact on the family and the child. The role and activity of "caring" for the child may become a means of distraction from the parents' emotions.

18.15   One reality for parents is that they may remain actively involved in the lives of children with disabilities until much later in life than usual, given the lack of services and opportunities for people with disabilities. It is no surprise, therefore, that they have deep concerns about their own responsibilities and how far they may extend.

18.16   When a family member becomes disabled much depends upon their age, how they adjust, and what type of coping skills existed in the family beforehand.

They need similar support and counselling to that required for parents of a child born with a disability. The person with the disability may need a considerable amount of support to help him/her to come to terms with the changing roles in the whole family or partnership.

No statistics are available in Ireland but research in Canada found that in marriages where the female partner became disabled 90% failed while 50% failed when the male partner acquired a disability. These figures are considerably higher than average marital breakdown rates.

18.17 Privacy and personal choices are often limited in institutional and residential settings. Institutions, both large and small, have rules and regulations which invade the privacy of individual residents and inhibit relationships. All service providers, particularly residential providers must have regard to the right of the individual and practices involving segregation rather than education which deliberately prevent informed, consensual relationships should be ended.

18.18 Access to support services for adult individuals and families, where required could be provided through the Disability Support Service, and would thereby be available in all residential centres as well.

Advice and Counselling

18.19 People with disabilities have been denied access to family planning services as a result of the familiar access problems (inaccessible venues, lack of information in suitable formats) as well as unwelcoming attitudes (disapproval, unaware staff). Like many other women, women with a disability have felt uncomfortable using their own GP for family planning and tend to use clinics for crisis management rather than prevention.

18.20 Counselling in sexual and reproductive health could be particularly useful for people with disabilities who face a wide range of barriers to expressing their sexuality. Given the lack of counselling available through the general medical services, however, attending a counsellor is a luxury. All the access problems apply in the case of counsellors, particularly discriminating against people with communication problems.

18.21 People with disabilities and parents clearly want and need access to appropriate genetic and medical counselling services, in order to make informed personal decisions about having children. The knowledge generated by the Human Genome Project has enormous potential for the management of our health but, if used unwisely, it also holds the danger of creating new forms of discrimination and new methods of oppression.

18.22   All women are entitled to ante and post natal health care free of charge but the facilities offered through the public health service are often inaccessible and inappropriate for women with disabilities. Some units do offer tailored services such as the ante-natal classes with a sign interpreter in the Rotunda Hospital in Dublin. However, there are insufficient examples of such initiatives.

18.23   The Adoption Board have no statistics on disabled parents adopting but it appears to be extremely difficult for a couple where one or both partners have a disability to adopt, especially to adopt a child without disabilities. Fostering children is an option available to them but, given the constant need for foster parents, the approach is quite different from the adoption process.

Sexual Abuse

18.24   Awareness of sexual abuse has increased greatly in recent years, both through media coverage of prosecutions of offenders and through research. Research outside of Ireland has highlighted the fact that children and adults with disabilities face an increased risk of sexual abuse. They were found to be most at risk in places where they live and work rather than in public places. The factors which make them more vulnerable include:

- their lack of control and choice over their lives.

- the encouragement of compliance and obedience rather than assertiveness.

- they come into contact with many more "caretakers" than the rest of the population.

- people with a physical disability are often exposed to intimate touching as a result of their disability and may find it difficult to establish what touches are appropriate.

- isolation and rejection increases their responsiveness to attention and affection and, therefore, their vulnerability.

- children with communication disabilities have been found to be at risk as they have difficulties describing their experiences.

18.25   The Commission recommends that programmes relating to sex education should be available in accessible formats, and include positive images of people with disabilities. These programmes should be provided as appropriate in all schools, training centres, workshops and residential centres for people with disabilities.

18.26   The legal system should be reformed so that it is better able to deal with cases of abuse involving people with disabilities. This may include mandatory reporting and addressing the issue of people with disabilities, especially those with learning disabilities, as credible witnesses. Sex offenders with previous convictions should not be given positions of trust with people with disabilities.

Sterilisation

18.27   There is no precise information about the extent of sterilisation of people with disabilities in Ireland. Although men are also sterilised, this issue more often concerns women. It is assumed that the sterilisations which do take place are authorised on the basis of medical and psychological opinion and with parental agreement. It is not known to what extent people with disabilities are consulted about such decisions.

This is a profoundly complex question with ethical, social, economic and legal implications. It is a question to be faced in the future, given the developing emphasis on people's rights and changing attitudes.

18.28   There is less discussion of hysterectomy, whether consensual or non-voluntary as a means of contraception, but such practices do exist and need to be investigated.

18.29   There is evidence, too, of non-consensual use of contraception by women with disabilities. While contraception does not have the same permanency as sterilisation, people with disabilities must be protected from non-voluntary and unnecessary medical interventions.

18.30   The abortion information legislation introduced in Ireland is also relevant to people with disabilities on two counts. Firstly, it is essential that any counselling services which are available should be accessible to people with disabilities. Secondly, care should be taken with the perception of counsellors about the lives of people with disabilities to ensure they do not encourage abortion in the case of foetal disability.

18.31   The Commission recommends that sterilisation of people with disabilities on the grounds of their disability alone should be legally prohibited. In any situation where sterilisation is being considered, every effort must be made to ensure that informed and free consent exists. Where informed consent is not possible, strict legal criteria must be adjudged to exist by a court of law before sterilisation can be carried out. These criteria should include the requirement to show:

- just and necessary cause;

- that other methods of contraception are unworkable;

- that fair procedures are observed, including medical and psychological assessment of the person's welfare and rights;

- independent advocacy on behalf of the person and full consultation with parents and carers where appropriate.

A Strategy for Equality Report of the Commission on the Status of People with Disabilities

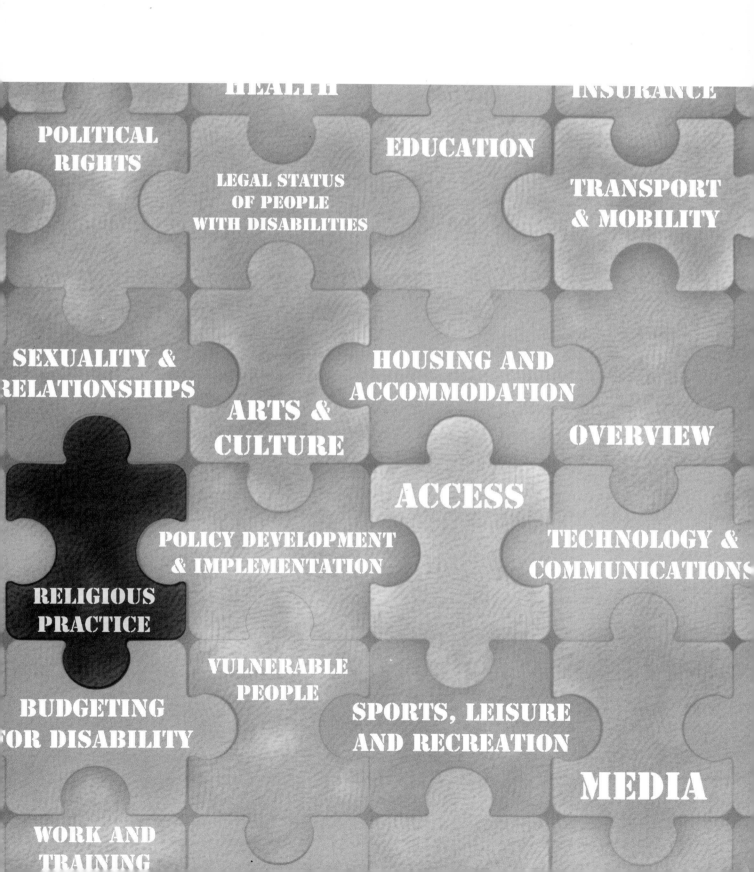

Chapter Nineteen
RELIGIOUS PRACTICE

HEALTH

INSURANCE

POLITICAL RIGHTS

EDUCATION

LEGAL STATUS OF PEOPLE WITH DISABILITIES

TRANSPORT & MOBILITY

SEXUALITY & RELATIONSHIPS

HOUSING AND ACCOMMODATION

ARTS & CULTURE

OVERVIEW

ACCESS

POLICY DEVELOPMENT & IMPLEMENTATION

TECHNOLOGY & COMMUNICATIONS

RELIGIOUS PRACTICE

VULNERABLE PEOPLE

BUDGETING FOR DISABILITY

SPORTS, LEISURE AND RECREATION

MEDIA

WORK AND TRAINING

19.1   Religion plays an important part in the lives of many Irish people, including people with disabilities. At present, however, barriers of attitude, communication and architecture prevent many of those people from participating fully in the worship, services and social activities of their respective congregations.

19.2   For those with a mobility problem - and this includes many older people - getting in to the place of worship of their choice may not be physically possible. Even when they do get in, they may not be able to negotiate narrow doorways, heavy doors or stairs or find print too small to read and not available on tape or in Braille. Sound systems may be inadequate, with no sign language interpretation for those who need it. Toilets, where they are available, may not be usable by wheelchair users.

19.3   For many, the biggest barrier may be the attitudes of others. Feelings of being ignored, isolated or rejected may be reinforced by not being included in activities in which other members of the congregation take part, by the language used by religious leaders, or in printed materials, by a general lack of awareness of the needs of people with disability in the community.

19.4   People with disabilities should be made to feel welcome and should be fully involved in every aspect of congregational life. To this end, the Commission recommends:

- that every religious community should set up a small task force or working group, which should include people with disabilities, to look at anything which could be a barrier to the inclusion of all in worship and to develop an action plan to eliminate those barriers;

- that disability awareness should be included in the formation of religious leaders at every level.

A Strategy for Equality Report of the Commission on the Status of People with Disabilities

Chapter Twenty

ARTS AND CULTURE

DELIVERING THE
CESSARY SERVICES

INCLUSION OF WOMEN
WITH DISABILITIES

HEALTH

INSURANCE

POLITICAL
RIGHTS

EDUCATION

LEGAL STATUS
OF PEOPLE
WITH DISABILITIES

TRANSPORT
& MOBILITY

SEXUALITY &
RELATIONSHIPS

HOUSING AND
ACCOMMODATION

ARTS &
CULTURE

OVERVIEW

ACCESS

POLICY DEVELOPMENT
& IMPLEMENTATION

TECHNOLOGY &
COMMUNICATIONS

RELIGIOUS
PRACTICE

VULNERABLE
PEOPLE

BUDGETING
OR DISABILITY

SPORTS, LEISURE
AND RECREATION

At the present moment in my own area I do not know of any culture.

-   excerpt from submission

20.1   While activity in the arts is on the increase in Ireland, not everyone participates equally, least of all people with disabilities. The main barriers to their participation are those already identified in other chapters of this report - lack of access to venues and to transport, inadequate information, and low economic status.

20.2   Demand for, and participation in, the arts is closely related to income and education; it increases as income increases and the higher the level of education and goes down as income and education levels decrease. The extra costs of disability and the low average level of income of people with disabilities in Ireland impacts disproportionately on their participation in the arts.

20.3   Arts education and arts approaches in education and training have a particular value for people with disabilities, including many people with learning disabilities, autism or mental health difficulties for whom other subjects and teaching methods are problematic or who have difficulty in using conventional ways of making or expressing choices. Being involved in arts activities can help people with disabilities to avail of other possibilities and thus function as a channel for achieving other personal objectives.

20.4   The marginal status of both arts and people with disabilities in each other's worlds can be measured by the fact that only 10% of the submissions received by the Commission mentioned the arts. Many of these only mentioned the arts in a general list to do with access. Very few submissions from organisations of or for people with disabilities mentioned arts or cultural issues and only two submissions were received from arts organisations (the Arts Council and Very Special Arts).

20.5   Those which did deal with the arts brimmed with suggestions for improvements, many of which have been incorporated into the recommendations of this report. While the prevailing view of the current state of affairs was negative, people with disabilities making submissions made it clear that they want to be involved in cultural activity. Several submissions also stressed the joy of discovering the arts.

20.6   The low participation rate of people with disabilities as arts practitioners is partly explained by the same factors which inhibit their participation as audiences - the lack of arts education and training, appropriate access and low income levels. While people with disabilities have always been notable practitioners in the arts in Ireland (Carolan and Joyce, for example), this aspect of their experiences has generally been unacknowledged, considered irrelevant or hidden. It is only in recent times that a generation of artists has emerged whose work is informed directly by their experience (e.g. Mary Duffy, Corban Walker).

20.7   On the whole, artists with disabilities are primarily concentrated in visual arts (e.g. George McCutcheon, Stephen Walsh, Maeve McCormack Nolan) and writing (e.g. Christopher Nolan, Maureen Charles, Davoren Hanna), rather than performance arts. A submission to the Commission suggested that this was not least because writing and visual arts can be created alone, in one's own space, while performance arts require access to public spaces, collaboration with teams of people, auditions and career structures, specialist education and training - all of which pose problems at present for people with disabilities.

20.8   Many of the Commission's earlier recommendations apply equally to the arts, particularly in the area of access. The review of the Building Regulations 1991, recommended in Chapter 9: Access, should include all arts venues and aim to make them as accessible as possible to as many people as possible. Among the facilities that should be available in all theatres, cinemas, auditoriums and concert halls are transfer places (which allow wheelchair users to sit in a seat) and wheelchair spaces (where the user can stay in their wheelchair). Induction loop systems, which amplify sound for hearing aid users, should be installed in all auditoriums, especially those in receipt of grant-aid, while infra-red systems are preferable in music venues. Stages may also require loop systems to facilitate deaf performers.

20.9   Box-office desks should be located at heights accessible to both wheelchair-users and ambulant people and should incorporate a counter loop system and a minicom or other text telephone system. Audio description systems - through which people with visual impairments can hear during pauses in dialogue descriptions of action taking place on stage or screen via a headset - should be installed in all cinemas and buildings where performances take place. The same equipment can be used for such services as simultaneous translation.

20.10   Super-titling equipment should be available for use in the Abbey Theatre, Siamsa Tire, the Municipal Theatre, Galway, Wexford Theatre Royal, Waterford Theatre Royal, Cork Opera House and any commercial theatre with more than 800 seats.

20.11   The Department of Arts, Culture and the Gaeltacht should draw up a code of practice for all the national cultural institutions and the heritage services to provide facilities and information at their institutions, sites and visitor centres for people with disabilities. The recent refurbishment of the National Gallery in Dublin is a good example of a serious effort to make it more accessible to people with a disability. Every level of the Gallery is now accessible, with chair-lifts strategically positioned in a number of locations. Staff have an appreciation of signing, and the overall impression is that people with a disability are made welcome in the Gallery at all times.

20.12   Strategies should be developed by the Arts Council, the Heritage Council and the National Monuments and Historic Properties Service to find ways of making accessible those arts and heritage activities which take place in existing buildings, including listed buildings. Operating in a building which cannot easily be made wheelchair-accessible should not prevent arts organisations from providing access features for people with sensory or other disabilities.

20.13   The Arts Council should disability proof the Arts Plan 1995-1997.

20.14   This is particularly important in the light of such general barriers as the uneven spread of arts activity throughout the country which can only be overcome by a proactive policy of inclusiveness allied to the priority zones strategy detailed in the plan.

20.15   The joint action research project by the Arts Council and the National Rehabilitation Board, mooted in the plan, should be expanded to include the Council for the Status of People with Disabilities as a third partner. Meanwhile, organisations in the field of disability should develop and implement arts policies in order to encourage and support access and opportunity in the arts for people with disabilities.

20.16   In order to increase access to, and participation in, the arts for people with disabilities, relevant state agencies should devise systems of incentives for them, both financial and otherwise. Along with local authorities, the Arts Council should provide adequate and clearly ring-fenced funding as a temporary strategic tool to increase access and opportunity in the arts for people with disabilities through grants to

- encourage the development of both disability arts and arts and disability practices, including integrated provision;

- ensure that venues become accessible to audiences and practitioners with disabilities.

20.17   The Arts Council should also develop a concessionary card system, through which people with disabilities in receipt of state benefits could obtain admission to arts venues and courses at concessionary rates. Priority seating in certain parts of auditoria (e.g. with level access for wheelchair-users, aisle seats for physically disabled people, near the stage for visually-impaired people, in good view of sign interpreters or super-titling for deaf people) should be offered to people with disabilities who need it, at the cheapest rate on offer. This is an access requirement which should be fulfilled at all times and should not be subject to the same conditions as financial concessions.

Education and Training

20.18   The Arts Council, local authorities, arts and disability organisations should introduce a system of bursaries for people with disabilities, with the aim of increasing their representation in all artforms and methods of cultural expression.

20.19   All children with disabilities should be given the opportunity to participate in a range of arts activities as part of their general education, including at pre-school level. This is of paramount importance, particularly for those children who have difficulty in using other, accepted ways of making or expressing choices or of learning.

20.20   People with disabilities who have missed out on arts education should be offered compensatory education through adult education programmes run or funded by the VECs. Providers of adult, second-chance and continuing education should ensure that arts education is made widely available to students with disabilities.

20.21   The training, including in-service training, of primary school teachers and secondary school art and music teachers should have an arts dimension as well as the disability dimension recommended in Chapter 11 on Education.

20.22   All arts organisations should institute disability equality training for their staff, members, and volunteers. Disability equality training is particularly vital for front-of-house and box office staff, whose offers of assistance, pro-activity, information-giving skills and knowledge are of paramount importance in dealing with customers with disabilities.

20.23   Arts awareness courses should be run in disability organisations, including for access experts. This is intended to ensure that disability organisations develop awareness of the arts and encourage their membership and client groups to seek involvement in the arts at all levels.

20.24   The Council for the Status of People with Disabilities should develop models and mechanisms for the identification of talent, leading to professional training in areas of disability arts or arts and disability practice where few role models exist and/or where the appropriate language and aesthetic are only in the process of development. The training itself should take place in mainstream settings.

20.25   Training in music, art and theatre for people with disabilities should be open in its entry policies, modular in structure, and lead to clearly-specified, national qualifications.

20.26   Artist-in-residence schemes should be organised to ensure that

- artists with disabilities work as artists-in-residence in both inclusive and disability-specific settings;

- artists-in-residence working with people with disabilities are of the same standard of excellence as those who work with other people.

20.27 The Irish Writers' Centre should develop training and standards for live and recorded audio description.

20.28 Theatre-in-education companies and others involved in outreach work in schools should ensure that their performances and workshops can be accessed by all children with disabilities in any class or school with which they work.

Information

20.29 Arts and cultural organisations should strive to make information on their facilities, services, events, or performances available in a wide range of formats (e.g. large print, tape, Braille, computer disk, signing). The Department of Arts, Culture and the Gaeltacht and the Arts Council should lead by example in providing information.

20.30 Information on arts and cultural facilities, events and performances should state clearly their arrangements for people with disabilities. This must include access information, pricing policy and any special features (such as the use of a strobe light or glitter ball which can have adverse effects on some people with epilepsy). Events and courses should be publicised by the widest possible range of media including Aertel, local radio, teletext, magazines for deaf people, specialist TV and radio programmes aimed at people with disabilities, the disability press and newsletters, and via disability organisations such as Deaf Clubs to ensure that the maximum number of people with disabilities have access to the information.

20.31 Arts and cultural organisations should provide scripts, précis, introductory talks, taped programmes, audio and sign language interpreted tours, touch tables, thermoforms and other means of ensuring maximum access for people with disabilities to venues, performances, exhibitions and events.

General

20.32 The Council for the Status of People with Disabilities should appoint an arts officer. This will ensure that arts and cultural matters assume a central position within the Council's work from the beginning. The Arts Council should nominate a professional member of staff to act as a link between artform officers and people with disabilities and their organisations.

20.33 The Council for the Status of People with Disabilities should also set up a talent bank of interested and suitably qualified people with disabilities to be recommended to the Minister for Arts, Culture and the Gaeltacht for consideration as nominees to state boards. The Arts Council should also have access to this talent bank and should ensure that people with disabilities are included as nominees to boards of management of arts organisations.

20.34 The Arts Council should commission the production of resource packs for arts organisations to assist them to implement ways of involving people with disabilities as audiences, participants or employees.

20.35 CAFE (Creative Activity for Everyone) should be developed as a central independent source of expert advice on arts and disability issues. CAFE and APIC (Awareness Publishing Information Communications) should co-operate more closely in order to facilitate such developments as the disability access coding of CAFE's extensive database. CAFE should also consider the establishment of a system of arts animateurs to facilitate the interface between arts and disability organisations.

20.36 County arts officers should conduct an immediate disability audit/inventory of all venues and arts organisations in their areas, reporting to the Arts Council, relevant city/county managers and regional authorities. This process should be repeated and updated in 1999 as part of a review of progress made arising from the recommendations of the Commission on the Status of People with Disabilities.

20.37 Application forms issued by the Arts Council, the Ireland Funds and other funding bodies for arts organisations should include a section requesting information about facilities for people with disabilities and arrangements made to ensure their full participation in the applicant organisation. As well as tracking progress made, this mechanism will also enable the Arts Council and other funding bodies to make disability-specific grants from time to time in respect of staffing and recruitment and numbers and types of exhibitions.

20.38 A touring "hothouse" roadshow should be developed by Very Special Arts to provide opportunities for people with disabilities, including those who live in institutions, to sample arts approaches in workshops and developmental projects.

20.39 The Arts Council should revise its handbooks for exhibition organisers to include sections on display, particularly as it affects people with disabilities. Exhibitions should be mounted in such a way that exhibits can be clearly appreciated by both wheelchair-users and ambulant people, with cord barriers, if used, at heights which do not present a trip hazard. All exhibition rooms and galleries should include seating to enable ambulant people with disabilities to rest.

20.40 The Minister for Arts, Culture and the Gaeltacht should propose an amendment to the Arts Act, 1951, Section 1, recognising "creative communication in sign language" as a specific artform. This will ensure the recognition of deaf arts and culture at the most formal level, alongside drama, literature and music. The drama officer of the Arts Council should provide a list of all sign interpreters qualified to work in theatre to all theatres and theatre companies.

20.41 Moltar don Roinn Comhionannais agus Athchóirithe Dlí, i gcomhar le hUdaras na Gaeltachta, staitisticí maidir leis an líon iomlán de dhaoine le mí-chumais sa nGaeltacht a chur le chéile, agus cláracha a fhorbairt chun cuidiú le daoine le mí-chumais bheith páirteach i saol cultúrtha agus soisialta na Gaeltachta tríd is tríd.

20.42 The Department of Enterprise and Employment should ensure that the legislation currently in the course of preparation by its Copyright Unit exempts from liability for copyright infringements any reproductions in formats other than print of copyright works, which are made for the use in education, or otherwise for the personal use, of people with visual impairments. Where the extent of such reproduction might conflict with a normal exploitation of the work, or risk prejudicing the legitimate interests of the author, the legislation should provide for the payment of equitable remuneration to a body representative of the rightsholders affected.

The second part of this recommendation may be necessary to ensure compliance by the state with its international obligations under the copyright conventions.

A Strategy for Equality Report of the Commission on the Status of People with Disabilities

Chapter Twenty-One
MEDIA

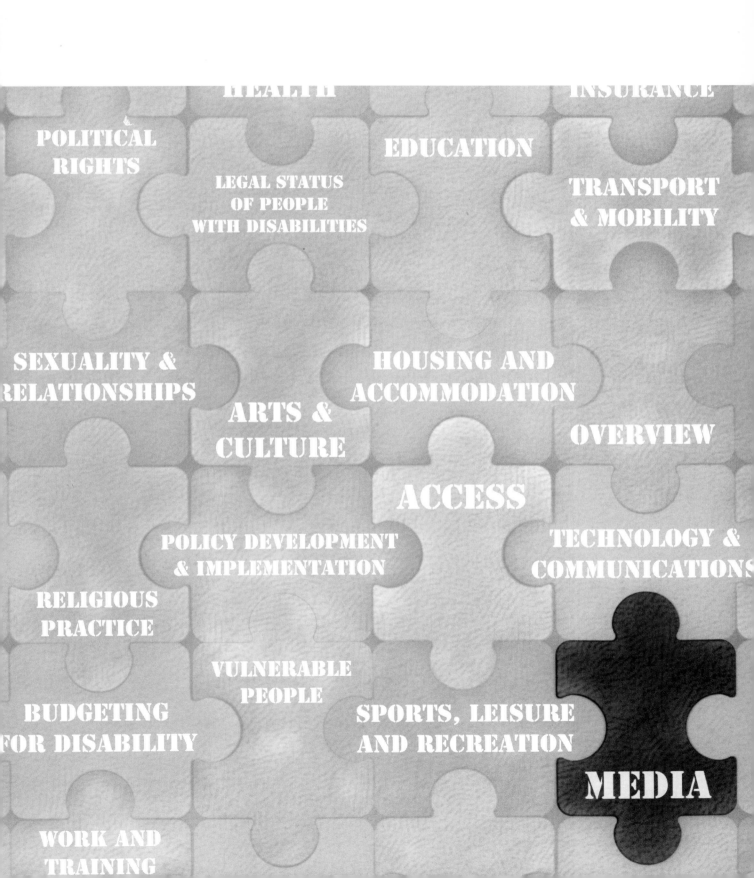

The media seems only to concentrate on the disabled when they are protesting for what they are entitled to.

— excerpt from submission

21.1   People with disabilities and their concerns are either invisible, marginalised, or depicted by negative stereotypes in the media. The world as represented on television fails to include the estimated 350,000 Irish people who have some form of disability as a significant element in society. They may feature occasionally in news or magazine programmes but they rarely appear in quiz shows or game shows or as regular characters in drama or other popular television forms.

21.2   When they do appear, it is generally seen by people with disabilities themselves as being in a negative or offensive stereotype. The media stereotypes them as being either pitiable and pathetic; objects of violence; sinister and evil; super cripples; objects of ridicule; their own worst and only enemies; burdens; sexually abnormal; and incapable of participating fully in community life. In short, it is the kind of stereotyping which has helped to marginalise people with disabilities and exclude them from equal participation in society.

21.3   The extent to which the media can influence self-images and change the public's attitude is not altogether clear. Other factors are also at work in these areas, including family, medical and educational factors. But the media's role should be of concern to broadcasters and journalists as well as to people with disabilities and those who campaign on their behalf.

21.4   Research into the effects of media representations of disability should be funded jointly by the Department of Equality and Law Reform and the Department of Arts, Culture and the Gaeltacht.

21.5   In the meantime, a number of steps should be taken to end the isolation and stereotyping of people with disabilities in the media. In post-primary schools, a section on the portrayal of people with disabilities should be included in media studies from the junior cycle onwards and in the film studies section in Leaving Certificate English. In-service training for teachers should provide the appropriate material and teaching strategies for this.

21.6   All courses and training in the media, journalism and public relations should include specific strands on disability issues. For those already working in the media, there should be workshops and seminars on disability issues. A style book to provide guidelines about negative, offensive and limiting language should be commissioned and published by the Department of Equality and Law Reform.

21.7   People with disabilities should be helped to participate in media and journalism courses by bursaries established by the Department of Education and the Department of Equality and Law Reform. They should also be given resources to enable them to attend training courses in public relations, lobbying and media management.

21.8 A database of available contributors and sources should be drawn up by the relevant officer of the National Union of Journalists. It could be modelled on Raidio na Life, the Irish-language community station in Dublin, which is currently compiling a database of Irish language contributors. While lobby groups would clearly benefit from an equivalent database, it would also be of interest to the media.

21.9 RTE, the Independent Radio and Television Commission and the National Newspapers of Ireland should provide ongoing funding for an independent Media and Disability Unit. This Unit would provide training and expertise to media organisations to ensure the full participation of people with disabilities in media services. It would provide advice about the portrayal of people with disabilities, the coverage of disability events, making programmes specifically for people with disabilities, and disability awareness training.

21.10 Media coverage of disability issues should be brought into the mainstream by, for instance, having them covered by general correspondents rather than by health correspondents. RTE should look at ways in which people with disabilities can be made more visible on television both as presenters and participants. The Advertising Standards Association of Ireland should stringently enforce the Guidance Note on the Portrayal of Disabled People in Advertising, lending particular weight to the views of people with disabilities.

21.11 Public funding to RTE and any other media funding should be dependent on the development by the funded organisation of an appropriate policy concerning people with disabilities. All media institutions and professional organisations should undertake positive measures to facilitate participation and membership by people with disabilities.

21.12 Submissions to the Commission included criticisms of the inadequacy of sign-language and sub-titling on television for the deaf community. The Commission recommends that RTE and other television stations with national licences should expand the number of hours and the range of programmes which are sub-titled. There should be a minimum of 50% of all programming hours captioned by 1998 and this should increase to all programming as soon as possible afterwards.

21.13 The National Rehabilitation Board or its successor should initiate a feasibility study into the establishment of a Disability Programmes Unit in association with appropriate partners such as RTE, the IRTC, FÁS, local radio stations and education institutions. Research should identify potential sources of funding and resources; whether it should operate within RTÉ or another organisation or as an independent company; and define its functions.

21.14 RTÉ should specify how it envisages using new information technologies as distribution mechanisms, feedback systems, and alternative media for people with disabilities. In the context of the Green Paper on Broadcasting, the establishment of any broadcasting authority should incorporate clear and accountable methods for dealing with complaints about programmes for or about people with disabilities and include appropriate enforcement mechanisms.

21.15 The use of the Internet as a forum for discussing Irish and international media and disability issues should also be examined. Disability groups should set up World Wide Web pages on the Internet to provide links to other relevant Web pages, to Television, Radio, Print and other news services. These sites should also include online archives of text-based documents relevant to radio and TV productions as well as software resources for computer-users with disabilities (such as text to speech conversion software and help files for people with visual difficulties using MAC and Windows operating systems).

21.16 The establishment of a Disability and Perception film or television programme should be initiated jointly by the Irish Film Board and RTÉ as part of their continuing commitment to and extension of equality principles. This could form a section of the "Short Cuts" initiative.

A Strategy for Equality Report of the Commission on the Status of People with Disabilities

Chapter Twenty-Two
SPORTS, LEISURE AND RECREATION

DELIVERING THE
NECESSARY SERVICES

INCLUSION OF WOMEN
WITH DISABILITIES

HEALTH

INSURANCE

POLITICAL
RIGHTS

EDUCATION

LEGAL STATUS
OF PEOPLE
WITH DISABILITIES

TRANSPORT
& MOBILITY

SEXUALITY &
RELATIONSHIPS

HOUSING AND
ACCOMMODATION

ARTS &
CULTURE

OVERVIEW

ACCESS

POLICY DEVELOPMENT
& IMPLEMENTATION

TECHNOLOGY &
COMMUNICATION

RELIGIOUS
PRACTICE

VULNERABLE
PEOPLE

BUDGETING

SPORTS, LEISURE

I suffer from spina bifida since birth ... I'm 16 years old and I feel my teenage life is over because there's lads that are 13 and 14 years old and they're going to discos that I can't go to because they've got narrow doors or steps. As well as that, on disco nights a bus collects people up at the crossroads. I can't get onto it.

- excerpt from submission

22.1 Sport plays a major role in the lives of many people, including people with disabilities, whether as participants, organisers or as spectators. Sport can and should also play a major role in integrating people with disabilities into society.

22.2 Sportsmen and sportswomen with physical, sensory and learning disabilities have done Ireland proud at home and abroad for many years. Many hold European and world records from the Paralympics and the Special Olympics. Their dedication and training is equal to that of other sports people competing at those levels. But there is little or no acknowledgement of their achievements in the media and it is only in recent years that some of these athletes have become members of mainstream clubs.

22.3 There is little appreciation either of the funding required to properly prepare and assist athletes to compete internationally. There is little or no statutory funding for the sporting bodies which represent them. Many athletes with disabilities have to raise their own funds to be able to compete. Few, if any, of them qualify for elite athletic grants given to some of their able bodied peers. This must change so that people with disabilities, wherever they live, can participate in the sport of their choice at the highest level at which they can compete.

22.4 Lottery funding should be made available to the governing bodies of these sports so that Irish athletes will be able to compete internationally on an equal footing with those of many other countries.

22.5 Ireland has applied to host the Special Olympics early in the next century and we hope that the Government will actively support and promote this application. Proper and adequate funding should be made available to ensure that Ireland could host such an event.

22.6 Every effort must be made to facilitate people with disabilities who are interested in sports as spectators. Major venues should not be inaccessible to people with physical or sensory disabilities nor should it be acceptable to have only a corner of stadiums set aside for wheelchair users and no facilities at all for people with other disabilities.

22.7 Planning permissions should not be granted to any sporting body for renovations or new buildings unless they include proper facilities for people with disabilities. Elsewhere in Europe, these include commentaries in sections of stands to assist those with visual impairments. Discussions should take place with the Council for the Status of People with a Disability to ensure that proper, adequate and safe facilities are made available to all people with disabilities.

22.8 Leisure and recreation, in the broadest sense, can cover most activities except those related to work, activities which are taken for granted by most people but which cannot be taken for granted by people with disabilities. Very few, for instance, can decide to take a weekend away from home without planning everything in minute detail. Going to the local pub is something which most Irish people do on a regular basis but very few public houses have toilet facilities for wheelchair users. In rural areas, many activities take place in community centres, few of which have facilities for people with disabilities. Not many organisations or associations, such as youth clubs, scouts or guides, sports clubs, women's groups, activity-based clubs and community groups, have a proactive policy of enlisting people with disabilities as members. Even a day out with their families on the beach or in local playgrounds can be impossible for people with disabilities because of inaccessibility.

The recommendations in earlier chapters, especially in Chapter 9: Access, cover many of these situations. However, the Council for the Status of People with Disabilities should commission a survey of all beaches in the country and try to ensure that only those that are accessible should qualify for Blue Flags.

22.9   Bord Failte and the regional tourism authorities should ensure that all tourist information includes details of the facilities for people with disabilities. There is a large potential market of tourists with disabilities. As Ireland markets itself ever more vigorously as a tourist destination, it is to the country's advantage to be able to cater for visitors with disabilities.

Tourist information centres should only receive state funding if they are accessible to all which, unfortunately, many are not. All information in them must be available in alternative media and all staff should receive disability awareness training.

22.10   Government must also ensure that all libraries under the control of local authorities are accessible and carry a range of books in large print or talking books. Within five years of the publication of this report each library should have an optical scanner.

22.11   Many voluntary groups, like Arch clubs, have done great work in promoting activities for disabled people as well as raising awareness about the contribution that people with disabilities can make to society. The clubs should be fully supported and have a mix of voluntary and paid staff as they cannot operate during holiday seasons, a time when many people with disabilities most need the social outlets they provide.

22.12   Workshops and other centres catering for people with disabilities, who need more structured leisure time, should be encouraged to open their facilities and centres in the evenings and at weekends, and to develop a policy on sport, leisure and recreation.

Part Five
VULNERABLE PEOPLE WITH DISABILITIES

Chapter Twenty-Three
VULNERABLE PEOPLE

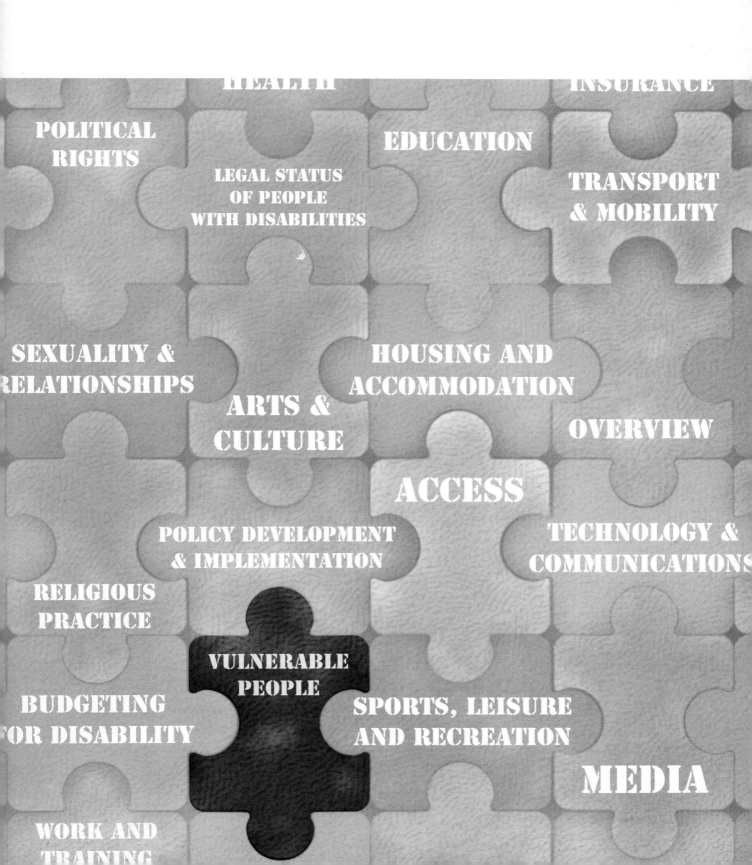

POLITICAL RIGHTS

HEALTH

INSURANCE

EDUCATION

LEGAL STATUS OF PEOPLE WITH DISABILITIES

TRANSPORT & MOBILITY

SEXUALITY & RELATIONSHIPS

HOUSING AND ACCOMMODATION

ARTS & CULTURE

OVERVIEW

ACCESS

POLICY DEVELOPMENT & IMPLEMENTATION

TECHNOLOGY & COMMUNICATIONS

RELIGIOUS PRACTICE

VULNERABLE PEOPLE

BUDGETING FOR DISABILITY

SPORTS, LEISURE AND RECREATION

MEDIA

WORK AND TRAINING

Parents do not expect the state or society to take over their responsibilities. They are prepared to make whatever sacrifices are necessary but with the best will in the world they cannot do it from beyond the grave.

- excerpt from submission

23.1   The Commission made a special commitment from the outset to give a high priority to the concerns of very vulnerable or marginalised groups of people with disabilities. Particular groups and individuals may be vulnerable on account of the severity of their disability; the low numbers with the particular disability; especially unhelpful public attitudes; a lack of public or professional awareness of special needs and concerns; or a combination of these factors.

23.2   Many of the recommendations already made in this report are of relevance to those who are especially vulnerable. But extra care should, and must, be taken to ensure that their rights are as well protected as those of any group in society.

23.3   In this part of the report, the Commission addresses the special concerns of four groups of people whom it regards as particularly vulnerable:

- highly dependent people with severe or profound disabilities (e.g. people with intellectual disability (mental handicap))

- people with rare disabilities

- people with spinal injuries

- people with head traumas

Highly Dependent People with Disabilities

23.4   People with intellectual disabilities who are very highly dependent as a result of severe and profound levels of intellectual disability are a particularly vulnerable group. They will inevitably be dependent on significant state support throughout their lives, irrespective of the resources of their families. Thus, the state has a special responsibility to act as guarantor of their health services, safety, and quality of life. Their vulnerability and dependency require special measures to protect their interests and maximise any possibilities that they may have for exercising personal choices.

23.5   The Commission's proposals in relation to personal support services are especially important for this group of people. They have the highest dependence on services and supports provided by both the state and non-governmental organisations. They often have little opportunity to make their own case.

23.6   For those highly dependent people living at home, high quality day activity services, with accessible transport, are an essential part of the necessary services. Day activity services tend to have a low priority and their availability differs widely between Health Boards and within Health Boards. The Commission has already recommended that day activity services should be part of the core personal support services to be provided as part of Community Action Plans (Chapter 3). The entitlement of a person with a severe disability to this service should be no less than that of more able people with disabilities to, say, work or vocational training. Health Boards should be adequately funded by the Department of Health to enable them to secure the development of the necessary quality day services for their area.

23.7 The well-being of people with severe or profound disabilities who are living at home is bound up inevitably with the well-being of their carers. Financial support for carers is an essential part of an equality strategy which aims at maximising independence for people with disabilities. Respite care is a requirement in every Health Board area.

23.8 Many elderly carers who attended the Commission's listening meetings were providing care, on their own, for a severely disabled family member, usually a son or daughter. These carers, unbelievably, are deprived of the living alone allowance and attendant benefits in such circumstances although it is obvious that the son or daughter can make no contribution whatever to the family income. The Commission recommends that where a carer is providing care for a family member in receipt of the Disability Allowance he or she should qualify for any allowances or benefits for which they would otherwise be eligible.

23.9 The Commission's recommendations aimed at safeguarding the rights and dignity of people with disabilities who are users of services are particularly relevant to highly dependent people with disabilities living in residential care. The proposals for a Charter of Rights for people in residential centres (Chapter 12: Housing and Accommodation) cover issues such as access to information and records; advocacy and representation; complaints procedures; the right to dignity and respect; and the right to a personal income.

23.10 These are important for all people with disabilities but the following have a special relevance for highly dependent people:

- a system of advocacy: it is important to put in place additional supports to maximise the independence and possibilities for choice for the residents of long-stay services. The sense of powerlessness of this group requires an investment in such measures. The post of advocate needs to be established by statute. Each Health Board should be required to appoint at least one trained advocate on behalf of residents in long-stay services.

- complaints procedures: every agency should be required to have a complaints procedure and to make it known to families and advocates.

- the right to a personal income: many people in residential care receive only a nominal discretionary payment and some receive no income at all, a situation which was strongly criticised by the Ombudsman in his 1992 report. The person with a disability in residential care should have the same entitlement to an income as the person living in the community. The personal income of a person with a disability in residential care should be paid directly to the individual, or an advocate or trustee on their behalf. A reasonable amount should then be charged to them for rent and board.

- the right to other services: the needs of people with disabilities living in residential institutions tend to be seen sometimes only in terms of accommodation or shelter. Individual service and support requirements - for day activity, employment, leisure, therapy or other services - must have equal standing with the service needs of people with disabilities living in the community. Consequently, the Commission proposes that the person with a disability in residential care should have appropriate access to the local Disability Support Service and a personal support co-ordinator.

- overseeing and monitoring standards: all types of residential services need a comprehensive and adequately resourced monitoring service with sufficient powers to ensure that standards are implemented in practice. Visiting committees should be established for residential care institutions. The National Disability Authority should have a clear brief in relation to the monitoring of standards in residential care services.

23.11 The allocation of a place to a person with a severe disability in a particular service should be done on foot of an independent assessment in which the person's family or advocate would participate fully. There should be statutory entitlement to this assessment process.

23.12 Where a recommendation has been made for a specific placement, any proposal to refuse admission to an individual should have to be referred to an arbitration process within the Health Board. Arbitration should be carried out by independent third parties with appropriate expertise. There must be a similar procedure for any proposal to terminate a particular placement against the wishes of the person with a disability or their family.

Funding Strategies for Service Delivery

23.13 The Commission welcomes the proposals in *Shaping a Healthier Future* (the Department of Health's strategy document) for funding service agreements between the voluntary sector and the health authorities. Within this framework, it is necessary to link funding to the service needs of individuals with disabilities.

23.14   The Commission recommends a two-tier funding structure in order to achieve this. The first tier should be a graded capitation grant which would take account of the level of severity of the person's disability. This grant should follow the person, irrespective of the source of the service.

The second tier should be related to the overhead costs of providing a particular service. It should be based on a formula which would take account of the size of the service, thus protecting smaller services or those with variable numbers from unreasonable fluctuations in their income.

23.15   The Commission also recommends that the revenue budgets of Health Boards should be structured in such a way that personal support services for people with disabilities should be ring-fenced. Such services should not have to compete with other areas like hospital services.

23.16   Funding restrictions in the past resulted in significant variations in the quality of services for people with severe and profound intellectual disabilities. Cuts in the late 1980s and early 1990s made it extremely difficult for Health Boards to implement the Planning for the Future policy. As a result there are still more than 1,200 people classed as having mental handicap in psychiatric hospitals. The transfer of such people to voluntary agencies envisaged in the Needs and Abilities Report did not happen.

In the main, the Health Boards have not been able to develop an appropriate service of their own although they are obliged to provide a "last resort" option for people with the most difficult and challenging behaviour. This option does not only apply to people with intellectual disabilities but also to people with multiple disabilities such as those who are deaf/blind.

23.17   The Commission strongly recommends that the proposals in Planning for the Future be implemented in full as a matter of urgency.

23.18   In addition, the situation of people with intellectual and other disabilities currently living in psychiatric hospitals warrants specific action. The Commission visited a number of these institutions and was greatly shocked by the poor standards of the physical accommodation in some of them.

23.19   After analysing the reasons for such grossly unsatisfactory conditions, the Commission is satisfied that the statutory authorities responsible for them were unable to implement their replacement plans mainly due to a lack of capital resources. The Commission appreciates fully the demands on national resources for funds to develop and improve services in all sectors of the economy. However, the funds available in this area have been too small and too thinly spread. The Commission is also aware of the potential demand for new revenue expenditure as a result of capital investment: in this area, capital spending on replacement projects would not generate large extra costs because existing staff would be redeployed.

23.20 The Commission believes that the time is opportune for a special programme to replace sub-standard facilities for people with disabilities. This programme must be protected from normal competition for scarce funds and should be managed by a special group of experienced professionals from within the Department of Health and the Health Boards.

Accordingly, the Commission strongly recommends:

- A special capital fund be created and designated for the replacement of existing sub-standard facilities being used by people with disabilities.

- The replacement programme should be managed by a special unit to be set up within the Department of Health.

23.21 The fund should be directed on a priority basis to the replacement of the worst facilities throughout the country.

23.22 The total programme should be completed within five years.

- The replacement facilities should reflect current thinking about design in terms of the lifestyle of the people with disabilities concerned.

- That these recommendations be implemented by the Government as a matter of urgency so that these unacceptable and degrading facilities can be eliminated.

23.23 Among the institutions visited by the Commission was St Ita's Hospital, Portrane where 347 people with intellectual disabilities are accommodated. The Commission was impressed by the Eastern Health Board's plans to improve these facilities but it has been unable to implement them because of a lack of funds. Because of the large number of people in St Ita's, the Commission is especially anxious that it should be among the first to be replaced under the programme recommended above.

People With Rare Disabilities

23.24 There are many recognised disabilities in Ireland. The majority of them are rare in that the number of people who have them is relatively small. But the effects of these disabilities is the same and the extent to which they affect individuals, their families and the community around them is intense. The consequences of many rare disabilities are compounded by the extra sense of isolation, lack of understanding, and lack of adequate research and back-up which are caused in many cases by the rarity of the condition.

23.25 The Commission recommends that a National Centre for rare disabilities be established and located in a modern teaching facility such as the new Tallaght hospital. It should have satellite centres, linked by computer, in different parts of the country.

23.26 Such centres exist in other countries, such as Norway where they are known as "Frambu" centres. Their purpose is to provide services to individuals, to their families and to the community, through research and the development of a data base.

23.27 The main functions of the National Centre should be:

- to improve the quality of life of people with rare disabilities;

- to provide counselling and advice to families from the moment of diagnosis (and to help families searching for diagnosis);

- to build up a national reservoir of knowledge about rare disabilities and to disseminate information about such conditions, their symptoms and consequences;

- to inculcate a high degree of consciousness and sensitivity among professional staff towards such disabilities;

- to act as a resource for professionals, especially in relation to diagnosis and course of treatment.

The National Centre should also encourage more awareness among and between families, to ease the isolation of those affected by rare disabilities, and to assist the formation of mutual support groups.

In some cases, it may be necessary to provide families with intensive training to help them cope with aspects of the disability. Such training should be available free at the National Centre and its satellite centres.

23.28 In the case of many forms of rare disabilities, families have to carry a disproportionate share of the burden. They often find themselves deprived of support simply because a disability is not adequately recognised. Many people with rare disabilities are denied the rights of people with more common disabilities, such as medical cards and free transport. There should be a fundamental review of entitlements to these facilities, and to family supports, to make sure that no form of long-term or life-long disability is arbitrarily excluded from them. A national database of rare disabilities would clearly be a valuable aid to policy in this area.

23.29 Many people with rare forms of disability have shorter life expectancies. All forms of counselling and support in such cases should therefore include the preparation of families for bereavement. This is especially important because of the emotional investment that families make in cases where the disability is not recognised sufficiently.

People With Spinal Injuries

23.30 Although there is considerable medical and paramedical expertise in the treatment of people with spinal injuries in Ireland, serious inadequacies remain in the support services for this group of people. They need the impetus to build the confidence to take charge of their lives again and individual planning should take place before their discharge from hospital.

23.31 A full assessment of their requirements must be made, with their involvement, and reasonable accommodations made to enable them to return home and live as they choose. Disability awareness training with particular emphasis on spinal injuries, including their affects on sexuality, should be made available to medical and paramedical staff. A team comprising medical, nursing and paramedical staff with special training in spinal injuries must be available in each Health Board region. Training should also be given to public health nurses on treating people with spinal injuries.

23.32 The Commission also recommends that the Department of Health should fund the establishment of a transitional housing facility, possibly linked to the National Rehabilitation Hospital in Dun Laoghaire and similar to the Transhouse model in the UK. Annual funding should be provided to run such a facility.

People With Head Traumas

23.33 Among the groups of people with disabilities who are not catered for adequately are those suffering from head traumas or brain damage which causes permanent disabilities like paralysis, speech difficulties, emotional lability, and intermittent intellectual disabilities. These may be the results of accidents, sub- arachnoid haemorrhage (similar to strokes in young adults), meningitis, carbon monoxide poisoning, chronic drug addiction, or other conditions.

23.34 There is a need to provide information to families and carers of people affected by such disabilities. More counsellors should be trained and made available at Beaumont Hospital in Dublin and other acute hospitals where brain injuries are treated, as well as at the National Rehabilitation Hospital. Adequate supports and trained staff should also be made available in regional hospitals and at community level. The Department of Health should ensure that an adequate number of neuropsychologists are trained and available.

23.35 Public awareness of the situation of people with head traumas needs to be increased by the National Rehabilitation Board and other appropriate agencies. Hospitals, GPs and public services generally should be targeted in this regard. It is important, for instance, that teachers in schools should be aware of the adverse effects on pupils who have somebody suffering from a head trauma in the family.

23.36 The Department of Education should draw up a policy for the future education of children with head traumas, including readmission to mainstream education if appropriate. Suitable supports in the classroom and counselling should be provided at local levels.

23.37 People who have survived head traumas and are judged to be mentally incapable of managing their own affairs are taken into wardship by courts. In this situation, independent advocates should be available, if required, to represent their rights.

23.38 Research into the long-term needs of people with head traumas should be funded by the Department of Health and should inform decisions about compensation arising from accidents. In the interim, the statute of limitations in relation to claims for compensation for head traumas should be extended to ten years to allow assessments of longer term affects which were not foreseen when the initial diagnosis was made. Any compensation due should be awarded in such a way that spouses have conditional access to it.

23.39 The Department of Health should make annual funds available for the establishment of a "Headway House" to provide counselling, telephone helplines, day and visiting services. Suitable respite care facilities should also be established and funded separately by the department.

Other Groups With Special Concerns

23.40 The Commission also identified other groups as having particular concerns and needs over and beyond those of the general population with disabilities. These include young people with disabilities, people who are deaf/blind, elderly people, travellers with disabilities, gays and lesbians with disabilities. All these groups would be helped by targeted awareness programmes aimed at professionals working in disability fields as well as at the general public.

23.41 Health and personal support services for elderly people with disabilities and for travellers have been reviewed and are the subjects of development planning. There has been no similar focus on the concerns of young people with disabilities: there is a need to explore the special issues affecting them. Health Boards should address their personal support needs within the framework of the health development sector programme which targets services to particular groups or areas. The Commission urges the National Youth Council, in conjunction with the Council for the Status of People with Disabilities, to undertake in-depth consultation with young people with disabilities to document their concerns and bring them to the attention of policy makers and service providers. In doing so, particular attention should be paid to young people with disabilities in rural communities and in institutional care.

A Strategy for Equality Report of the Commission on the Status of People with Disabilities

Part Six
RESEARCH

Chapter Twenty-Four
RESEARCH

WITH DISABILITIES

& MOBILITY

SEXUALITY &
RELATIONSHIPS

HOUSING AND
ACCOMMODATION

ARTS &
CULTURE

OVERVIEW

ACCESS

POLICY DEVELOPMENT
& IMPLEMENTATION

TECHNOLOGY &
COMMUNICATIONS

RELIGIOUS
PRACTICE

VULNERABLE
PEOPLE

BUDGETING
OR DISABILITY

SPORTS, LEISURE
AND RECREATION

MEDIA

WORK AND
TRAINING

RESEARCH

THE LAW AND
THE LEGAL SYSTEM

INCOME
AND
DISABILITY

24.1   The Commission was hampered in its consideration of many issues by the lack of data. In addition to the surveys and data bases referred to in Appendix A, it had the results of other small scale surveys and case studies and a wealth of qualitative, impressionistic and anecdotal data to draw on, where appropriate, in preparing this report.

24.2   According to the Economic and Social Research Institute, there is widespread agreement on the inadequacy of information on the numbers, characteristics and needs of people with disabilities in Ireland. The ESRI, in its report for the Commission (see Appendix A), added that

> *comparative statistical information published by Eurostat also indicate that there are a number of important gaps in the Irish data (notably regarding the circumstances of second and third-level students with disabilities, people with disabilities in the workplace, the level and nature of impairment) which limit the effectiveness of public policy in this area. Statistical information is needed in order to plan and evaluate*
>
> - *the provision of special services for people with a disability and, where appropriate, their carers; and*
>
> - *strategies to increase the opportunities of people with disabilities to participate in generally available services and opportunities (including health, education, employment and leisure activities).*

24.3   Funding for research into disability issues is small, there appears to be little if any co-ordination or prioritisation, and the dissemination of information on current and completed projects is patchy.

24.4   The Commission considered the advantages and disadvantages of establishing a specially designed Disability Research Body but concluded that it might lead to a further segregation of disability issues which would run counter to the general principle of social, economic and scientific integration. Instead, the Commission recommends that the proposed National Disability Authority be empowered to conduct and commission research on disability issues and that adequate funding be allocated to extend both the scope and volume of current research.

24.5   The Commission further recommends that a Research Co-ordination Group be established under the auspices of the National Disability Authority to provide a forum in which interested bodies could exchange information, agree priorities, avoid overlaps and help to construct joint projects, streamline the dissemination of results and identify and pursue funding options at home and abroad.

A Strategy for Equality Report of the Commission on the Status of People with Disabilities

APPENDICES

APPENDIX A

Statistics

A.1   The absence of overall statistics about the number of people with disabilities in Ireland and the lack of research into specific areas of disability has been commented upon repeatedly in this report.

A.2   There are several difficulties involved in compiling accurate statistics about the number of people with disabilities. These include the definition of disability: whether it is based on a medical definition or, the definition favoured by the Commission, based on a social definition which sees disability as something that arises from society's failure to adapt itself to the different ways in which people with impairments accomplish activities. Another difficulty is that disability is a relative concept and therefore requires a cut-off point as to the degree of severity of disability (however defined) which would be included or excluded.

A.3   In addition, it is difficult in practice to distinguish between sickness or illness, on the one hand, and disability on the other hand and this means that for many purposes the two categories are combined. In general, sickness or ill-health are regarded as temporary while disability is thought of as being more permanent but for many purposes the two categories are combined.

A.4   The perception of a disability and its extent, whether by a person with a disability him/herself or another, also depends on a complex and inter-related combination of considerations including the following:

(a)   their perception of what constitutes a physical, intellectual or psychological impairment;

(b)   their personal attitudes and expectations;

(c)   what they consider "normal" for people of a particular age in a particular setting;

(d)   the financial and other resources of the individuals involved;

(e)   the cultural, physical, communication and other hidden barriers - especially those of prejudice or discrimination.

A.5   In relation to (c), for example, there is a considerable overlap between "people with disabilities" and "the elderly": whether particular older people are considered as having disabilities depends on a lot of factors, including subjective ones. This subjectivity applies whether disability is defined by experts, medical or otherwise, or by people with disabilities themselves.

A.6   Even when definitions and cut-off points are agreed, the problem remains of estimating the numbers of persons in the categories corresponding to the definitions. This would require a major survey of the population.

A.7   The Commission asked the Economic and Social Research Institute to assist it by collating existing quantitative data on disability which might enable it to arrive at some overall estimates. The ESRI's report suggested that the prevalence and incidence of disabilities could be estimated from existing data in three ways:

- by reference to statistics on disability-related income support schemes;

- on the basis of data from the Census and from the Labour Force Survey on people who are outside the labour force for reasons of permanent sickness on disability;

- from the results of sample surveys in which people themselves estimate

    (a)   the extent to which they are "hampered in [their] daily activities by any chronic physical or mental health problem, illness or disability" (The Living in Ireland Survey, 1994); or

    (b)   the degree of difficulty they have in carrying out certain daily activities (Survey of the Over-65s, 1993).

A.8   The ESRI report analysed these different data bases in some detail. The estimates arrived at on the basis of these three methods, and the disadvantages of each method from the point of view of arriving at a reliable overall figure, are set out in Table 1, at sections 1 to 3 overleaf.

A.9   The area of mental handicap, or intellectual disability, is the only area of disability in which comprehensive statistics are collected systematically on a census basis for administrative purposes. The Department of Health established a computerised national mental handicap database in 1995 and the first statistics became available in 1995. These show, in general terms, that there are approximately 26,000 persons with intellectual disabilities, from mild disability to profound disability, known to the Health Boards of whom over 6,000 are children under 15 years of age (Mulcahy, Mulvany and Timmons, 1996).

TABLE 1: ESTIMATES OF NUMBERS OF PEOPLE WITH DISABILITIES

Methods of Estimation	Estimated Numbers and/or percentages	Limitations of Method
1. Statistics on disability-related income support schemes.	106,000 long-term recipients (1994) of Department of Social Payments & DPMA (4.9% of population aged 15-64)	1. People *in* the labour force, whether employed or unemployed, not included. 2. Non-insured people who do not pass DPMA family means-test not included, e.g. many married women. 3. People over 65 and children not included. 4. Most people in residential care not included.
2. The Census and Labour Force Survey (LFS) **NB** *(a) The Census is based on self-reporting;* *(b) LFS is a sample survey done by interviewers*	(a) 80,000 "unable to work due to sickness or disability" (*Census*, 1991) (b) 66,000, as above, (Labour Force Survey, 1995)	1. Underestimates disability among older middle aged people who are more likely to describe themselves are "retired". 2. Underestimates disability among women, especially married women, who are more likely to describe themselves as "engaged in home duties". 3. Children not included
3. Surveys of people estimating their own disabilities.	(a) 11.3% of all age-groups experienced restrictions of activities due to illness, injury or emotional/mental health problems (*Living in Ireland Survey,* 1994) (b) 15.4% of over-65s could not do at least one "daily activity" (ERSRI *Survey of over-65s,* 1993)	1. Underestimates disability which is thought by people to be a part of growing old. 2. Underestimates extent of mental illness. 3. People in residential care not included. 4. Children not included.
4. European Averages (Eurostat, 1995, *Disabled Persons, Statistical Data,* Second Edition)	(a) c. 12% of total population disabled (b) 6-8% of people aged under 60 disabled (c) 4-5% of people aged under 60 receiving disability-related payments.	The rates of disability vary from one country to another depending on: • the structure of the population by age; • methodological differences concerning the definition and method of identifying persons with a disability; • technological and industrial characteristics of countries and their experiences of war

European Statistics

A.10 Another approach to estimating the numbers of people with disabilities in Ireland is to rely on estimates arrived at in other countries, including the UK, where comprehensive surveys have been done. However, differences between Ireland and these other countries in terms of demographic structure, historical experience, economic conditions, and public attitudes make such an exercise hazardous.

A.11 Fortunately, a volume became available in 1995 which collates statistics on disability from the twelve EU Member State (as they were before the last accessions). Grammenos (1995) in his Disabled Persons: Statistical Data, published by the Statistical Office of the European Communities presents detailed tables based on censuses, surveys and administrative data (ie, social security data) in each country. Ireland is included but, generally speaking, there are more comprehensive data bases for most other countries.

Most of this report is devoted to tabular data from individual countries but it identifies (pp. 324 - 327) patterns across countries which enables it to arrive at some general conclusions about the prevalence of disability in EU countries. The main estimates are in the fourth section of Table 1.

A.12 The most striking finding is that the "analysis of the percentage of disabled persons by age group revealed a stable and uniform relationship in the Member States". Disability is related to age: "the rate of disability rises from 1% for the very young to around 90% for the very elderly". The data also shows that the rate of disability is higher among women than among men, which can be partly explained by their greater longevity. Another unsurprising result is that "as the degree of disability increases, the number of persons [affected] declines": in other words fewer people have more significant (serious) disabilities; more people have less significant (serious) disabilities. The distribution by degree of disability is the same for men and women.

A.13 In relation to types of disability, the conclusions in the report, which are approximate, are as follows:

One might say that persons with an intellectual or psychiatric impairment account for 5 to 15% [of all people with disabilities], with a sensory impairment for 10 to 18% and a physical impairment for 50 - 80%. Locomotor impairmens predominate among this latter.

A.14 The Commission attached some importance to these general conclusions since they represent the results of data collection in eleven other countries as well as Ireland. There is no reason to think that these general conclusions do not apply to Ireland too, although all the relevant data is not available for Ireland.

Overall Numbers in Ireland

A.15   The Commission concluded that one can, on the basis of the data presented in Table 1, arrive at reasonably reliable estimates of the numbers of people with disabilities in Ireland. This has been done by trying to fit the figures in Table 1 together like pieces of a jigsaw. In fact, the pieces overlap instead of fitting neatly together and it becomes a question of presenting rounded overall figures that are:

- consistent with the gross numbers and percentages of the Irish data (Table 1, parts 1, 2 and 3) and

- consistent with the patterns of prevalence indicated by the European percentages (Table 1, part 4).

A.16   Where these data still allow for variations in estimates, the Commission tended to adopt conservative ones. Overall rounded estimates are presented in Table 2 below on the basis that these figures, despite their limitations, give a reasonably accurate picture. It notionally covers different types and degrees of disability and includes both people in the labour force and people outside the labour force who are usually categorised as "engaged in home duties" or "retired".

TABLE 2: THE PREVALENCE OF DISABILITY IN IRELAND			
Age Group	No. in Population (2)	% with Disabilities	No. with Disabilities (3)
0-14	1,000,000	3	30,000
15-59	2,000,000	7.5	150,000
60+	550,000	33	180,000
All Ages	3,550,000	10	360,000

Notes
(1)   These estimates are based on the results presented in Table 1 and are consistent with them.
(2)   The total in this column corresponds to the CSO population figure for 1992; it has since increased. The distribution by age-group is not exact: the figures are rounded for easy calculation.
(3)   The figures here are rounded too.

A.17   The estimated overall number of people with disabilities, at 360,000, represents 10% of the population as compared with an average of 12% for EU countries (Grammenos, 1995, p. 325; see Table 1). It is interesting to note that recent surveys in Northern Ireland estimated that 17.4% of the adult population had disabilities (McCoy and Smith, 1992) as were 3.5% of the child population (Smith et al., 1992). Our own estimates suggest that half of all people with disabilities are aged 60 and over.

A.18   It is worth nothing that only a small minority of people with disabilities are in residential care although, as we have said in the body of our Report, they are likely to be most disadvantaged. For example, available official statistics indicate that about 500 children with mental handicap or intellectual disability are in residential care, there are about 34,000 adults in residential care, including hostels and "community residences", i.e. 7,000 persons with mental handicap, 12,000 with mental illness and 15,000, mainly older people, with various levels of dependency, in residential facilities for the elderly.

APPENDIX B

EQUALITY, STATUS AND DISABILITY - A PAPER PREPARED FOR THE COMMISSION BY THE EQUALITY STUDIES CENTRE, UNIVERSITY COLLEGE, DUBLIN

Summary of Contents

SECTION 1

Definition of Status

The status of a group refers essentially to the level of esteem in which it is held by society at large. It refers therefore to the social standing of a group: it connotes the level of esteem, honour and social regard accorded to a particular group, and to its individual members.

To establish the status of disabled people therefore, one must identify all the factors which positively or negatively affect its social standing. The status of the group is derived therefore from its standing in all the major social institutions, structures and systems within the society.

The status of disabled people, in this general sense, refers to their social standing as a whole group and as individual members of that group. It also refers to their social standing in general throughout society.

Because disabled people are a heterogeneous group, divided along gender, wealth, age, power and other lines, there will be considerable status differences between disabled people themselves which are not necessarily related to their disability but which derive from their social standing arising from such factors as gender, age, occupation, sexual orientation, ethnicity and wealth.

In addition, there will also be status differences between disabled people themselves arising from the nature of their disability. Within any given society, certain human attributes are likely to be accorded higher status than others, depending on the way in which that society is organised. A society or group which relies on hunting skills and will obviously place a high value on sensori-motor skills related to such tasks. Because of the sedentary nature of many occupations in our society, mobility skills are not as crucial for survival and therefore the person who has a mobility impairment is likely to have considerably higher status than in a society where mobility-skills are essential for survival. However, our society does place high value on literacy and numeracy skills, for example, and people who are disabled in these areas will be accorded lower status in many contexts.

Finally, the status of a disabled person can and will vary across contexts, although the status of the person in one context will naturally interact with that in another. A person who is deaf and whose natural language is sign, for example, could be a highly successful athlete or sportsperson although they might have low status in an educational context which required the use of spoken language. It is self-evident that the status of people in any given context (such as education) is also related to the level of equality which exists in society at large for disabled people. In that sense, the factors which affect status can be subject to change depending on the legal, educational and policy interventions which are made.

SECTION 2

The Principal Determinants of Status

A major purpose of this paper is to identify the principal processes, practices and institutions which positively or negatively affect the social status of disabled people. We know from research that there are **a number of institutions and systems which have a crucial bearing on social status** in our society and a number of these will be given particular attention.

For example, the status of all people in Irish society is strongly influenced by the level and nature of their employment, the level and nature of their education, and by the amount of wealth which they own and control. Status is also influenced by the cultural images portrayed about particular groups (in the media for example), by the legal rights and protection accorded to particular groups, and by the presence or absence of education about a particular group aimed at combating prejudicial and discriminatory attitudes. The level and nature of one's involvement in personal relationships and in political life also affect one's status. So too does the level and nature of one's involvement in cultural institutions such as the media, sport, the arts and entertainment.

In all of the above, **gaining status in one area significantly increases the likelihood of achieving it in another.** High status in a given area generally increases the person's sense of self worth. This feeling of self worth acts back upon the public self and enables the person to initiate involvements in areas outside those in which she/he has high status initially; this, in turn, increases their opportunities for status enhancement. For example, if a disabled person is successful in a particular sport, the sense of achievement which she/he gets from this will increase her/his sense of self worth; this will, boost self confidence which will enable the person to get involved and succeed in new areas and will improve their general social status accordingly.

The status of disabled people is also **influenced by the level and amount of social differentiation which exists in society at large.** The more egalitarian the political, economic, social and cultural organisation of a society as a whole, the more egalitarian it is likely to be for any given group, including disabled people. For example, the more equal the distribution of goods and services in society as a whole, the more equal their distribution is likely to be between disabled and able-bodied people.

The conditions and factors which affect the status of a given group may **change over time.** While the core factors such as level and nature of employment, and level and nature of education are quite likely to exercise a key influence on the status of a particular group for the foreseeable future, it is conceivable that the relative importance of these factors may change over time.

The status of a particular group is established in a **comparative** context vis-á-vis another group. A group such as disabled people has either high, medium or low status vis-á-vis able-bodied groups in society. We recognise, however, as noted above in Section 1, that as long as society itself is stratified along lines of age, gender, social class, etc., there will be status distinctions along these lines between disabled people themselves; there will also be status distinctions related to the nature and extent of their disabilities. The focus of our analysis in this paper, however, will be between the disabled and able-bodied people as that is what is required from the terms of reference of the Commission.

Because **disabled people are a highly differentiated group** in terms of the nature of their disabilities, it will also be necessary to take account of these differences in identifying practical measures to raise the status of disabled people. For example, the methods employed to enable people with mobility impairments to participate successfully in higher education, will be very different from the methods necessary to enable those with hearing impairments to participate fully. Also, disabled travellers, for example, will have different needs in education from disabled settled people.

Given that one of the tasks of the Commission is to advise on "practical measures to ensure that people with a disability can exercise their rights to participate, to the fullest extent of their potential, in economic, social and cultural life", this goal cannot be realistically achieved without the identification of ways in which the status of disabled people can be raised in society to a level comparable in general with that of the able-bodied.

In this paper, therefore, we will examine a number of ways in which the status of disabled people can be raised. We have chosen to focus on four key areas, namely education, employment, political life and personal relationships. We fully appreciate the need to address the issue of status in other areas but time constraints do not allow for this.

Before we begin our analysis of each of the four areas, we will outline the conceptual framework used throughout.

SECTION 3

What is equal status?

In this section, we outline four different criteria which have been suggested for determining whether citizens have equal status. The first three criteria are concerned with whether disabled people have equal status with able-bodied people. It is important to recognise, however, that there is a great variability among disabled people, in terms of type of disability, degree of disability, multiple disability, and the interaction of disability with such factors as social class and gender. In principle, the first three criteria apply to the status of each specific group of disabled people relative to able-bodied people, and our examples later on are chosen to illustrate this. The criteria can also be applied to the status of each group of disabled people relative to other disabled groups; we consider this to be an important question but we do not address it here. The fourth criterion is in a way the logical extension of this process of disaggregating and concerns the equal status of every individual citizen.

The Equal Status of Disabled vis-á-vis Able-bodied People

First criterion: Equal Formal Rights and Opportunities

Equal status is sometimes thought to be guaranteed by the provision of equal rights to participate in economic, social, political, and cultural life, where such rights are construed as the absence of legal and institutionalised barriers to such participation. This view is linked to the idea of formal equality of opportunity, i.e. the idea that no one should be prevented from participating in education, employment, politics, etc., or in advancing from one level of participation to another, on the grounds of sex, race, ethnicity, disability, or any other irrelevant characteristic, and that access to and advancement within such forms of participation should be based on merit.

Equality of Formal Rights and Direct and Indirect Discrimination

The most common way of establishing equality of formal rights and opportunities for disabled people is by means of legislation and policies prohibiting direct or indirect discrimination. Both forms of discrimination concern the way disabled people can be disadvantaged by the criteria used for admission into or advancement within some area of activity. Direct discrimination occurs when someone is treated differently when they should be treated the same and when as a result they experience a disadvantage. Direct discrimination is defined in the Australian Disability Discrimination Act (Cth) 1992, Section 5(1) as occurring where because of the aggrieved person's disability, the discriminator treats or proposes to treat the aggrieved person less favourably than, in circumstances that are the same or not materially different, the discriminator treats or would treat a person without the disability.

Indirect discrimination refers to the differential impact of the same treatment where the differential is not justified. It is defined in the Australian Disability Discrimination Act (Cth) 1992, Section 6 as occurring where the discriminator requires the aggrieved person to comply with a requirement or condition:

(a)   with which a substantially higher proportion of persons without the disability comply or are able to comply; and

(b)   which is not reasonable having regard to the circumstances of the case; and

(c)   with which the aggrieved person does not or is not able to comply (McDonagh, 1993:129).

Second criterion: Actual participation

It is now widely recognised that equality of formal rights and opportunities is not enough to secure equal status, because a person's status depends not simply on their formal rights to participate in society but on the actual exercise by them of those rights, that is, their actual participation in society. This clearly requires that all citizens are able to participate, by possessing both adequate financial, educational and other resources and by having overcome non-legal barriers to participation. Another way of expressing this idea is to say that equal status depends on ensuring that **the basic material needs and the basic psychological, educational and other needs** of disabled people are fully provided for, since to provide for a person's basic needs is precisely to provide those things necessary for their full participation in society.

Providing for basic needs **enables** participation, but to have equal participation, it is necessary to **encourage** participation. Actual participation depends therefore on ensuring that disabled people are **motivated to participate and are accepted by others as full participants.** This means going beyond mere provision for basic needs. It could mean adopting proactive policies such as access programmes to encourage disabled people to participate in particular sports or artistic activities or the undertaking of disability equality training and education for staff in public service areas such as transport and communication systems to overcome prejudice and ignorance.

Addressing inequalities in participation varies according to the nature and scope of a person's disability and according to context. In particular, policies which allow one group of disabled people to participate may do nothing to foster the participation of another group, and so may generate inequalities of status between groups of disabled people. It is clear, for example, that many of the strategies adopted to improve the participation of people with mobility impairments will not assist people who are mentally impaired.

Third criterion: Equal success in participation

Undoubtedly it would be a major step forward for disabled people to be guaranteed adequate means to participate in economic, social, political, and cultural life. Such a change could only come about as a result of a substantial redistribution of resources towards disabled people; it would in turn have major effects on those inequalities which affect status.

Nevertheless, status is in fact strongly affected not just by participation in society but by the degree of success people experience in the course of their participation, that is, by their relative place in the distribution of income and wealth, in organisational hierarchies, in educational attainment, in political power, etc. If society was not hierarchically stratified in terms of wealth, power and privilege, then the question of equality of success would not be so significant. However, society is currently stratified so if disabled people are to be equal to able-bodied people in terms of success, this means that they must be enabled to succeed at the same rates as able-bodied people.

It follows that equality of status between disabled people and the able-bodied as groups depends on achieving overall equality between these groups in terms of access to, and the distribution of, economic, educational, cultural and other benefits. Similarly, equal status between groups of disabled people depends on overall of success between these groups.

International experience shows that there is no easy mechanism for realising equal success for different social groups, but that any serious attempt to redress the problem involves policies commonly referred to as 'affirmative action', 'preferential treatment' or 'reverse discrimination' and 'quotas'.

It should be noted, however, that a number of these strategies could also be employed to achieve equality of participation as outlined in number two above. For example, affirmative action could include the running of a special university access programme for disabled students to enable them to participate on equal terms with able-bodied students when in the university system. Affirmative action might also include the development of a training policy in a given company which was directed at developing senior management skills among disabled staff. In the latter case affirmative action is oriented towards achieving equality of success while in the former case the intention is to achieve equal participation.

Quotas are more obviously a strategy for achieving equal success for disabled people as they **ensure** rather than merely enable or encourage equal rates of success vis-á-vis the able-bodied.

Fourth criteria: Equal status of all citizens: equality of condition

The third criterion represents a radical challenge to existing policies. However, like the first two criteria, it operates by comparing the disabled and the able-bodied as groups, and allows for substantial inequalities of status within these groups.

By contrast an egalitarian society would be committed to the equal status of all citizens, and not simply to the equal status of particular groups. If a person's status is dependent on their social standing in various key contexts, then it follows that the equal status of all citizens depends on substantial equality in the living conditions of all citizens.

This criterion calls for widespread changes throughout society. It would involve the equalisation of wealth distribution; substantial equality in the working conditions; job satisfactions, and income across different occupations, an educational system devoted to developing the potentials of every member of society; a radically democratic politics which aimed at the equal participation and influence of all citizens; and a restructuring of family and personal life for the sake of enriching the personal relationships of every individual. Policies based on the second and third criteria of equal status could clearly contribute substantially to satisfying this fourth criterion, although they would continue to fall short of it.

Criteria of equal status: Summary

Four criteria of equal status have been outlined here: three of these are concerned with whether disabled people have equal status vis-á-vis able-bodied people, namely equal formal opportunities, equal participation and equal success, while the fourth, equality of condition, is concerned with equality of status between all citizens.

1. Equal formal rights and opportunities

2. Equal participation

3. Equal success in participation

4. Equal status of all citizens: equality of condition

SECTION 4

Equal status for disabled people in four key contexts: education, employment, political life and personal life

This is the core part of the paper in policy terms. In each section we will identify the type of legal and social framework which is necessary to ensure that disabled people of all types have equal status with able-bodied people while also addressing the implications of equality of condition.

We wish to emphasise that we are offering these examples as illustrations of policies, rather than as specific or comprehensive recommendations. In our view the only adequate source of information on the needs of disabled people and the restrictions they currently experience are disabled people themselves; we see our role as providing a conceptual framework which the Commission may be able to use in discussions with disabled people. In the development of our framework for this paper we are indebted to the writings and research of a number of disabled people including Barnes (1991), Duffy (1993), Mason (1981) and Oliver, (1990); they have helped inform and develop our thinking in the Equality Studies Centre at UCD.

Education, Status and Equality

The key question about education is that it operates at different levels. One must examine education as a series of interrelated systems, the most obvious of which are the first, second and third-level systems. Adult, continuing and second-chance education also form centres of education around which policies have to be developed. Within each of those systems one can look at equality for disabled people in four ways: in terms of formal rights and opportunities, participation, outcome/success and in terms of the implications of having equality of condition. Although, space will not allow us to develop an account of what each type of equality would require at each level of education, it is useful to bear the framework in mind for the purposes of policy-making.

1. Equal Formal Rights and Opportunities in Education

One cannot examine the issue of formal rights to education without taking account of the interrelationships between formal rights in one sector and that in another. For example, participation in third-level education is related to having access to and success in relevant second-level and primary education. For a variety of reasons, a considerable number of disabled students are not now prepared for public examinations such as the leaving certificate. The result is that a number of these young people are not in a position to apply for or participate in third-level education. Any proposal for change in educational policy therefore, must take account of the need to facilitate movement from one education sector to another. It must also enable disabled mature students who have been denied appropriate second-level education to enter third-level education through alternative routes such as adult access programmes.

Direct Discrimination

Formal equality of educational opportunity, defined in terms of access, exists when there is no legal or quasi-legal barrier to a person's entry to education because of their disability. With the exception of Rule 155 (4) (a) of the Rules for National Schools which formally states that

"Before a candidate is admitted to a Training College, the medical officer of the College must certify that he is of sound and healthy constitution and free from any physical disability or mental defect likely to impair his usefulness as a teacher; the medical certificate shall include such details as the Minister may require".

there are no regulations in first, second or third-level education in Ireland which formally discriminate against disabled people. The Disability Discrimination Act (Cth) 1992 (DDA, section 22) in Australia outlaws direct discrimination such as that which exists in teacher training colleges in Ireland (McDonagh, 1993:136). Discrimination in relation to the admission of students, denial of benefits, expulsion and subjection of the student to any detriment is also prohibited (ibid).

Indirect Discrimination

Although there may is little evidence of direct discrimination, there are a number of ways in which disabled people are indirectly discriminated against in terms of access to education. One example is through **the use of entry tests.** Secondary schools (as opposed to vocational, comprehensive and community schools and community colleges) are privately owned and controlled educational institutions. At present, a number of secondary schools use entry tests to select pupils. These are normally written tests in Irish, English and Mathematics, although some schools also use written aptitude and intelligence tests. Such tests are not normally available in Braille. Those who write in Braille therefore would be unable to take the test and would thereby be unable to attend the school in question. Also, such tests indirectly discriminate against all those who have a writing disability. If a person is only able to express themselves orally for example, then they could not do written tests and would not be able to attend a school where successful performance on a written entry test is a requirement of entry.

Indirect discrimination could also occur due to the requirements of some disabled people for **personal assistants.** If a potential pupil needed a personal assistant and was prepared to provide their own, the school could argue that there is no provision for such arrangements within the rules of the school. For example, they could claim that such a person would not be an employee of the school and would create problems for them in terms of insurance or in terms of discipline.

Strategies for Action

There is a clear need to outlaw direct discrimination in relation to education by enacting legislation prohibiting it. This has already been done in the United States through the Individuals with Disabilities in Education Act, 1990 and in Australia through The Disability Discrimination Act (Cth) 1992 (DDA, section 22).

In the cases cited above where indirect discrimination could occur, the particular needs of disabled people could be met if resources were made available. If the schools is to have tests available in multimedia form or to hire its own personal assistants for disabled pupils, considerable expense in involved. The policy question which arises here is whether the individual, the school/college or the State is to meet such costs. Because most schools receive over 90% of their current and capital expenditure from the State, in practice, the option is between the State paying or the individual paying. The exception to this may be those fee-paying primary and secondary schools which charge fees. In these latter cases individuals have chosen to enter a fee-paying system and it could be argued that the state had no immediate responsibility to pay the full cost for them in schools where the outlay is higher because of its exclusive nature.

As noted below in the **Section 3 on Equality of Success in Employment, Strategies for Action,** there needs to be some sanctioning system for educational institutions which continue to discriminate. It is also necessary to have a monitoring body with statutory powers to enforce sanctions.

2. Equality of Educational Participation

To enable disabled students to participate in education on equal terms with able-bodied students requires the school or educational institution and the state (as provider of educational services) to take account of their needs. If disabled people are to participate in schools or colleges then the institution must provide 'reasonable accommodation for the needs of disabled students'. What this accommodation would mean would vary with the disability and the educational context.

Reasonable Accommodation in Education: Basic Material Needs

This would involve making the **physical environment** readily accessible and usable for those with mobility impairments. It would mean allowing guide dogs in schools or colleges for those with visual impairments. If the student needed a **personal assistant** to participate, it could mean providing such an assistant or allowing the person to have their own personal assistant in the school but providing some financial aid towards their support. If a person is reliant on the use of sign language for communication purposes, it could mean the provision of an interpreter to enable them to participate; for those children with lesser hearing impairments it could mean the provision of appropriate hearing aids suited to a teaching situation with background noise. For those with a visual impairment, equality of participation could mean the provision of teaching and learning materials in large print, or, if necessary, in Braille and the availability of a resource person/teachers who could interpret Braille. Alternatively, and perhaps more satisfactorily (because most teachers cannot read Braille) equality of participation would mean the availability of a computer workstation for each child where they could type in Braille but which would translate the Braille into standard text. For a student who had to write with her feet, equality of participation could mean the provision of appropriate seating and desks which were comfortable and at an appropriate height. It could also mean the provision of a trolley if the desk had to be moved from one classroom to another.

Reasonable Accommodation of Basic Material Needs: Subject Choice, Examinations and Extracurricular Activities

Equality of participation also means **being able to opt for particular subjects** in schools on the same terms as able-bodied students. For example, if laboratories or workshops in schools are constructed in such a way that students in wheelchairs cannot move around the rooms to undertake the essential tasks of the subject, then such students are indirectly discriminated against in terms of their ability to participate on equal terms with able-bodied students. They are effectively precluded from exercising their rights to full participation by being excluded from taking particular subjects.

To participate on equal terms with able-bodied people in school one must be able to participate in **examinations and assessments**. The provision of special facilities for examinations such as scribes, individual rooms, or microcomputers would all be essential in different circumstances depending on the disability.

One must also be able to participate in **extracurricular activities** if one is to participate equally with others in education. There is a need therefore for schools and colleges to make reasonable accommodation for their disabled students in the extracurricular area. This means having appropriate equipment so that pupils with mobility difficulties can participate in physical education, enter and exit swimming pools easily, travel on school buses etc. It also means enabling students to participate in games or activities which are of interest and accessible to them, or providing such activities in the extracurricular programme as were appropriate for disabled students.

Reasonable Accommodation in Education: Social, Psychological and Other Needs

If students who are disabled are to participate on equal terms with others, then there must also **be provision made to educate teachers, lecturers and other students about disability** issues. The pre-service and, more particularly in the Irish case, the in-service education of teachers and lecturers about disability is crucial here. If teachers are not educated, and therefore not fully apprised of the needs and interests of their disabled students, the students cannot participate on equal terms with others in schools and colleges. Teachers who are ignorant about disability will not understand the needs of disabled pupils. There is evidence that they may even feel resentful or threatened by them in class with all the attendant negative implications that this has for their pupils and students themselves (Booth and Swann, 1987).

In addition, if disabled students are to participate equally with others then there is a need to **breakdown misconceptions and ignorance about disability in all schools or colleges**. This can be done by incorporating more material by disabled people across the curricula, by having **role models** who are disabled (e.g. teachers, administrative staff, etc.), by including systematic education in relevant subject areas about different disabilities and by developing whole-school/college policies about disability in the context on an overall equality policy.

Specialised Centres of Education and Inclusive Education

One question which has to be addressed here is whether provision for disabled students should be made in all schools and colleges, in some regionally-based schools and colleges, in a selected number of specialised national centres, or by providing a mixture of services which allow for some special centres but generally pursue inclusive education policies. Clearly the views on this question will vary with the disability as well as with the level and type of education required and the age of the person in question.

The limitations of concentrating provision in specialised segregated schools are as follows:

1. the disabled students do not have the opportunity to mix with able-bodied students and vice-versa. This limits both the social and educational opportunities available to both types of students about one another.

    The best way to overcome prejudice about disability is to have disabled and able-bodied people working together as equals. By having segregated as opposed to inclusive education, there is little scope for real confrontation of prejudicial attitudes towards disability among the able-bodied. By inclusive education, we do not mean simply locating able-bodied and disabled people in the same schools and then ignoring the reality of difference. We mean taking account of differences and developing a school/college policy which addresses differences in an open and honest way. Inclusive education is about making the system suit the pupils not just making the pupils 'fit the system' which has often been what integration has meant in the past.

2. specialised units often cannot afford to offer students a full range of subjects owing to their size. This can seriously limit the educational opportunities available to students at third level.

3. when specialised education is highly centralised, it means that a considerable number of students have to go to boarding schools at a young age. This can put the disabled student at an emotional disadvantage vis-á-vis able-bodied students as

they lack the experience of warmth and caring which can be provided in a loving family context. The emotional trauma involved in separation at a young age can inhibit the young person's educational development as well.

The potential inequalities that young disabled people may experience as a result of their segregation into special schools does not mean that there are not potential dangers involved in integrated education.

Young disabled people may not be able to participate fully in inclusive schools especially if their disability is one which isolates them from other pupils in a significant way, or where it would be extraordinarily difficult to accommodate their difference in a way that would allow them to participate equally with able-bodied children. One obvious example are pupils who are deaf and whose natural language is sign. Such students may only experience equality in educational participation by being educated in a school where sign is the medium of communication.

3. Equality of Success in Education

If disabled students are to succeed at the same rate as able-bodied students in schools and colleges not only must they be able to access and participate in schools on equal terms, they must also be given whatever resources they require to succeed on equal terms. What one would be aiming for here is the same rate of educational success (as measured by the proportion of disabled people sitting and attaining success in school, public and college examinations among disabled people as in the population generally). Success could also be measured in terms of the level of satisfaction which disabled people experienced with their education; it should be the same level of satisfaction as in the population generally.

Ongoing measures to ensure success would mean the provision of extra resources and support services to enable the disabled person to achieve comparable grades in public examinations and to enable them to experience comparable levels of satisfaction.

In particular, if disabled people are to attain equal levels of success in third-level education, they would, in certain cases, needs special tutors to enable them succeed at a comparable level with able-bodied students.

Quotas, Reserved Places and Affirmative Action in Higher Education

Because disabled people are significantly under-represented in higher education at present, there is a need to operate a quota or to have reserved places if their participation rates are to be brought into line with those of able-bodied students. There may even be a need to have a reserved places policy over a long period of time as many of the disadvantages which disabled people experience in attaining equal rates of participation in higher education cannot be realistically overcome for the foreseeable future.

Special attention would have to be paid to **disabled women** in the operation of a quota system or reserved places policy. At present disabled women may experience a double disadvantage of being women and by being disabled. There would be a need to ensure that quotas or reserved places were equally balanced between the women and men.

Disabled women, like women generally, are significantly under-represented in fields such as technology, engineering and computer science, yet these are growth areas of employment. If disabled women are to be attracted in to these areas, there would be a need for an affirmative action strategy such as an pre-university access programme, as without it disabled women would simply not be available in sufficient numbers to meet the quotas. For disabled women to access fields of study where able-bodied women are now well represented, such as law, medicine or the arts, would also probably require access programmes owing to the non-gender-related disadvantages such women experience.

If equality of success or indeed of access or participation were to be achieved, it would be essential that such policies were monitored on an ongoing basis and that sanctions would apply to institutions which did not meet targets. **(See Section 3 on Equality of Success in Employment, Strategies for Action below).**

4. Education and Equality of Condition

Even if there is equality of access, participation and success for disabled students in education, it must be realised that they very same inequalities in outcome which now exist between able-bodied students will also occur between disabled students. This will mean that just as students from the lowest socio-economic group (unskilled manual workers) are now under-represented by a factor of 6:1 in higher education and students from higher professional families are over-represented by a factor of 3:1, the same divisions will exist between disabled people (Clancy, 1988). Those disabled people whose parents are professionals would be over-represented while those whose parents were unskilled manual workers would be significantly under-represented even if there was equality of access, participation and success. Equally just as women in general are significantly under-represented in the fields of technology and engineering, so also will disabled women be under-represented in these areas.

For equality of condition to operate in education, it would have to operate in all other major institutions in society. Indeed it would be impossible to have equality of condition in education without equalising the distribution of wealth and power throughout society. This is a factor which has not generally been recognised in education yet it is of profound importance. If certain sectors of society own and control most of its wealth and power, then they will always be in a position to use their wealth and power to offset or challenge any equalisation policy in education. For example, those who own and control significantly more financial resources are in a powerful position to pursue cases through the courts and to challenge equality rulings if they deem them not to be in their interests. In addition, those who are wealthy are in a position to ignore financial sanctions unless the sanctions unless the sanctions are such that they seriously jeopardise their institution.

That is to say, it is only when there is an even distribution of wealth and power that all types of disabled people will have an equal chance to develop their talents in education and acquire the type and level of credential they want. If wealth and power are unequally distributed in society generally, then they will be unequally distributed between disabled people.

While having equality of condition in other institutions is a pre-requisite for having equality of condition in education, it is not the only consideration. Schools and colleges are the principal institutions in our society for transmitting and legitimating cultural forms. At present, much of what is incorporated in the formal curricula of schools and colleges does not take account of the life world of disabled people. Equality of condition would require not just that disabled people be enabled to access, participate and succeed on equal terms with able-bodied people in education, but that **the organisation of school life (what is referred to in educational circles as the hidden curriculum of schooling) and the formal curriculum took account of their life style and culture and recognise it fully in the school/college.** It would mean, for example, having a full subject on offer in 'Sign Language' at the leaving certificate for example. It would include the incorporation of 'Disability Studies' as a subject as well. It would mean **recognising fully the multiple forms of human intelligence which exist,** and not just the linguistic and mathematically-based abilities which so dominate education in terms of subject matter and in terms of modes of assessment at present (Gardner, 1985).

The pre-occupation of so much of formal education with credentialising those forms of knowledge and human understanding which can be assessed and measured through the medium of written language and mathematics is, in fact, a factor creating disability and inequality in education. For example, many people have insights, competencies, skills and abilities which cannot be measured through the linguistic medium, yet such people are heavily penalised and often labelled disabled in education; examples include people whose primary interests are in the visual/spatial sphere, those who work through the oral rather than the written medium, those who are primarily oriented to the bodily-kinesthetic sphere and those whose principal competencies are in the inter-personal and intra-personal spheres. The problem is not that such people are disabled but that the education system does not allow them the means of expression or the opportunity to develop the fields of competence and interest which they have. In effect, equality of condition would mean changing the school and curricula, not just making disabled students fit the system as it stands.

Employment and Disability

As noted above in Section 2 the level and nature of one's employment is a key determinant of status. There are a number of issues which must be considered in relation to improving the status of disabled people through employment.

First there is the nature of the work that disabled people do, the sector and occupation in which they are employed. Because the paid labour market is stratified both between occupations (e.g. hotel managers versus waitresses) and between sectors (e.g. pharmaceutical industry versus cleaning industry), some sectors and occupations give one an opportunity to have higher status and income than others. For example, the average industrial wage is much lower in the textile industry than it is in the telecommunications industry; workers in the medical profession have an aggregate much higher status and income than workers in the cleaning profession. If the status of disabled people is to be equal to that of able-bodied people generally, then it is clear that they must not be concentrated in low status and low paid sectors of employment or low status and low paid occupations within particular sectors.

Secondly, occupations are also internally stratified; that is to say there are senior and junior positions within most occupations with attendant differences in pay and status. If disabled people are concentrated in areas of employment where there is little opportunity for promotion, or in junior positions within occupations with promotional opportunities, this will have an adverse effect on their status.

Thirdly, entry to paid employment, in Ireland is strongly correlated with one's level of educational attainment; in other words, the higher the level of education attained the more likely one is to be employed (Department of Labour/Enterprise and Employment, Annual School Leavers Surveys). In addition, promotion within employment is also related to level of education attained. Because of this one cannot separate out the issue of employment from education in the discussion of status: the two are closely interwoven and this will be taken in to account in our discussion here.

1. Equal Formal Rights and Employment

To have equal formal rights in employment all legal and quasi-legal barriers which prohibit disabled people from either entering employment or from being promoted within employment would have to be removed.

Direct Discrimination

There is need to provide protection for disabled people in Ireland against direct discrimination arising out of quasi-legal barriers to employment. The fact that medical examinations and enquiries can lead to discrimination has been recognised in Title I of The Americans With Disabilities Act (ADA) 1990. "The general rule which applies in the pre-employment context is that a covered entity is not allowed to conduct pre-offer medical examinations or make enquiries with a view to establishing if a person has a disability (section 102(c)(2) ADA" (Quinn, 1993:72). Neither can the prospective employer inquire about the applicant's compensation history nor can questions which identify or assess a disability be asked at interview (ibid). Given current practices in relation to application and entry procedures to employment in Ireland there is need for a similar provision here.

A related issue is when an educational or professional body controls entry to an occupation and when they specify conditions of entry to the profession, occupational group or institution which discriminate against disabled people. One specific and well known example of this in Ireland is that of Rule 155 (4) (a) of the Rules for National Schools which we referred to above in the Education Section which precludes people from entering unless the medical officer of the College certifies that " he is of sound and healthy constitution and free from any physical disability or mental defect likely to impair his usefulness as a teacher".

The case above applies to entry to an educational institution but it has direct implications for one's ability to enter employment as a primary teacher if one is disabled. As noted above in the Education Section, this type of discrimination is outlawed in Australia by the Disability Discrimination Act (Cth) 1992 (DDA, section 22).

Indirect Discrimination

Indirect discrimination is experienced by disabled people in accessing employment also. Using educational credentials which disabled people are less likely to possess than able-bodied people, and which are not justified in terms of the skills required for the job, indirectly discriminates against disabled people. For example, educational credentials such as a leaving certificate or third-level diploma or degree are widely used to screen candidates prior to short-listing or interviewing for particular jobs in Ireland. Indeed, there is a very close correlation between the level of one's educational qualifications and one's employment/unemployment status (Department of Labour/Enterprise and Employment, Economic Status of School Leavers Surveys). Yet, many of the jobs for which educational credentials are used as a selection device do not really require the skills/competencies tested by the examination. A well known example is that of supermarket outlets which specify that applicants for jobs such as check-out operators must have the leaving certificate although there is ample evidence that one could perform this job in a wholly satisfactory way without a leaving certificate. The precondition of having to have a credential for a job where it is not occupationally necessary indirectly discriminates against a number of educationally disadvantaged groups including the disabled because there is considerable circumstantial evidence that disabled people in particular do not acquire the same level of educational qualifications as able-bodied people (Murray and Whyte, 1993:9). The reasons why disabled people do not achieve as highly as able-bodied people are undoubtedly related to the lack of equality of opportunity which they have had in the education and related sectors as we have noted above.

Just as the use of occupationally irrelevant educational credentials for occupational selection indirectly discriminates against disabled people at entry to employment, so too does it discriminate against them when it comes to promotion. Indirect discrimination could also occur at the promotional level by the laying down of other criteria such as having occupied certain positions in the organisation (for example, the requirement that one has worked as a management accountant to become chief executive) when it is known that disabled people are highly unlikely to have occupied such positions, and when experience in such positions is not essential for success in the promotional post.

Action to Prohibit Direct and Indirect Discrimination

To ensure the realisation of formal rights for disabled people in employment, there is a need to introduce legislation which outlaws direct discrimination. This means introducing legislation which prohibits the treatment of disabled people in a less favourable way than able-bodied people in circumstances which are the same or not materially different (McDonagh, 1993:129, citing the Australian Disability Discrimination Act (Cth) 1992 , DDA, section 5 (1) definition of direct discrimination).

There is also a need for legal and other provisions to prohibit indirect discriminations. As the experience of the Fair Employment (Northern Ireland) Act, 1976, shows (which did not cover indirect discrimination) prohibiting direct discrimination alone will make little change in the status of a given disadvantaged group. For example, there was little evidence that the proportion of Catholics employed in certain major private companies in Northern Ireland increased to any significant degree after the 1976 Act. One of the major problems here appeared to be the operation of indirect discrimination practices e.g. using educational credentials to select candidates for posts which Catholics were less likely to have) (Smith and Chambers, 1991:235-329).

Provision could take legislative, policy and educational forms. For example, it could be stated in law that educational credentials or a particular ability (e.g. having a current driver's licence) could only be used to select candidates where they were job-relevant. (It is obvious that such a regulation would have implications for educationally disadvantaged groups other than the disabled as well). Organisations or bodies which did not adhere to such principles could be sanctioned financially. Sanctions could take the form of tax penalties, the withdrawal of government subsidies or supports or ineligibility for government contracts where those applied. In addition, there could be educational programmes for potential employers and their agents showing them the arbitrariousness of using irrelevant credentials in selecting applicants with a view to encouraging them to discontinue their practices.

2. Equality of Participation in Employment

Gaining access to employment is only the first step on the road to equality of status. There is also the need to ensure that disabled people are able to participate in employment on equal terms with able-bodied people. Having a formal right to participate in employment is not enough, one must also be enabled to exercise this right.

The Needs of Disabled People and the Provision of Reasonable Accommodation: Material Needs including Transport

One of the clear issues at stake here is the need for employers to take account of the needs of disabled people within the employment context. There is a need for the employer to provide 'reasonable accommodation' for the needs of the disabled person to enable them to participate in employment. The Americans With Disabilities Act, 1990, Section 102(b)(5)(A) spells out precisely what discrimination in this area means: it includes…not making a reasonable accommodation to the known physical or mental limitations of an otherwise qualified individual with a disability who is an applicant or an employee, unless such covered entity [i.e. the employer and/or her or his agent]* can demonstrate that the accommodation would impose an undue hardship on the operation of the business of such covered entity (cited in Quinn, 1993:68).

* inset in brackets [ ] is ours.

The precise meaning of undue hardship is spelt out in section 101(10)(B)1-1V of the ADA (ibid: 79).

What this would mean in terms of different disabilities depends on the disability and the context. It obviously could mean providing ramps to enter buildings for people on wheelchairs as well as accessible work-related facilities such as toilets, rest areas and canteens. For those who have a visual impairment, it could mean providing written instructions in large type-face or in Braille, or providing extra lighting. For those who are deaf, it could mean the provision of access to communication systems other than spoken language or the provision of appropriate hearing-related equipment such as relay systems if such were appropriate. For people who do not have the use of hands or arms for writing, it could mean the provision of some kind of accessible Dictaphone and/or appropriate computer and seating facilities so that they could type or write with their feet. For people with writing difficulties, the provision of a Dictaphone would obviously enable them to prepare reports and write letters if the job required this.

If people are to participate in work, then they must be enabled to get to work. The critical nature of public transport has been underlined in the Americans With Disabilities Act (ADA, Subtitle B, Part 1 of Title II) (Quinn, 1993:91). To be denied effective transportation is to be denied the full benefits of employment. There is need clearly for appropriate transport systems for all types of disabled people. This would mean that public transport would have to be made readily accessible to and usable by all disabled people including those using wheelchairs. If existing transport could not be altered without undue cost, then the relevant public authority would have to be enabled to provide alternative accessible and usable transport. In addition, all new stock such as trains and buses would have to be easily accessible to and usable by disabled people including those using wheelchairs.

Reasonable Accommodation: Psychological, Educational and Other Needs

Reasonable accommodation for people who have a mental disorder would vary with the disorder or the illness experienced. For example, if the person was a teacher and her/his mental state was seriously disturbed by having to take the most demanding class/stream then it would seem reasonable that she/he would not be given such a group. If a person experienced claustrophobia, providing reasonable accommodation could mean giving them an office or room for work which had a good sense of space and lighting so that they did not feel confined.

To enable disabled people to participate on equal terms in employment with able-bodied people, account must also be taken of their educational and developmental needs. For example, if skills within the particular sector were subject to constant obsolescence problems (as is the case with jobs requiring the use of computer software) then disabled people must be enabled to participate in staff upgrading programmes in that field at an equal rate with able-bodied people and, if necessary enabled to acquire new educational credentials if equal participation demands this.

Disabled people cannot participate on equal terms with able-bodied people in employment if there is ignorance and prejudice about disabilities in the work context. Ignorance creates fear and fear, in turn, can lead to isolation of the disabled person with its attendant negative effects on their employment experience. Equal participation in employment would require that an educational programme be provided about disability in the employment context to ensure the breakdown of prejudicial attitudes and thereby to provide an equal working environment for the disabled person(s).

3. Equality of Success in Employment

Being able to participate in employment is in itself no guarantee that one will be able to participate equally with able-bodied people in relation to different sectors of employment or that one will be able to succeed at the same rate within a given occupation or job as able-bodied people.

As noted at the outset of this section on employment, paid work is segregated both within and between sectors and within and between occupations. Equality of success for disabled people means enabling them to succeed on equal terms with able-bodied people both within and between occupations and sectors.

We will address the question of sector and occupational differences in employment first. Certain sectors of employment enjoy higher status than others: for example, being in the pharmaceutical sector accords one higher income and status than being in the cleaning sector. Also, certain occupations clearly enjoy higher status than others; medical doctors enjoy higher status and income on average than telephonists.

The sectoral and occupational breakdown of employment for disabled people is not available nationally. However, given the fact that disabled people do not attain the same level of education, on average, as able-bodied people, it is quite likely therefore that they are concentrated in sectors of employment (sheltered workshops doing assembly work for manufacturing industry for example) and in occupations (telephonists) where their chances of career mobility are greatly circumscribed. There is well documented evidence that segregation can also lead to lower pay and poorer working conditions for weaker groups as has happened in the case of women (Second Commission on the Status of Women Report, 1993).

Equality of success within employment therefore would mean ensuring that disabled people were enabled, not just to access employment or to participate equally within given employments. It would mean enabling them to get employment in sectors and occupations which were well paid and with good career prospects at comparable levels with able-bodied people.

Equality of success within occupations would also mean enabling disabled people to gain equal status within occupations with able-bodied people. Because of educational disadvantages for example, disabled people are not generally in a position to compete on equal terms with able-bodied people for promotional posts no matter how 'reasonable the accommodations made'. Consequently, the argument would be that there is need for policies which would guarantee the same representation of disabled people in senior or promotional posts as able-bodied people. Furthermore, different types of disabled people should also be represented in senior or promotional posts taking account of their proportion in the general population.

Strategies for Action

It is self evident that if there is to be proportionate representation for disabled people, even on an approximate basis, across sectors, occupations and senior posts, there must be an accurate and disaggregated statistical profile available of the disabled population in society. Such data is not available at present. **One of the most obvious requirements in relation to any policy-making with and for disabled people is the availability of comprehensive, up-to-date statistical and qualitative research data. The lack of adequate data is itself a major barrier to promoting all types of equality policies as there is simply no basis for comparison with able-bodied groups.**

To ensure equality of success for disabled people within employment would require both long-term strategies for those who have not yet entered the paid labour market and short-term strategies for those who are in employment at present .

In the long term, it is clear that major changes would have to occur in the educational opportunities available to disabled people if they are to enter the broad range of jobs and to succeed within jobs at the same rate as the able-bodied. In particular, there would have to be proactive educational campaigns to encourage disabled people to enter third-level education and in particular to enter third-level education sectors such as technology, engineering, medicine, architecture, law and computer science where the limited evidence available suggests they are particularly poorly represented at present. Unless disabled people enter these sectors of higher education, then they are not likely to be qualified to enter and succeed in the related employment sectors.

Affirmative action would be also required such as the provision of specially designed access courses for disabled people who wanted to enter higher education. Research in the U.S. indicates that it was only when affirmative action was required, through the Individuals With Disabilities in Education Act, 1990, that the participation of disabled people began to increase significantly in higher education.

Gaining the educational credentials necessary to succeed on equal terms with able-bodied people for jobs is a long term strategy. In addition, it is fraught with difficulties as the experience of women shows. Although women now attain higher grades than men in public examinations across most countries in Europe, and although they are even entering faculties such as medicine and law at the same rates as men, they are not achieving the high status positions at comparable rates to men (U.S. Department of Education, 1991; Wilson, 1991). It would appear essential, in the short term at the very least, that there would be some system of quotas introduced both within sectors and occupations and for particular posts if disabled people are to have rates of success in employment comparable to those of able-bodied people. A disaggregated quota system would be required so that disabled people would be represented in each sector, occupation and level. The details of the employment sectors and the occupational categories are available from the Central Statistics Office (CSO) and are used in analysing the paid labour force annually (CSO, Annual Labour Force Surveys).

If affirmative action strategies and quota systems are to be effective it is essential that they be implemented. This means that there must be agency which has the statutory authority to oversee the implementation of affirmative action programmes and quota systems and which has the **authority to sanction** individuals, organisations and bodies which fail to comply with the regulations. There is a useful example in the Fair Employment (Northern Ireland) Act, 1989. Section 27 of this Act enables the Fair Employment Commission to monitor employment practices and Sections 10 and 11 allow for surveys of employment and investigation of employment practices. It is also possible **to encourage** organisations to implement quotas and affirmative action strategies through financial incentive schemes such as grants and reduced tax liabilities. One obvious difficulty here would be in establishing the liability of any given employer in terms of meeting the quota.

4. Equality of Condition for all Citizens and Employment

Neither equality of access, participation or success in employment will alter the fact that inequalities in income, power and prestige will continue to exist across and between sectors and occupations unless equality of condition exists for all citizens. Even if one has equality of success, disabled people will be stratified occupationally, with some having high status occupations and others low status occupations with attendant differences in income. The equalisation of formal rights, participation and success will not alter the hierarchical structure of the paid labour market; this means that some disabled people will work in poorly paid occupations and in low status occupations in just the same way that able-bodied people do.

Only in a society where there is equality of conditions for all citizens can all disabled people have equal status with one another and with all able-bodied people.

Political participation

Political participation in this context includes voting, standing for and holding positions as public representatives, participating in political discussion and policy formation, and participating in organisations such as residents' and tenants' associations, political parties, trade unions, farming organisations and single-issue campaigning groups. Such participation contributes to social status both by influencing the way disabled people are seen by others and by raising the self-esteem of disabled people through a sense of political membership and efficacy.

1. Equal formal rights and opportunities

Under the Irish constitution, all citizens have the same rights to vote, stand for office, engage in political discussion and belong to political associations. The rights of disabled people to these forms of political participation could be reinforced by legislation against direct or indirect discrimination in membership rules and qualifications for office but this does not seem to be a major problem as things now stand.

2. Equal Participation

Some legal provisions exist to ensure that disabled people are able to vote, such as provision for 'special voters' to vote at home and for physically disabled voters to vote at accessible voting stations (Electoral (Amendment) (No. 2) Act, 1986). It may be advisable to conduct a systematic review of provisions in relation to the whole range of disabilities.

It must ensured in particular that any new procedure which is enacted does not introduce new discriminations in to the system between disabled people themselves.

Undoubtedly disabled people face greater barriers in connection with standing for and holding public office. To some extent these stem from barriers to participation in political associations (see below) but specific problems may include the inaccessibility of public buildings, and practices and procedures which make office-holding by disabled people practically impossible. For example, a deaf or hearing-impaired person might not be able to operate effectively as a public representative without appropriate provisions such as simultaneous signing of others' contributions. Public representatives without speech need appropriate provisions for expressing their contributions to a meeting. A blind public representative needs to have reports, bills, etc. available orally, in large print or in Braille. Without **firm guarantees that such needs will be provided for,** disabled people cannot make use of their right to stand for public office.

Political discussion, orally and in print, is the life blood of political participation, yet such discussion is largely inaccessible to those with speech, hearing, and visual impairments. This clearly forms part of the **wider communication needs of disabled people,** raising educational, technical, and financial issues. In mass communication contexts, policies might involve the use of teletext subtitles, simultaneous signing, and written transcripts of broadcast material, of audio and Braille versions of printed material, etc.

The barriers to participation are in most ways exacerbated at the level of political associations such as residents' associations, political parties, trade unions, and voluntary groups. Such associations often meet in inaccessible locations, and they are usually even less geared to meeting the communication needs related to specific disabilities than public bodies are. Although their more intimate character may in some circumstances serve to make disabled people feel more welcome as participants, they are also capable of being more thoughtless or even intolerant of disabilities. A major campaign of public education directed at the members of such groups could help them to review their own provisions and attitudes. Policies directed towards a wider availability to such associations of accessible public buildings (including state-financed buildings such as schools) would have the benefit not only of ensuring access but of encouraging the sense that participation is a basic right of all citizens and not a private privilege. State funding to allow large organisations such as parties and unions to provide material in alternative media could be considered.

Political participation is impossible without **adequate educational and financial resources.** The rate of political participation of disabled people is therefore closely connected with participation in education and employment.

3. Equal success in participation

In politics, equal success means equal power and influence. Although the right to vote gives every citizen a formally equal say in elections, how this operates even at the electoral level depends on the electoral system. Under the Irish system of proportional representation by single transferable vote, which operates in relatively small constituencies (for most elections no more than 5 seats), a quota of votes (i.e. 17% or more of the poll) is the minimum threshold for direct political representation. Since disabled people, particularly when disaggregated by disability, constitute less than a quota in all constituencies in all current local, national, and European elections, the current electoral system cannot be expected to provide direct political representation for disabled people. Indirect influence by way of voting for parties committed to the needs of the disabled is hard to assess, but there is no obvious evidence of it.

There is no straightforward policy within the current electoral system for increasing the number of disabled people elected as public representatives. The use of quotas among nominees, for instance, which has a clear application to gender equality. **Quotas** could be used to increase the political representation of disabled people although some system would have to be devised for representing different types of disability within the quota; it could not be a simple quota, it would have to be a representative quota. The use of direct nominations to public bodies, particularly to the Seanad, could also be used to increase the number of disabled people in public office. Without imposing a strict quota, political parties could nevertheless set themselves targets in terms of the number of disabled people they hoped to get elected to councils, the Dáil, and the Seanad. Irish political parties are sufficiently centralised that such a policy could be effectively planned in association with local activists. Thus although ensuring the election of a minimum proportion of disabled people to public bodies does not have a mechanical solution, targets could be effectively set and achieved if there were the political commitment to do so. Given the small size of most elected bodies and the heterogeneity of disability, no system of targets on its own would give equal influence to all disabled people at a given time, but it would be a step in the right direction.

Independently of the direct election of disabled people, the electoral influence of disabled people would be enhanced by **taking steps to develop the organisational capacities and resources of groups representing the interests of disabled people,** so that individual voters had more systematic information on the policies of political parties towards disabilities and were in a stronger position to vote in a co-ordinated way within particular constituencies.

State financial and organisational support for groups representing disabled people would also enhance their ability to take part in political debates and to influence public policy. We emphasise that the object of such support would be to ensure equality of influence for groups which are currently politically marginalised, partly at least by the electoral system itself, and so in no way shows 'favouritism' towards disabled people. At present the resources of groups representing disabled people are severely stretched and may in some cases be caught in a tension between being used for political purposes and being used to meet the needs of disabled people directly. Under-resourcing can also lead to disabled people being represented by an organisation in which they have little real involvement. It should be seen as a major purpose of representative organisations to encourage and support the participation of disabled people in other political associations as well.

In contemporary politics a great deal of influence is exercised by **appointed boards, committees, and commissions.** These provide another area in which the political influence of disabled people could be made more equal. The general principle for such bodies ought to be that disabled people be appointed roughly proportionately to the impact on disabled people of the committee in question. Thus, bodies which have a general impact on citizens at large would be expected to have disabled members roughly proportional to the proportion of disabled people in the Irish population. Committees which have a special impact on particular groups of disabled people would be expected to have an especially high membership from those groups. Appointments need to be sensitive to the differences among disabled people; for example, it would be appropriate to try to ensure that at least 40% of appointees were women. Inviting groups which represent the interests of disabled people to nominate representatives to public bodies would help to ensure that the voice of disabled people was genuinely representative.

Another factor in political influence is **media coverage in news and current affairs programmes and publications and in particular the participation of disabled people in such programmes and publications.** Not only would a proportionate participation (for example, among the panellists in RTÉ's Questions and Answers) help to raise the importance of issues affecting disabled people, but the visible participation of disabled people would directly contribute to equal status.

The relative political power of different social groups is expressed institutionally through the organisation of parliamentary committees, special commissions, government departments, and responsibilities and procedures within government departments. Attention to how **the machinery of government could be restructured to provide disabled people with a more equal influence over public policy** might suggest the desirability of one or more of the following: a joint committee of the Oireachtais on the Rights of Disabled People, a new government department or a division within an existing department to deal explicitly with the needs of disabled people, improved guide-lines for ensuring the recruitment of disabled people to all levels of the civil service and procedures to ensure that the impact of particular policies on the needs of disabled people were addressed as a matter of routine. As always, our aim here is not to make a firm recommendation but to point out opportunities for achieving equal status.

4. Equality of condition

Enhancing the influence of disabled groups does not itself ensure that disabled individuals are equally politically influential. In particular, the degree of inequality among disabled people will be influenced by the degree to which the relative influence of some disabled people stems from broadly based, democratic organisations. Policies aimed at extending democratic participation and control throughout society would help to make the influence of all citizens more equal. More immediately, it seems appropriate to consider the degree of democratic participation and accountability within organisations specifically dedicated to promoting the interests of disabled people themselves.

Equality and Personal Relationships

In this section we discuss ways in which the participation of disabled people in intimate personal relationships contributes to equal status. Among the relationships we have in mind are personal friendships, family relationships including marriage, long-term partnerships and parenthood, and relations of sexual intimacy. As with other forms of participation, the establishment and development of personal relationships serve both to enhance the status of disabled people in the eyes of others and to sustain the self-esteem of disabled people themselves.

1. Equal formal rights and opportunities

In the area of personal relationships, the concept of discrimination applies, informally, in the way in which able-bodied people treat disabled people as potential friends, partners, and lovers. Obviously there is no straightforward legal solution to the prejudice able-bodied people exercise in developing their personal relationships, but some of the other policy tools we have highlighted have an important role to play. For example, the way disability is treated in educational contexts can have an important bearing on whether or not able-bodied people find it perfectly natural or highly problematic to make friends with disabled people. Whatever the value might be of segregated education for children with special needs, one of the key arguments in favour of some degree of integration is to reduce the barriers between disabled and able-bodied people. Social policy can play a similar role in helping disabled people to be integrated into the social life of local communities as against being isolated and institutionalised. The role of the mass media in portraying disabled people as friends, family members, and sexual intimates can also have an influence on popular prejudice.

Some disabled people face another, **more institutional barrier to personal relationships** through their dependency on caring agencies which may have the authority to restrict or discourage certain kinds of relationship. Although it might not be possible to defend absolute rights to have intimate sexual relationships or to have children, regardless of disability, it seems to us that these ought to be considered at least prima facie rights which could only be restricted under very special circumstances. As in other areas, dependency creates a vulnerability to the power of others which needs to be carefully and self-consciously reviewed.

The officially sanctioned removal of some disabled people from their families or other households is another way in which opportunities to form or maintain personal relationships are sometimes curtailed. In some cases such actions may be unavoidable, but as before this very serious form of power over some disabled people needs to be carefully controlled and monitored.

2. Actual participation

For many disabled people, **the difficulty of establishing and maintaining personal relationships stems from difficulties in satisfying their other basic needs.** Developing personal relationships is by its very nature a communicative process; those with special communication needs may therefore experience severe problems in developing personal relationships. Friendships and long-term partnerships often develop out of shared activities, at work, in education, in political associations, in sports or cultural pursuits. All the obstacles which society places in the way of the participation of disabled people in these activities also affect their opportunities for developing personal relationships out of them.

In many cases, people may only be able to pursue a social, educational and work life independently if they have a **personal assistant.** Obviously most disabled people would not be in a position to hire such an assistant out of their own resources; equality of participation would mean state support or provision of such an assistant so that one could equally participate in social life and have the time and opportunity to make friends and form satisfying personal relationships.

The impact of a person's disability on the able-bodied members of their family or household and on their friends can also have severe repercussions on the character and sustainability of these relationships. **Adequate state support for carers** would answer to the needs of both disabled people and carers, both at the material level and at the level of sustaining and enhancing their relationship to each other. For example, the needs of a paraplegic and her/his carers can be considerably eased by appropriate help from visiting nurses and auxiliaries. Policies to enhance the independence of disabled people would help to ensure that they can develop personal relations with others on the basis of freedom and equality rather than severe dependency. Personal inter-dependency is a characteristic feature of deep human relationships, but severely unequal dependency can also strongly limit relationships.

Parenthood offers tremendous satisfactions to most people, and carries a significant status in the wider society. Disabled people often face substantial obstacles in having and rearing children; yet most forms of disability are perfectly compatible with successful parenting, provided that the special needs related to the disability are catered for. Mental illness constitutes one of the most widespread forms of disability in our society, and is often manifested in difficulties in developing and sustaining personal relationships. An adequate mental health service would itself undoubtedly contribute opportunities and support for developing personal relationships through the use, where appropriate, of group therapy, day centres, counselling services, etc.

3. Equal Success in Participation

Unlike employment, education, or politics, the sphere of personal relationships is not organised in institutional hierarchies. We could not establish quotas to ensure that disabled people on the whole had just the same quality of personal relationships as able-bodied people, or insist that everyone should have at least one disabled person as a friend or lover. At the same time, however, it is possible to use some broad statistical measures of whether or not particular groups of disabled people are doing as well as able-bodied people in their personal relationships. For instance, if people with certain types of disability have a significantly lower marriage/stable partnership rate, or a significantly higher rate of marriage breakdown, than able-bodied people, this may point to ways in which their needs are being inadequately supported. If certain groups have higher rates of treatment for depression or higher suicide rates, this is a likely indication that their personal relationships are not going so well as the rest of the population's. We cannot intervene directly to change a group's marriage or suicide rate, but we can use this information to highlight unmet needs and to spur further research and policy initiatives.

4. Equality of condition

Acting to change the conditions under which personal relationships can develop is for the most part an indirect and long-term strategy. Although it may be possible to intervene in ways which help to narrow the gaps between disabled and able-bodied people, the character of our society sets severe obstacles in the way of nearly everyone's ability to develop close, loving relationships, and makes it inevitable that there will be wide inequalities in the degree to which people find their personal relationships satisfying and fulfilling. The additional support which disabled people need for developing personal relationships is thus closely connected with the additional support which all of us need in this regard. Although no conceivable social policy can ensure that everyone has a satisfying life, we believe that everyone's ability to make and sustain satisfying personal ties could be enhanced by the development of a more egalitarian society. That project would meet a common need of disabled and able-bodied people alike.

SECTION 5

References

Barnes, C. (1991) *Disabled People in Britain and Discrimination.* London: Hurst.

Booth, T. and W. Swann (1985*) Including Pupils With Disabilities: Curricula For All.* Milton Keynes: Open University Press.

Clancy, P. (1988) *Who Goes to College.* Dublin. Higher Education Authority.

Duffy, M., (1993) *Integration or Segregation: Does It Make a Difference?* Unpublished Master of Equality Studies thesis, University College Dublin, Equality Studies Centre.

Gardner, H., (1985) *Frames of Mind: The Theory of Multiple Intelligences.* London, Paladin.

Government Publications Office (1993) *Second Commission on the Status of Women,* Report to Government. Dublin.

McDonagh, M. (1993) Disability Discrimination Law in Australia, in G.Quinn (ed.) *Disability Discrimination Law in the United States, Australia and Canada.* Dublin, National Rehabilitation Board.

Mason, M. (1981) 'Michelene' in J. Campling (ed.) *Images of Ourselves.* London, Routledge and Kegan Paul.

APPENDIX C

OUTLINE PRINCIPLES OF A DISABILITIES ACT

The Commission gave consideration to the problem of discrimination in Irish society against people with disabilities. It came to a very specific and definite conclusion namely:

Specific legislation will be required to effectively eradicate discrimination against people with disabilities.

In the context of the Commission's conclusions a person with a disability means:

(a) A person with a physical, mental, intellectual, emotional or sensory impairment and who, due to a lack of receptiveness and adaptability in existing social structures and otherwise, encounters obstacles to participation on equal and equally effective terms with all others in all aspects of the life of the community

   or

(b) A person with a record of such impairment

   or

(c) A person who is so regarded by third parties.

The term also includes:

(a) A person who has such an impairment but whose condition is controlled by medication

(b) Persons who are substance abusers, but who are currently enrolled in rehabilitation programmes.

"Discrimination" means any distinction, exclusion, restriction or denial of reasonable accommodation based on disability which has the effect of nullifying or impairing the recognition, enjoyment or exercise of rights, liberties, and privileges of the person concerned including the provision of different or separate services to persons with disabilities unless such provision is absolutely necessary to provide such person with services that are as effective as those provided to others.

Discrimination also refers to indirect discrimination which includes requiring a person with a disability to comply with a condition or a requirement

(a) with which a substantially higher proportion of persons without the disability comply or are able to comply

(b) is not reasonable in all circumstances and

(c) is one with which the aggrieved person does not or is not able to comply.

The Commission identified five main areas in which discrimination was manifest or where it quite frequently occurred. Those areas were:

1. The provision of services to the public by Departments of State, Statutory Local Authorities, Statutory Boards, semi-state companies, other State agencies and delegated agents.

2. Private amenities including commercial, leisure and sporting concerns (whether operated by individuals or corporate bodies) which offer services to the public at large.

3. Insurance and assurance companies which offer to provide insurance and assurance facilities to members of the public.

4. The employer/employee relationship.

5. Education and the provision of educational opportunities.

In relation to these five areas and others the Commission's goal is:

(a) To see discrimination against any person with a disability outlawed.

(b) To see in place an effective sanction for those who are in breach of anti-discrimination legislation.

DISCRIMINATION BY DEPARTMENTS OF STATE, STATUTORY OR LOCAL AUTHORITIES, STATUTORY BOARDS, SEMI-STATE COMPANIES AND OTHER STATE AGENCIES/BODIES PROVIDING SERVICES TO THE PUBLIC, INCLUDING PEOPLE WITH DISABILITIES

These bodies provide services to the public, including people with disabilities, over a wide range of activities. These activities include:

(a) the need to visit offices or premises of such bodies in relation to private and commercial affairs

(b) the use of telecommunication services

(c) the use of public transport, access to health clinics or the offices of various social welfare agencies and other public amenities such as beaches and parks

(d) the exercising of the right to use the services provided by the civil and criminal courts and other relevant administrative bodies for ventilating or defending rights or privileges.

(e) participating in the administration of justice by acting on juries

(f) exercising their franchise in local, national and European elections.

The Commission has found that discrimination has arisen from the failure of such bodies to make reasonable accommodation in the provision of their services, to ensure that a person with a disability could make use of or participate in and enjoy the benefits of such services. For example, there is little point, as far as a person with a disability is concerned, in having a public telephone service provided which he or she cannot use by reason of it being above the height to which he/she can reach or in a telephone box which they cannot enter or which, by reason of their disability, has inadequate facilities to enable them to use it. There is also little point in a person with a disability going to a health centre which, by reason of his or her particular disability, they cannot enter because of the physical approach and access. There is also a failure in providing persons with sensory impairments with information in appropriate forms.

To put it very simply, the Commission sees a need to make all services accessible and usable by persons with disabilities.

The Commission would wish to see the authorities concerned:

(a) Carry out a self evaluation of the quality and status of existing services within a period of two years from the commencement of a Disability Discrimination Act. Such evaluation should be based on compliance with guidelines prescribed by such Act.

(b)   Carry out modifications necessary to comply with the said guidelines within a clear cut statutory timescale.

(c)   Conduct audits at regular intervals to ensure continued compliance with the guidelines prescribed by statute.

The Commission also wishes to ensure that failure to comply with the guidelines should give rise to the sanctions prescribed by the Act and that the sanctions be such as to maximise compliance with the law.

DISCRIMINATION BY PRIVATE AMENITIES

The Commission found major areas of discrimination in the private commercial world. These amenities include:

- Hotels, motels and places of lodging

- Establishments serving food and drink including restaurants, bars and fast-food outlets

- Places of exhibition, entertainment including theatres, cinemas, concert halls and sports stadiums

- Places of public gathering including auditoriums and conference centres

- Retail establishments including shopping centres, department stores, shops and grocery stores

- Services including automatic teller machines, offices of physicians, pharmacies, banks, insurance offices, petrol stations

- Places of public display such as art galleries

- Places of private education including pre-schools, colleges and other learning centres

- Places of recreation including bowling alleys, private commercial beaches and the like

- Places of exercise including gymnasiums and fitness centres.

- Places of worship.

The Commission is of the view that it is necessary by statutory provision to require the proprietors of such establishments and services to make them user friendly to persons with disabilities with a result that they are, to the maximum extent feasible, readily accessible to and by persons with disabilities. Again the Commission would wish to see this state of affairs achieved within a timescale and in accordance with guidelines established under the Discrimination Act.

INSURANCE AND ASSURANCE - PROVIDING INSURANCE AND ASSURANCE TO THE PUBLIC

The third area in which the Commission identified discrimination was in relation to the terms in which insurance and assurance cover is provided to persons with disabilities. In the view of the Commission no person or company providing insurance/assurance should be entitled to refuse cover outright or effectively outright to any person or class of persons, on the basis of disability. The mere existence of disability should not be a ground to require premiums in excess of those required from other members of the public where the same or like cover is required. In the view of the Commission cover for specific disabilities and in relation to specific benefits may be excluded or provided at a higher charge if the party providing insurance cover can establish that such exclusion, higher charge or limitation is

(a)   based on sound and current actuarial data or

(b)   necessary for the realisation of the fair and reasonable rate of return on investment by the party providing insurance.

Subject to the foregoing provisions, insurers should be obliged by law to deal with people with disabilities on the same basis as other members of the community.

DISCRIMINATION IN RELATION TO CONTRACTS AND TERMS OF EMPLOYMENT

In the Commission's view where a person with a disability can, with or without reasonable accommodation, perform the essential functions of the job, or such person holds or desires to hold it, it should be unlawful to discriminate against that person either

(a)   when a person applies for a job or

(b)   in relation to promotion within employment or other terms and conditions.

The "essential functions" of any given job means the fundamental job/duties of the employment/position which the person with a disability holds or seeks to hold. The term does not include the marginal functions of the position.

The Commission would see any pre-selection system which is adapted to screening out persons with disabilities or tests likely to render people with disabilities ineligible (whether for appointment or for promotion) in a job as discrimination.

The Commission would see it as reasonable accommodation to

(a)   allow a qualified employee with disability to bring and use his own aid, assistive devices, guide dogs, hearing assistance dogs or other trained animals on the job

(b)   provide such ancillary aids and services as may be reasonable and necessary to facilitate the employee with disability in performing the essential functions of the job

(c)   move all physical barriers so that any relevant work space is readily accessible to and usable by the person with a disability. The Commission would see it appropriate that within a period of time from the date of commencement of the Act an appropriate authority should prescribe, after due consultation with employer organisations, standards of good practice.

The Commission considers that there should be ready access to a rights officer with a right to appeal to a tribunal and to the circuit or high court on the lines of the procedures which apply to the Employment Appeals Tribunal and its ancillary services. It should be possible to extend the jurisdiction of the Employment Appeals Tribunal to cover discrimination against people with disabilities. This system is a simple, prompt and effective remedy. It could be adapted for the purpose envisaged in this situation.

EDUCATION AND EDUCATIONAL OPPORTUNITIES

The Commission believes that all children and adults with disabilities have an equal right to education and related services as all others. In this context related services means any service which is necessary to allow access to education and includes:

- Speech and occupational therapy

- physical education

- Support and counselling for parents

- Psychological support

- Technical aids and supports

- Communications support

- School transport, including escort where necessary

- Classroom assistants

- Resource and remedial teaching

- Personal assistants.

It shall be presumed that all children with disabilities shall be placed in mainstream schools and within mainstream classes of such schools unless the parents or guardians request otherwise or unless it can be shown that such placement is inappropriate.

All decisions on placement shall be taken by the school authorities concerned together with the child's parents or guardians, all relevant independent professionals and the child himself or herself wherever appropriate.

The onus of proof for showing that placement, or continued placement, in mainstream schools and classes is inappropriate rests with the school authorities concerned. This presumption may only be rebutted by adducing clear and concrete evidence that either

(a)   such placement would be impossible due to the kind and quantum of related services needed and after making all reasonable efforts to obtain technical assistance and advice from all relevant State, semi-State and private agencies, or

(b)   such placement would not be in the best educational interests of the child concerned and that such has been independently verified, or

(c)   such placement would objectively hinder the advancement of the educational needs and rights of the other children in the class and where no reasonable arrangements can be found after all due enquiries to meet them.

Examples of discriminatory behaviour would in the opinion of the Commission include the following:

(a)   insisting on conditions for entry and participation that generally apply but which cannot be met by the child in question and for which he/she should not reasonably be expected to comply

(b)   the imposition of conditions for entry and participation which do not ordinarily apply and which cannot be objectively justified

(c)   failing to admit the physical presence and use of the child's technical aids and assistive devices including guide dogs, hearing assistance dogs and other trained animals

(d)   failing to provide such ancillary aids and services as are reasonable and may be necessary and appropriate to ensure that the child concerned can benefit from the full range of educational opportunities as are available to others

(e)   failing to remove architectural barriers where such are readily removable

(f)   failing to adequately involve the parents in all discussions affecting entry, placement, suspension, dismissal as well as in the formulation, review and revision (if any) of the individual education plan in relation to the child.

(g)   failing to provide related services where such are necessary to enable the child to enjoy meaningful education.

The Commission gave consideration to the mode and manner in which such legislation would be enforced.

The Commission takes the view that the complaints procedure should be simple and accessible and made known to all parents. In default of an appropriate response the Minster for Equality and Law Reform or his successor should have a statutory obligation, after all conciliatory efforts have proved negative, to take proceedings against the Department of Education for an order of mandamus to provide a suitable educational plan in respect of the child concerned.

Finally, where a Department, Statutory Authority, Local Authority, semi-state body, individual or corporate entity is required to carry out some act or activity in a given timescale prescribed in the statute aimed at eliminating an area of discrimination the purpose of any sanction to obey the law must be positive. It must be aimed at getting the act required to be in fact carried out and not merely to penalise the offending party. An appropriate range of remedies should be provided within the statute including the right to apply to the High Court for an order of mandamus.

APPENDIX D

DEFINITIONS OF KEY POSITIONS

D.1   Throughout the report the Commission has referred to a number of important positions which it believes are necessary to ensure that people with disabilities are guaranteed their rights. These include patient advocates, rights advisers and key workers and the functions of such positions are explained in this Appendix.

Patient Advocate

D.2   The Patient Advocate should be employed by the Department of Equality and Law reform and have total access to psychiatric hospitals and the 25 to 50 bed psychiatric units in regional general hospitals.

D.3   The Advocate would respond to requests from a patient directly (or via a Rights Adviser) to:

- put a review (by the Review Body) in process;

- find and instruct legal advice;

- articulate the patient's concerns at a review hearing;

- represent the patient in court if necessary;

- arrange meetings with senior clinical and administrative personnel and support and, if necessary, articulate the patient's views.

Rights Adviser

D.4   The Rights Adviser would be employed by a psychiatric hospital or the psychiatric unit in a general hospital. He/she should consult with every patient within 48 hours of their admission and make sure that they are fully aware of their rights, e.g. to have an involuntary admission reviewed, to have access to private telephones, to see their clinical files, etc.

Key Worker

D.5   In hospital, the Key Worker would be a member of the nursing staff who would:

- ensure that the patient's personal needs are met, e.g. in relation to clothing, cosmetics etc.

- ensure that the patient's concerns are understood and appreciated by other staff at shift changes;

- facilitate the patient to contact and socialise with relatives and visitors;

- co-ordinate programmes of activities like group therapy, art therapy and neurological consultations.

APPENDIX E

MEMBERSHIP OF WORKING GROUPS

EDUCATION
Chairperson
Dr Sheelagh Drudy,   Maynooth College

Commission Members
Ms Jacqui Browne (Convenor)
Mr David Leydon
Ms Frieda Finlay
Sister Angela Magee
Dr Paul McCarthy

Advisory Group Member
Mr Frank Maguire

Other Members:

Ms Noirin Hayes	Catha Brugha Street (Pre-School Perspective)
Ms Deirdre Walsh	Representative, Ballymun Comprehensive School (2nd Level Perspective)
Ms Nora Friel	Parent - Physical/Sensory Disability Perspective
Mr Mícheál O Flannagáin	Department of Education
Ms Elaine Howley	National Council for the Blind of Ireland

Background Paper/Research Support
Mr Sean Griffin
Jacqui Browne (Technical Rapporteur)

ARTS/CULTURE
Chairperson
Dr Colm Ó Briain   Department of Arts, Culture and the Gaeltacht

Commission Members
Ms Anne Coogan
Ms Frieda Finlay

Other Members:
Ms Eilish Butler   Interested consumer - physical disability
Ms Josephine O'Leary   Sensory disability
Mr Steven Daunt   Physical disability
Ms Katie Woollett   Art Therapist
Mr Francis Murphy   NI Arts Council - Disability Brief
Mr Sandy Fitzgerald   City Arts Centre
Mr Gene Lambert   Photographer - physical disability
Mr Aiden Shortt   Disability Action

Background Paper/Research Support
Ms Maureen Gilbert   National Rehabilitation Board

WORK/TRAINING
Chairperson
Ms Carmel Foley   Chief Executive, Employment Equality Agency

Commission Members
Ms Anne Coogan
Dr Arthur O'Reilly (Convenor)
Mr Michael Gogarty
Ms Margaret O'Leary
Mr John A Cooney

Advisory Group Members
Ms Anne Dinnegan   Aer Rianta
Mr Cearbhaill O Meadhra   Disability Advisor

Other Members
Ms Catherine Kearney   Consumer Representative, Mental Health Alliance
Mr Donal Devenny   Cneasta
Ms Siobhan Lynam   County Enterprise Partnership Boards
Ms Mary Boyd   Parent - Learning Difficulty Perspective

Background Paper/Research Support
Dr Barbara Murray

The Commission wish to acknowledge with gratitude the input of Mr. Larry Murtagh, NEC Ireland Ltd. with regard to the chapter on Work and Training.

FAMILY SUPPORTS/PERSONAL SUPPORTS
Chairperson
Professor Joyce O'Connor

Commission Members
Ms Kathleen O'Flaherty
Mr Conn Mac Cinngamhna (Convenor)
Ms Annie Ryan

Other Members
Ms Vera Mulcahy	Carers Association
Ms Florence Dougall	Incare
Ms Mary Cody	Headway
Mr Michael Mullally	Parent - Physical/Sensory Handicap Perspective
Ms Maire Ni Chorcora	Community Care Services Perspective

Background Paper/Research Support
Dr Jean Tubridy

INCOME SUPPORT
Chairperson
Mr Seamus O Cinnéide

Commission Members
Mr Seamus O Cinnéide
Mr John Bohan (Convenor)
Ms Frances Spillane
Mr Paddy Doyle

Advisory Group Members
Mr Colman Patton
Dr Austin O'Carroll

Other Members
Ms Helen Johnson,	Combat Poverty Agency
Ms Mary McAnaney	Parent Representative - Physical/Sensory Disability
Perspective	
Mr John Dolan	Disability Federation of Ireland
Mr Joseph Cody	Forum, Kilkenny (rural Perspective)

Background Paper/Research Support
Mr Mel Cousins

HOUSING/ACCOMMODATION
Chairperson
Mr Frank Mulcahy

Commission Members
Mr Mark Blake-Knox
Ms Fidelma Ryan
Mr Frank Mulcahy (Convenor)
Mr Allen O'Connor

Other Members
Mr Martin Naughton   Incare
Mr Sean O'Brien   MS Society
Mr Michael Dooley   Galway County Association for the Mentally Handicapped
Mr Bernard Thompson   Irish Council for Social Housing
Ms Elaine O'Neill   DET Cork

Background Paper/Research Support
Dr Pauline Faughnan

HEALTH
Chairperson
Mr P J Madden   General Secretary, Irish Nurses Organisation

Commission Members
Mr Conn Mac Cinngamhna
Sister Angela Magee
Mr John Cooney
Ms Frances Spillane
Dr Paul McCarthy

Advisory Group Member
Dr Austin O'Carroll

Other Members
Ms Winifred Bligh   Alzheimer Society of Ireland
Ms Wendy Murray   Parent with Sensory Disability
Mr Padraig O'Morain   Irish Times
Mr Criostóir Mac Brádaigh
Ms Mary Coveney   OT Cork University Hospital Irish
                                       College of General Practitioners

Background Paper/Research Support
Mr Andrew Logue

MOBILITY/TRANSPORT

Chairperson

Ms Mary Darley   Dublin Corporation, Irish Life Centre

Commission Members

Mr Michael Gogarty
Ms Kathleen O'Flaherty

Other Members

Mr David Egan	Spinal Injuries Association
Mr Gerard Ellis	
Mr Martin Naughton	Centre for Independent Living
Mr James Dukes	Irish Wheelchair Association
Mr Brian Crummy	Disabled Drivers Association
Mr Dermot Purcell	
Ms Aideen Kelly	
Mr Des Murphy	
Ms Niamh O'Doherty	National Rehabilitation Board
Mr Rory Boland	Roads and Traffic Section, Civic Offices
Mr Graham Lightfoot	Transport Consultant

Background Paper/Research Support

Ms Mairide Woods

RIGHTS OF PEOPLE WITH DISABILITIES

Chairperson
Mr Michael Mills

Commission Members
Ms Annie Ryan
Ms Margaret O'Leary
Ms Fidelma Ryan
Mr Frank Mulcahy

Advisory Group Members
Mr Kevin Power
Mr Sean Megahy

Other Members

Mr Kevin Coyle	Psychologist, St Michael's House
Ms Martina Murphy	Physical Disability, Richmond Cheshire House
Mr Michael Coote	The Alzheimer Society of Ireland
Mr John Costello	Solicitor
Mr Colm Whooley	Physical Disability
Mr John Bosco Conama	Sensory Disability
Ms Helen Faughnan	Department of Social Welfare

Background/Research Support
Mr Mel Cousins

SEXUALITY AND RELATIONSHIPS
Commission Members
Mr Frank Mulcahy
Ms Jacqui Browne
Ms Frieda Finlay
Ms Annie Ryan

Advisory Group Member
Dr Austin O'Carroll

Other Members
Mr Colm Whooley	Spinal Injuries Association
Ms Joan Carthy	Spinal Injuries Association
Dr Brendan McCormack	Mental Handicap Centre,Cheeverstown House
Mr Kevin Coyle	Psychologist, St Michael's House
Ms Eileen Rowan	St Vincent's Centre

Background/Research Support
Ms Rachel Martin

TECHNOLOGY/TELECOMMUNICATIONS
Chairperson
Professor D P Burton   University of Limerick

Commission Members
Mr Michael Gogarty
Mr Allen O'Connor
Ms Jacqui Browne
Mr Paddy Doyle

Advisory Group Members
Dr Patricia Noonan-Walsh
Mr Frank Maguire
Mr Cearbhaill O Meadhra

Others Members
Ms Mary Kirk-Allen   Physical Disability
Mr Bob Allen   Central Remedial Clinic
Mr Derek Farrell   Disabled Drivers Association of Ireland
Mr Barry Dunne   Sensory Disability
Dr John O'Flaherty   National Microelectronics Research Centre
Mr Carl Magee   Telecom
Mr Donie O'Shea   National Rehabilitation Board
Professor Aonnrai de Paor   National Medical Rehabilitation Centre

Background Paper/Research Support
Mr Kevin Cullen   Work Research Centre

CONSULTATIVE PROCESS
Chairperson
Mr Pat Wylie

Commission Member
Mr Frank Mulcahy

Advisory Group Members
Mr Gerry Ryan
Mr Donal Toolin
Ms Helena Saunders

Others Members
Ms Maureen Gilbert   National Rehabilitation Board

LEGAL RESOURCE GROUP
Commission Members
Dr Gerard Quinn
Ms Annie Ryan
Dr Arthur O'Reilly
Mr Frank Mulcahy
Ms Jacqui Browne
Mr Michael Gogarty

ADVISORS TO THE COMMISSION

Mr Gerry Ryan	General Secretary, National Association for Mental Handicap in Ireland
Mr Niall Keane	Chief Executive, National Association for the Deaf
Mr Donal Toolin	Journalist & Advocate
Mr Cearbhaill O Meadhra	Disability Advisor, Information Technology Specialist
Mr Sean Megahey	Forum of People with Disabilities
Dr Austin O'Carroll	Irish College of General Practitioners and Forum of People with Disabilities
Mr Des Kenny	Chief Executive, National Council for the Blind
Dr Pauline Faughnan	Social Science Research Unit, UCD
Dr Patricia Noonan Walsh	Director of Research & Service Evaluation, St Michael's House Research Department
Ms Deirdre O'Carroll	
Mr Roger Acton	Chief Executive, Disability Federation of Ireland
Mr Frank Maguire	St Joseph's School for Deaf Boys, Cabra
Ms Helena Saunders	Irish Deaf Society
Mr Kevin Power	Wexford Community Workshops
Ms Mary O'Mahony	Chief Executive, Mental Health Association of Ireland
Mr Martin Rogan	Alliance for Mental Health
Ms Anne Dinnegan	Disability Access Officer, Aer Rianta